Beatrix Campbell has been a journalist, both in print and in broadcasting, for thirty years. Her work has appeared in the *Independent*, the *Guardian*, the *Scotsman*, the *New Statesman*, *Marxism Today* and *Time Out*; amd she co-founded the co-operatively owned *City Limits* and the journal *Red Rag*. Her award-winning books and documentaries include *Wigan Pier Revisited* (winner of the Cheltenham Festival literary prize), 'Listen to the Children', a documentary about the watershed Nottingham child abuse case, and *The Iron Ladies* (winner of the Fawcett Society Prize). Her book *Goliath: Britain's Dangerous Places* was adapted by Bryony Lavery into a successful one-woman play for the Sphinx Theatre Company. Beatrix Campbell is Visiting Professor of Women's Studies at the Univeristy of Newcastle-upon-Tyne.

DIANA
Princess of Wales

HOW SEXUAL POLITICS
SHOOK THE MONARCHY

Beatrix Campbell

First published by The Women's Press Ltd, 1988
A member of the Namara Group
34 Great Sutton Street, London EC1V 0DX

Reprinted 1998

Extract on p9 from *For Coloured Girls Who Have Considered Suicide
When the Rainbow Is Enuf* by Ntozake Shange. Reprinted by
permission of Methuen, London.

British Library Cataloguing-in-Publication Data
A catalogue record for this book is available from the British Library.

ISBN 0 7043 4585 4

Typeset in Trump Mediaeval 10/12pt by FSH Ltd, London
Printed and bound in Great Britain by Cox & Wyman Ltd,
Reading, Berkshire

To the Memory of Bobby Campbell

(July 1942–September 1997)

who brought his big but fragile heart and mind to some of the great themes of our time, not least men's ways of being with women and children. His confident knowledge that this *is* a historic theme engaged him in the struggle to sort out what it means to be a man. His life showed that it was all worth it. He exemplified the cultural courage of our generation. Fortunately we came into each other's lives and changed them.

Contents

Part III – Seen and Heard

Acknowledgements

This book began one Sunday morning in June 1992 when my companion Judith Jones and I were out walking in Northumberland, relishing the *Sunday Times* serialisation of Andrew Morton's sensational book on Diana and the monarchy. We knew that we were learning something very important about the royal family and its dissident daughters-in-law. That conversation never ceased, indeed it became this book – it was Judith's suggestion and its ideas are as much hers as they are mine.

Thanks, too, for advice to the Northern Initiative on Women and Eating, Anna Clark of the University of North Carolina and James Knowles of the University of Newcastle-upon-Tyne; to Kath Webb and Jim Webb for newspaper research; to Charter 88 director Andrew Puddephatt for discussion about royalism and republicanism; to Anthony Holden, Andrew Morton, James Whitaker and other tabloid journalists for their interviews and their help; and finally to those who cared about Diana, who knew her worth and who privately shared their thoughts.

Preface

Another book about Diana, her death, and the meaning of life in *fin de siècle* Britain? There can never be enough books about the emblematic moments in which we rediscover ourselves as a society, and there can never be too many books which engage in society's conversation with itself about who we are, why and when we are renewed or ruptured, and how searing moments are lived in our psyche and in our politics. These debates are forms of self-expression, they are warnings, they are a wish for recovery and reform. This book is an argument against the notion that the personal is personal and that the private lives of monarchs should mean nothing to their subjects. It is also an argument against the plea that the royal family should be left in peace. It is my belief that the enlightenment and interest of their 'subjects' offers the best chance that Charles and his sons, William and Harry, may ever get of discovering how best to be human.

This book is also a reinstatement of the role sexual politics had to play in the drama of Diana's life and death. The traumas, the hounding, the celebrity and the public's mourning can only be fully understood when the issue of gender infuses the discussion. Diana suffered as a woman, because she was a woman and a product of her class. She was hunted as female quarry, first by the prince in search of a wife, and then to feed the lusty lenses of the so-called 'rat-pack'. The massive popular response was testimony to the fact that the public understood that this was a woman who had already lost so much during her lifetime. Yet in the wake of Diana's death, the issue of her suffering *as a woman* was totally eclipsed by the debate over media intrusion and privacy laws.

The personal behaviour of this sovereign family, and in particular its sexual politics, consummates the constitutional and economic case against the monarchy. How long can this society sustain such an antiquated institution?

Introduction

The death of Diana, Princess of Wales, at the end of August 1997 presented British politicians and the royal family not only with a tragedy, but with the task of translation – of interpreting the rise and rise of criticism of the royal family as a family, and of understanding the massive swell of support for this woman who had been so effectively banished from the royal entourage. Television, newspapers and magazines were filled with Diana. The public flocked to Kensington Palace and Buckingham Palace with an estimated £50 million worth of flowers, with candles, poems, cards, balloons and personal letters. People who never knew the woman queued for over eight hours to sign the books of condolence. The tributes were endless. So was the criticism.

Diana had been the jewel in the royal crown who refurbished fading, *fin de siècle* royalism. And yet her ill-treatment and finally her death ignited a republican sentiment that was unprecedented in the twentieth century. Diana's death may have initiated criticism of the royal family, but it was the burgeoning wave of republican feeling that sustained the debates and opened up a new dialogue about the dissonance between the royals and the society of the 1990s.

Sexual politics had detonated the reputation of the royal family. Cynics protested that this was nothing new – monarchs' morals may have disgraced them before, but they didn't destroy them. This was to miss the point. The contours of politics had changed. Diana was the first person to enter the royal family from another world that was being transformed – by women. Her revolt against her arranged marriage, the discovery of the deceit and duplicity of her husband, the heir to the throne, and the complicity of his relatives, exposed them as an atavistic family, a family *manqué*. But there was more – Diana's struggle within the royal family resonated with the stuff that British society was also trying to sort out. Royal manners mattered not because people required of them a Rupert Bear model of respectability, but because the royal family claimed to represent a society struggling with a new settlement between men, women and children; a historic new deal that promised to replace patriarchal power with domestic democracy.

The royal family is uniquely patriarchal. Until recently, primogeniture prevailed. Even when Diana was giving birth to her babies, she was relieved when they were boys. It was the royal family's own patriarchal predicates that produced its '*annus horribilis*', which was misattributed to its daughters-in-law. It was not the daughters-in-law themselves, it was their dissent that caused the crisis.

In the aftermath of Diana's death the royal family had to confront the criticism head-on. In late February 1998, it was announced that the Queen would not be against changing the law of succession, primogeniture. However, it was obvious that the Queen had not generated this idea herself and that this was no heartfelt embrace of feminist politics or the issues raised by her daughter-in-law's life.

But the 1990s also exposed Britain's political system as

unsettled by the attempts to modernise the sexual contract. Both Majorism and the *beau* Blair's New Labour benefited from Thatcherism's 'regressive modernisation', its repudiation of the insurgent social movements of the 1960s and '70s and their campaigns for a redistribution of both resources and respect.

The reluctance of political society to challenge the monarchy about anything was repeated throughout the 1990s. Margaret Thatcher announced in 1990 that the Civil List would be settled until the year 2000, relieving the royals of unseemly financial scrutiny. The Labour front bench agreed. In the twentieth century the Windsors, Elizabeth and her father to be precise, have evaded the duty they share with their 'subjects' – paying tax. The debate about royal taxation did not take off until 1992 after the publication of Philip Hall's forensic audit of Windsor finances, *Royal Fortune*. Hall's research, which had been the basis of a *World in Action* documentary by Paul Lashmar a year earlier, showed that although the Queen is one of the richest people in the world, she and her family cost the country more than they contribute. The idea of taxing the monarch, endorsed by the mass media, did not translate into Parliamentary pressure until 1992, after Andrew Morton rocked royal reputations and fire ravaged the family home, Windsor Castle. The government said the people would pay for the restoration. Oh no, said the people. Less than a week later the royal family decided to pay themselves, but they decided to recoup the costs – from the *people* paying to see Buckingham Palace. The Prime Minister also announced that Elizabeth and Charles would start paying tax. After the death of Diana republican sentiment was palpable in public opinion: 72 per cent believed that Elizabeth was out of touch and 58 per cent reckoned that the monarchy would not exist in its current form in 30 years' time. (*Sunday Times*, 14 September 1997). The government recoiled, however, from reforming the monarchy and its political power.

In the wake of Diana's death it was sexual politics that
initially animated alienation from the monarchy. But
parliamentary culture had no feel for this new mood –
Parliament remained one of the most sexist institutions in
the political firmament. It could only contextualise the
unprecedented public response to the tragedy within an
attack on press intrusion and the paparazzi. Parliament
was also irredeemably royalist. Our parliamentary
tradition is centralist, unionist and monarchist. It made no
difference that Diana died in the long, lovely summer of a
new national spirit released by the 1 May general election.
Labour has, throughout the twentieth century, been the
royal family's great friend. So, despite the election of the
largest number of women ever to Parliament, and despite
New Labour's commitment to constitutional reform,
political society failed to register the connection between
constitutional and sexual politics. It failed, therefore, to
appreciate how Diana's defence of herself as a woman had
disturbed the royal family's stability as a monarchy; it
failed to grasp how Diana's determination to salvage her
self-respect, call a future king to account, shook the royals
to their very core.

Andrew Morton's book was the first intimation of the
Windsor's corporate complicity in the deception of this
woman about her destiny. The public understood this to be
a great disgrace. The Windsors' response to their daughter-
in-law's distress merely reminded us that the aristocracy
has always maligned troubled and troublesome women and
confidently dispatched them to the Tower, the guillotine or
the asylum. What was revealed in the 1990s was the
monarchy's estrangement from women and thus from
contemporary civil society; a space that is familiar with
women's pain and protest, that is itself engaged in the
reform of relations between genders and generations.
Diana's testimony on *Panorama* cemented her connection
to the concerns that are alive in popular culture. In naming
her suffering, she also gained the empathy of the thousands

of women who had survived or were going through similar experiences.

But still political parties could not bring themselves to address the substance of her lament. It is supposedly the function of political parties to give institutional and ideological form to feelings, but the meaning of Diana's death did not find expression in the centralist, unionist and monarchist soul of the father of parliaments. Instead the great debate was codified as a crisis of public and private, a crisis of the public person's privacy.

The argument in this book is that the patriarchal foundations of the monarchy have lost their legitimacy. They are the cause of its current crisis. This book begins, therefore, with a discussion of the patriarchal culture of the royal family. Looking back at the historical precedents set for the royals by their ancestors, we can see the roots of their modern-day crisis; we can see the cult that is the royal family. This environment moulded Charles, both as a man and as a future sovereign, but, paradoxically, in doing so, it created the conditions for his own demise. It also laid the foundations for the unhappy alliance between Charles and Diana and the inevitable rupture of the marriage. The economic and political power of the monarchy, albeit limited by its form as a constitutional monarchy, cast an authoritarian shadow over our society. But it was only the inflammatory sexual politics ignited by Diana's life and death that created the conditions for a great debate about royalism and republicanism.

This book begins, therefore, with a discussion of the patriarchal culture of the royal family, its princes and its queen. It looks at the production of Charles as a man and a sovereign within the cult of the royal family. It then explores the endemic sexism of the aristocracy that delivered Diana to her doom; the preoccupation with Diana's sexual status; Charles and Diana's barren, brisk courtship, the duplicitous wedding; and Diana's decline. In the third part, the book considers the paradoxical play of the tabloid press both as sexual harassers and as instruments of a democratic wrangle with the royal family over the limits of what might or might not be known, and Diana's imperative to bear witness to her own tragedy. Finally there is a discussion of the democracy of the crowd, its cosmopolitanism and the complexity of its grief.

It was Diana's treatment as a woman, and her sense that she was sustained by the sympathy and strength of women, that made her dangerous. She spoke out in order to save her sanity, to warn her enemies, and to share her troubles with millions of people who recognised them, because they, too, endured them or knew someone who did. The people understood: she had been done down by the bad behaviour of a man who behaved like a king. The connection between sexism and monarchism was not lost on the people.

For Colored Girls
Who Have Considered
Suicide When the Rainbow
Is Enuf

Somebody almost walked off wid alla my stuff
not my poems or a dance i gave up in the street
but somebody almost walked off wid all my stuff
like a kleptomaniac workin hard & forgetting while stealin
this is mine
this aint yr stuff
now why don't you put me back & let me hang out my own
   self

Ntozake Shange

Part I
Men in Waiting

1. Pointless Princes

The present Prince of Wales is the latest in a long and dishonourable tradition of ageing sons who were provided for, their futures prescribed, while they loitered on the threshold of power, waiting, waiting for their parents to die. They have always presented the palace with a problem – themselves. Kings and queens prayed that they would be spared their sons' ruinous reputations. These princes were given their first experience of sovereignty: they were given Wales, England's first colony. The first sons of English monarchs were apprenticed to their royal craft by their appointment to England's most successfully conquered country, after centuries of raids, insurrections, race wars, civil wars and colonial wars.

Edward I of England had first declared his own infant son Prince of Wales at Caernarvon Castle in 1301. Edward had already commissioned an inquiry into Welsh law, which uncovered a 'people's law' in which rights were rooted in kindred and community. Although, like the rest of Europe, Wales was dominated by male interests, the English system of primogeniture was regarded by the Welsh as 'alien'.

(Williams, 1985, p74) England's conquest was the beginning of the end of a social system in which women's position was, at least, ambiguous. They were deemed inferior, they didn't wage war and they had a price on their virginity. Yet there was no concept of bastardy, and the preoccupation with descent was qualified by civilised embrace of 'the children of the brake and brush'. Welsh women were freer than their European sisters, they had access to land, and widows were respected and seem to have 'acted as remembrancers to their community which so badly needed a collective memory'. (Williams, 1985 p52)

Wales had already been occupied by England when its own great *national* prince, Owain Glyn Dwr, led its last, long rebellion in 1400. Amazingly, there was still resistance in a landscape garrisoned by a trail of castles, where the English patrolled communities who had become foreigners in their own territory, and peopled little towns 'by an organised transplantation of English endowed with a sense of racial superiority'. (Williams, 1985, p89) During Glyn Dwr's rebellion England's 'ferociously racist' penal laws turned the people into unpersons. Eventually old Owain Glyn Dwr vanished. He didn't die. Wales didn't die. Around its edges and up its hills Welsh people went on speaking Welsh, despite a terrifying purge of their language and their law. Wales was, for sure, not England, but after Glyn Dwr, it developed a schizoid sense of self that was muted by dignified, literate but injured accommodation to the omnipotent English. Wales was more successfully subdued than any other nation in these islands.

England gave the defeated people a prince who was as English as he was pointless. Princes of Wales became renowned as being rich, reluctant, indulged, capricious and petulant. Walter Bagehot, in his 1867 rumination *The English Constitution*, warned that 'all the world and all the glory of it, whatever is most attractive, whatever is most seductive, has always been offered to the Prince of Wales'. It would be unreasonable, he concluded, 'to expect the best virtue'.

Bagehot's law can be discerned through the behaviour of a long line of princes-in-waiting. Before Charles, the role had been defined by some memorable princes of Wales: the Duke of Windsor, lover and Nazi sympathiser; Bertie, later Edward VII, lover and shooter; and George IV, bigamist and big spender.

The principality over which they exercised strange, ceremonial, distant dominion had little or no administrative autonomy, and thus didn't really exist, except in its diasporic travels and in its thoughts. The subjects were usually polite but sceptical spectators at investitures that were made up as the monarchy went along, their country an empty proscenium in which the monarchy practised the art of 'inventing tradition' – improvising rituals which, by repetition, implied inevitability. (Hobsbawm and Ranger, 1983, p1)

The domination of Wales also echoed through the princes' relationships to their wives, who were expected to be similarly sentimentalised, duped and subdued.

Bigamist and Big Spender

Perhaps because the British monarchy has enjoyed an easy life for most of the twentieth century, with remarkably few republican flutters, monarchists inside and outside the royal family have forgotten that it was often the shameless, unacceptable face of patriarchy that produced the royal family's troubles. Charles' great-uncle Louis Mountbatten warned him that he was acquiring a reputation as a playboy prince, that he was following the bad example of his Uncle David, whose abdication *for love* caused the only significant royal crisis in the twentieth century. (Dimbleby, 1994, p316) But the great-uncle was being selective in his evocation of historical precedent – he ignored the *strategic* and stabilising impact of George III's domestic regime during an era ravaged by revolutionary rupture, and also ignored the reversals caused by the amazing sexual scandals that defined George IV's interregnum as Prince of Wales and his subsequent tenure of the throne.

George was broke. Marriage was his only route to money and, ultimately, secure kingship. In his early twenties he regularly fell into debt, into drink, and in and out of love. His great love, however, was the widowed Catholic Maria Fitzherbert, a star in the Prince's Whig firmament and a reassuringly rich woman. After mounting a formidable campaign against her respectable defences, he wooed and won her. In a secret ceremony they were wed in 1775.

According to her church there had been a marriage. According to his there was no marriage. The Act of Settlement in 1701 stated that the heir to the throne could neither be a Catholic nor marry one. The 1772 Royal Marriages Act required his father's or Parliament's consent to any marriage. On all counts George was either perpetrating a grave deception – not least upon Mrs Fitzherbert – or disinheriting himself.

Since he had not secured his father's permission, the Prince, as the king's son, was not properly married but the Prince, as a man, could have his way and have it paid for by the duped Mrs Fitzherbert. He was never to be seen in society without her until Frances, Lady Jersey, appeared and made it her mission to win him. Maria Fitzherbert was, for the time being, ousted. Lady Jersey triumphed. The daughter of a bishop, she was mature, married, a mother and grandmother. She was also clever, fascinating, without scruples but with great schemes; she was, it was said, an utter 'bitch'. (Fraser, 1997, p41) And she had an obliging husband: Lord Jersey was rewarded, and controlled, by his appointment as Master of the Horse. She was, therefore, the perfect mistress.

Despite his illicit marriage and his access to Mrs Fitzherbert's plentiful means, the Prince of Wales was still broke. Lady Jersey encouraged him to make up his mind to marry a 'suitable' girl, a device by which he could reap the rise in his income from the Civil List due to a married man and invoke Parliament's promise to pay his debts.

Princess Caroline of Brunswick was to be his sacrificial lamb. Letters and cameos were exchanged. But he didn't know her, and when he met her, he didn't like her. She, naturally, was a virgin. She had been sequestered in Brunswick by her parents who regarded her boisterous behaviour as a sign of rebelliousness and a tendency to passion. Their response was to treat her as a prisoner: she was not allowed to dine or keep company at court. Her friends were her servants. She was, however, educated, erudite and a great enthusiast for life. She had been kept 'tidy' for a longed-for marriage to a needy prince, and she and her parents welcomed the proposal from the Prince of Wales, which promised a beneficial alliance between their two families. She was described by her British chaperones as good-looking but slightly smelly – Brunswickians didn't go in for personal hygiene at that time. Lord Malmesbury commented that she had many strong qualities and although her education was of the 'nonsensical' type that combined 'privation, injunction and menace', she was bright and brave.

But when the Prince of Wales laid eyes upon her, he called for a glass of brandy, and fled. He walked up the aisle desperate and drunk, and had to be supported on either side by equally drunk dukes. The Archbishop of Canterbury 'looked earnestly at the king, as well as the bridegroom' when he asked if there was any lawful impediment to lawful matrimony, 'giving unequivocal proof of his apprehension that some previous marriage had taken place'. (Fraser, 1997, p61) Caroline was sacrificed to a conspiracy of silence: everyone knew. Their first night together was disastrous 'even by the traditionally low standards of such occasions' and although she soon became pregnant, the pair were no longer living as man and wife within a few short weeks of the wedding.

The Prince of Wales pestered Parliament for money and

publicly humiliated the brave, bewildered princess with his
contempt and his flagrant liaisons. When Caroline dared to
complain, he adopted the position of the injured, persecuted
party; the perpetrator presenting himself as the victim. The
Prince of Wales was provoked by Caroline's very stamina
and social self-sufficiency. Marooned outside his court, she
created her own parallel, progressive universe. He forced the
House of Lords Commissioners to conduct a 'delicate
investigation' into her alleged affairs, engineered her exile,
and upon his father's death determined to divorce her. His
impending coronation galvanised him: if he was king, then
Caroline would be his queen. 'The horror of having the
Queen made an object of the prayers of his people haunted
his imagination,' wrote Lord Castlereagh. (p347) A Bill of
Pains and Penalties, an ancient device regularly invoked by
monarchs to discipline their challengers, was introduced in
the House of Lords to deprive Caroline of her royal titles and
bannish her from England. The device evoked the tumbrils
– the mere mention of this Parliamentary manoeuvre sent a
chill through a society that remembered how it had been
used against Jacobites after the 1745 rebellion. Lady Cowper
thought its use against the wronged queen sounded 'to the
ignorant as as if she was going to be fried or tortured'. (p399)

But his action harvested a counter-action: Caroline was
at the centre of a resistance movement welding disparate
interests, from Whigs to Radicals and dispossessed
plebeians, the 'constituency of the rejected', all of them
activated by his bad behaviour as a *man*, whose tyrannies
were both kingly and manly. The Carolinian resistance
movement created a new kind of politics in the public
realm: *sexual politics*.

The Lords' inquisition into Caroline's robust survival
strategies as a wronged but indefatigably independent
woman inaugurated a great public debate about royal
oppression which connected sexual politics with a
discourse of rights. George had invited a critique of his
tyranny as a man and thus opened a political space in

which radical republicanism was compelled to engage with sex and gender.

This was a watershed in republican and popular politics, a moment that transformed the movement for constitutional reform. According to the feminist historian Anna Clark, radical republicanism in Britain 'learned to draw upon the vitality of plebeian popular literature to create a new political language that could speak both of high royal politics and of family crises in the same breath. Instead of trivialising radical politics, the transformation of popular literature into overt political language made mass mobilisation possible.' (1995, p165) Radicals were chastened and changed by the plebeian fascination with Caroline and by the vast popular literature caricaturing and critiquing a dissolute and disrespectful aristocracy – a repertoire found in shop windows and popular melodrama that was legible to the semi-literate. This transformed what could be voiced in public. It also shook up the radicals themselves, 'pushing them out into the community and forcing a responsiveness to women's concerns'. Women's experience became the measure by which to judge kingly oppression. Power and corruption, the use and abuse of Parliament, and the infringement of subjects' liberties, all became 'central constitutional issues'. (p165)

George's campaign against Caroline took place in riotous times. Britain was a society of mass movements, insurgent street protests, petitions, mass meetings, colonial rebellion, mutiny and, of course, massacre. The King's pursuit of Caroline was shadowed by the Peterloo massacre only the year before, in which women as well as men had been martyred. Now a heterogeneous span of masculinities, from artisans, mechanics and labourers to middle-class respectable men, began to connect their own concerns with women. All were able to address her as a subject, like them, as a victim: 'the same power which scourged us is now oppressing you.' (p165) The Caroline case took radical republicanism's priorities and practices beyond 'abstract constitutional issues' composed in smoke-filled rooms and coffee shops. Sexuality and gender politics were introduced – on the side of women. Having endorsed the experience of women, radical republicanism created a new social base. A concept of the people emerged, comprising all classes, the rough, the raunchy, the respectable – and inclusive of both genders.

Lover and Shooter

In 1842 Queen Victoria bestowed the title Prince of Wales upon her unloved son Edward when he was one year old. He finally became king in 1901 after enduring the longest internship in the history of the Princes of Wales. Unlike his prolific father, the German Prince Albert, the interested and interesting consort whose enterprise transformed the landscape of Victorian Britain, the boy known as Bertie unsettled his disappointed parents with his passions: dressing up, gambling, eating, socialising, shooting and sex.

He did find time to lend himself to a royal commission on the conditions of the aged poor, which pioneered state provision of old-age pensions, and he supported the reform of the royal requirement to repudiate Roman Catholicism, but otherwise he famously committed his life to pleasure and promiscuity while loitering in the wings of history, waiting for his unyielding mother to die. Despite his father's best efforts, he proved remarkable in his resistance to education, expeditions and intellectual improvement. He regarded history and ancient monuments as the 'mouldering stones' of 'the temple of something', and preferred the ruder entertainments of 'society'.

He made his mark on the map not in Wales but in Norfolk. In 1864 his parents bought him his own estate, Sandringham, in the hope that he might do something useful. It became his winter retreat before he threw himself back into the city for the London 'season'. After a modest beginning, Bertie made Sandringham into something special; its grounds were planted to produce the greatest possible pleasure for hunters and shooters – an ersatz landscape designed to maximise the production of game and the provision of cover across its mellow killing fields. The Prince of Wales was a committed and congenial socialite and shooter, and Sandringham was the perfect project for a man with time on his hands. Although it did not rival other aristocratic estates for the sport or the volume of corpses, 'a day's shooting there was unrivalled for the sheer scale and pageantry'. (Plumtre, 1995, p95) It gave Bertie much to do – fashion a landscape, arrange uniforms, menus, guests, sanitation, plates, orchestrate spectacular house parties, entertain prime ministers ...

Ambassadors and sport-mad dukes, 'big-shots' such as Lord Walsingham, a champion among obsessive shooters, were enthusiastic guests. Disraeli, however, was less impressed by 'the strong brigade of the darker sex', the toadies, 'buffoons and butts' and 'Polish Counts picked up at the Roulette Baths'. Sandringham became a station in the royal season, an episode in the creation of a 'tradition'. The sporting estate institutionalised tweeds, horses, guns, stag and game as part of 'the public perception of a royal life, as it has remained ever since'. (Plumtre, 1995, p90)

When hunting declined as an 'upper class obsession', shooting, transformed by new ordnance technology and the mass production of tame birds, took its place. The shooting party, when 'smart' society evacuated the city for the countryside, became an institutionalised aristocratic pastime. The Prince of Wales took to this 'with alacrity'. (Cannadine, 1990, p364)

By the end of the century English aristocrats were moving 'out of land and into business' (p443) and the Prince of Wales exemplified this dramatic realignment between land and capitalism. His wealth was protected and expanded not by landed enterprise but by investment in the financial markets – brilliantly organised on his behalf by the financier Sir Ernest Cassell. The countryside was therefore being reinvented as a place for the super-rich to go out and play, 'a place of rest and repose, where money was spent not made and they were fully contented with the amenities of rural living – riding, hunting, shooting and entertaining'. (p359) Sandringham, then, was the epitome of the metamorphosis of the countryside in the aristocratic imagination.

During the six months of his betrothal to Princess Alexandra, Bertie's mother contrived to keep them separate for all but three days. They began their married life together as amiable strangers. She lent poise and beauty to the family firm. However, the writer Rebecca West described her wasting away in an exhausting 'torrent of royal fertility' producing an army of children, while her husband sought other great beauties among the flock of bright and bold women in 'society'. (West, 1996, p54)

One of Bertie's achievements, then, was to animate aristocratic society with his increasingly portly presence amidst the 'Marlborough House set' during the dreary decades of Queen Victoria's mourning. Despite her reign's reputation for sexual repression, he entertained his milieu – and its audience – with the frisson of impropriety: famous affairs that were sanctioned and settled into the routines of his private and public life. Bertie's liaisons were not only *not* secret, nor repressed, they were a feature of the 'society' created by Princes of Wales, in which the circulation of romance, and the distribution of the royal person among favoured women, was constitutive of their alternative courts.

Unlike those of Bertie's predecessor George, his sexual scandals did not particularly pitch him against his parliamentary paymasters. So they were not 'political' in that sense – although he lacked political acuity. Still, his public presentation as a pleasure-seeker functioned as an irrepressible challenge to the respectable middle class and to his mother. His affairs and loutish company attracted attention, the intensity of which was to prefigure the crises of publicity that vexed royals and their acolytes a century later. Scrutiny of royal standards is not a new sport, nor is it a function of modern technology and its techniques of surveillance. It is incited by the way *they* live, and the mirage of national identity narrated through royal rhetoric.

Bertie and Alexandra entertained on a grand scale, in the country and the city; he adored the theatre, he loved gentlemen's clubs and illegal gambling, he coveted actresses, showgirls and society ladies, and he enlisted plutocratic financial enterprise to multiply his personal wealth. The Prince of Wales exemplified the new class convergence between the aristocracy and the insurgent plutocracy – a reciprocal alliance which bankrolled the declining aristos, 'parasites on the plutocracy', and lent social prestige to the plutocrats seeking a niche in their remote eyrie. (Cannadine, 1990, p444)

His clique was predictably and publicly promiscuous. The Prince came close to notoriety himself when Sir Charles Mordaunt embarked on a marathon attempt to divorce his wife, Harriet, citing her admitted affairs with several men in the Prince's circle. Poor Harriet lived in an asylum until 1906, only one of many society women wrecked by use and abuse. The divorce case came close to the Prince of Wales in another sense – he had a relationship with one of Harriet's sisters, by whom he is reported to have had a daughter, of whom he seemed eternally fond.

Queen Victoria supported Bertie in the Mordaunt affair but warned that his 'intimate acquaintance with a young married woman being publicly proclaimed, will show an amount of imprudence which cannot but damage him in the eyes of the middle and lower classes'. Note, damage in the eyes of the *useful* classes, but not the aristocracy. Victoria added that this was 'most deeply to be lamented in these days when the higher classes, in their frivolous, selfish and pleasure-seeking lives do more to increase the spirit of democracy than anything else'. (Plumtre, 1995, p65) The progressive *Reynolds News* noted that even the the most robust royalists worried whether he would 'have the tact and talent to keep royalty upon its legs and out of the gutter'. (Plumtre, 1995, p65)

The Prince of Wales had a serious love affair with Lillie Langtry, a young star in London theatre and high society, whose husband hovered while she was installed as Bertie's companion. Lillie ended her days as a vagrant. Amidst a resurgence of republicanism in Britain, the Prince of Wales' affair with Daisy Brooke again took him to notoriety, this time implicating him not only in sex but in illegal gambling. He 'swept her into his life' and abandoned her only when she advocated socialism as 'the salvation of our country'. Libertine though he might be, 'like fidelity, homosexuality and suffrage, socialism was not a concept of which Bertie approved'. (Souhami, 1997, p47)

Finally, Bertie 'settled in late middle age for staid infidelity' with young Alice Keppel, who consolidated a synergistic alliance with Bertie's financier friend Sir Ernest Cassel. 'Kingship, politics, business, adultery and personal profit intertwined.' (p58) Alice Keppel's life spiced and sustained the whims of the ageing King. Keppel was on his arm, in his bed and in his life, while Queen Alexandra was consigned to child care and royal ceremony. It was Keppel who went racing, shooting, socialising, dining and gossiping with the King; it was she who played bridge, holidayed in Biarritz, and was courted by politicians. 'Politicians knew that to win the King's approval they must first please her.' She was 'compliant, available, flattering, firm, dominated him with her charm.' (p61) Alice Keppel, the married royal mistress, whose children were her audience during her intermittent presence, was addicted to the appearances of respectability, bequeathing to her own daughter a sense that 'marriage was a socially acceptable cover for socially unacceptable sex.' (Souhami, 1997, p137) But marriage had left Queen Alexandra marooned and marginal.

Nothing was what it seemed, which didn't matter because *seeming* was the substance of royal style. Perhaps unexpectedly, Bertie was to make his mark on the monarchy as the apotheosis of appearances. He loved showing off the 'attributes of sovereignty' and it was therefore 'entirely characteristic that one of Edward's earliest acts as king was to revive the state opening of parliament as a full-dress ceremonial occasion' including the presentation of his speech from the throne, a spectacle not seen for 40 years. (Cannadine, 1983, p136) David Cannadine has argued that for 30 years before the coronation of Edward VII, more and more elaborate ceremonials were becoming part of the technology of power to enhance statehood. Elsewhere 'this efflorescence of ceremonial' focused on heads of state with *real* power, but only in England 'while the ceremonial shadow of power was cast over the monarch, the substance increasingly lay elsewhere'. The monarchy's love of ceremony demonstrated the glorification of appearance over substance. In little more than a decade, half a dozen coronations and funerals, and a burgeoning culture of civic ceremonial in the regions which gave redundant or bankrupt aristocrats something to do, refined a national language of symbols. Old and new institutions 'were clothed with all the anachronistic allure of archaic but invented spectacle'. (p138)

Edward proved to be the perfect player. He had been a stickler for protocol, a martyr to empty excess and princely pointlessness, and so by the time he inherited the throne he had had a lifetime of practice. He brought enthusiasm and flair for the *rituals* of royalty to his kingship, which made him more than a roué, rescued his reputation, and redeemed royalism as pageant.

The Abdicator

Like all Princes of Wales, David, the future Edward VIII, endured a brutalised, bullying boyhood; he was unloved by his father, George V. He was invested as Prince of Wales in 1911 when he was 17 years old, dressed in a madly medieval confection to celebrate a palpably precarious union – designated 'Ukania' in Tom Nairn's marvellous republican polemic *The Enchanted Glass*.

Britain was re-inventing itself, new political conflicts and coalitions were emerging between classes, regions, races and genders. Already working-class advocates had been elected to Parliament for their own party, the Labour Party. Despite their electoral landslide in 1906, the Liberals were bleeding support over their eternal failure to address women's suffrage and Home Rule for Ireland. Lloyd George's 1909 budget – the People's Budget – was pledged to 'wage implacable warfare against poverty'. The peers regarded the budget as nothing short of socialism and during the summer the Chancellor threw a warning at the land-owning peerage. In a speech made in London's Limehouse in July he urged that they submit and share the cost of social welfare or the people would 'reconsider the conditions' of their land ownership. By the autumn the budget crisis rolled on and encouraged Lloyd George to challenge the aristocracy again, in a speech in Newcastle-upon-Tyne:

> The question will be asked whether five hundred men, ordinary men chosen from among the unemployed, should override the judgement – the deliberate judgement – of millions of people who are engaged in the industry which makes the wealth of this country. That is one question. Another will be: who ordained that a few should have the land of Britain as a prerequisite? Who made ten thousand people the owners of the soil, and the rest of us trespassers in the land of our birth?

The answers to his questions were, he added, 'charged with peril for the order of things the peers represent'. (Pugh, 1988, p50)

The aristocracy was again testing the limits of its political power. The royal family and the new king, who was crowned in 1910, listened hard and shivered. No parliamentary leader had talked like this for nearly 30 years. Having once chilled the royal family and chided the peerage, he changed his position and now decided the time was ripe for an orgy of improvised ceremony to cement royalism as the courier of continuity. Lloyd George, the Caernarvon MP and former Home Ruler, was settled far, far away from Wales in Westminster – a majestic radical now in service to the elite. He embodied his country's crisis of identity, always 'referential and deferential', struggling for and against Welsh sensibilities mired in puritanism; literate and poetic in their polemics. He typified the humiliating but rewarding fate of those Welsh and Scots parliamentarians who from their 'half-foreign periphery simply furnished a more acute, Faustian awareness of certain realities fogged over by metropolitan complacency'. (Nairn, 1994, p220) Nairn locates the tragedy and triumph of Lloyd George in the crisis of a state with 'no democratic-popular identity' in which 'democratic-popular individuals end by learning to trade their souls for power', which is why 'semi-outsiders can so easily turn into the ablest and most odious servants of any Establishment'. (Nairn, 1994, p221)

The royal family never forgot his assault on inherited privilege, but they were reassured and roused by his proposal that the royal family and the Welsh people would be captivated by an investiture. Lloyd George himself coached the young Prince in speaking some sentences in Welsh – something that still invited punishment in Welsh schools. One of these sentences, the Prince recalled, was 'Mor o gan yw Cymu i gyd' 'All Wales is a sea of song.' (Nairn, 1994, p221) Such happy natives!

The Prince was to be invested at Caernarvon Castle. Although, like other royal men, he loved dressing up, he protested when he was sent for a fitting for a new costume of white satin breeches and a robe of purple velvet and ermine, 'a preposterous rig'. His mother, Mary, the 'decisive vector' of royal manners, insisted that his friends would understand how he, being a prince, might have to do things that 'may seem a little silly'. At Caernarvon Castle his father, George V, placed on his head a 'coronet cap' and led him towards the battlements, where he was presented to the people of Wales. 'The dear boy did it all remarkably well, and looked so nice,' his father wrote in his diary; virtually the only compliment George bestowed on his eldest son during their long 'acquaintance'. (Tomlinson, 1994, p74)

David claimed that although he would submit to pomp, he recoiled from his position as a person deserving homage. He appeared to mean it when, in the early 1930s, he met impoverished steelworkers in the Welsh valleys and announced, 'Something must be done to find them work.' This 'something must be done' speech is often invoked in his defence, implying a concerned and compassionate commitment to his people. Anthony Holden reminds us, however, that by then he was already King Edward VIII, 'privately aware that his abdication was likely in a few weeks. So his words were deeply hypocritical. But they were also unconstitutional.' He was only the king, after all. For Holden 'such royal concern for social conditions have in recent history been little more than well meaning *en passant* gestures'. (1989, p181)

Despite his protestations about pomp, the Prince of Wales loved the life and the access it gave him to lots of women. He particularly loved the shelter of married women. Lady Thelma Furness was his lover and the woman his playmates blamed for the 'modernisation' of the Prince, making him a tad too democratic, 'casual and a little common'. It was Furness who introduced the Prince to Wallis Simpson, a twice married rich American with whom he fell in love.

In 1936 the crunch came when David's father died and he became Edward VIII. During the summer he cruised around the Dalmatian coast with Wallis Simpson. He was photographed canoodling by the European press, although the pictures never appeared in the British media. Panicky rumour raged around the Establishment and some of his friends quarried their circle for an alternative candidate for queen. In the winter he finally told his mother that he intended to marry Wallis. She was distraught but determined: he must do his duty and Wallis must go. The prime minister, Stanley Baldwin, was unequivocal and announced the King's abdication to parliament in December. David later explained that what was at stake was not a choice between love and duty, but a 'different concept of kingship'. He had married for love, 'but I abdicated because I chose the path of duty'. He had surrendered the crown, he said, 'rather than risk any impairment of its prestige'. (Tomlinson, 1994, p78) This, of course, was pious, but he was making a point about love, women and kingship that was erased by his later life as a useless aristocrat, a kept man paid off by the public purse, who lent his connections and his class to a dangerous liaison with Hitler.

'Uncle David', later the Duke of Windsor, had carried on the long and dishonourable tradition of princely pointlessness and philandering. But he concentrated the mind when he revealed the emptiness of his destiny – by repudiating that destiny. Impaled between love and duty, he insisted that love *was* his duty.

A Worried Man

Towards the end of the 1970s Charles' great-uncle Louis Mountbatten was a worried man. His protégé was fast becoming a typical Prince of Wales – a playboy prince (Dimbleby, 1994, p317). The time had come, he thought, to find a 'suitable girl'. He chided Charles and reminded him to beware of the ghost of 'Uncle David' and in doing so concentrated Charles' mind on the 'impossible' coupling of love and duty. It is surprising that such an obsessive genealogist should forget the equally explosive nature of duty without love. The political tumult provoked by the marriage of George and Caroline of Brunswick should have been warning enough.

In 1969 all of Wales was wondering whether the investiture of Charles at Caernarvon Castle would be bombed. When the ceremony was first conceived, Wales was not yet seething. But by the late 1960s Wales was being invigorated by cultural and political radicalisms, and riveted, fascinated and appalled, by sects of bombers and flame-throwers. As in the days of 'Uncle David', issues of sex, nationality and democracy were once more under scrutiny.

Since the spectacle was all about *seeing* the Prince of Wales, the show had been designed to maximise visibility. Designed by Lord Snowdon, (described by Tom Nairn as a 'vexing novelty', an arty working commoner married to Elizabeth's sister Margaret Rose), the ceremony mixed and matched the ancient and modern. The act of investiture itself was to take place under a Perspex canopy. Visibility meant vulnerability, however. Already Prince Charles was an unwelcome visitor to the 'principality'. When he arrived for a term at Aberystwyth University before the investiture, he was confronted by a student protest and placards he couldn't read: they were in Welsh.

The royals were worried about bombs and while Charles' audience was waiting, Lord Snowdon paced restlessly, guarding his set. Then the audience heard the sound of explosives. The talk travelling through the crowd was that there had indeed been a bomb. Two young men had blown themselves up while trying to hit the royal train. To this day their deaths are commemorated by masked military nationalists at their graveside in north Wales.

A section of the audience was drawn from schools. One of the pupils, Judith Jones, recalled:

> Many of us didn't want to be there. We felt a mixture of disinterest, hatred of the royal family, and shame. Shame

at being participants.When we realised there had been an explosion we became quite excited and wondered whether someone really could pull it off – blowing *them* up. I remember thinking that once they came into the castle the royals would have to assume that the thousand or so people inside were not going to hurt them. It was a completely confident thing to do. The newspapers said later that the Queen looked terrified.

When the audience had to sing 'God Bless the Prince of Wales', the young people didn't sing, we felt terrible. The feelings that I had then were of a bilingual, Anglo-Welsh person, but not a nationalist, the feelings were of our humiliation.

Charles addressed his audience in Welsh, a language he would never speak except as a performance. The British press congratulated him on his respectable effort, but to the Welsh speakers the very sound was a stab. I felt sick, because it had an English accent. In any case everybody at the ceremony spoke English, so why did he need to speak Welsh? This was a time when Welsh-speaking people still had to go to a court of law and have their case heard in English. At school we were coached to speak the English of Prince Charles.

The investiture was a warning. Wales was rediscovering itself. Within a couple of decades the political devolution that had been so scorned by both Labour and Tory politicians at Westminster was finally to be delivered. Charles might have been a man for all these seasons. But he wasn't. His presentation as a progressive Prince of Wales did not extend to his principality. His reputation in the 1980s as 'forward-thinking' worked only when set against the British government's rush to the right at the time. This was after Charles emerged from his playboy period, got married and got serious.

Only a year before the investiture, the House of Windsor had first allowed television cameras on to its domestic stage. The people had not been allowed to see the sacred moment of Elizabeth's coronation but they were now allowed to observe the private life of the most public family. Millions watched, relieved by the evidence that they were, after all, virtually human. The Windsors seemed to exemplify the model of modern monarchy as a 'royal family' which had been prefigured by George III (despite the ruinous behaviour of his son). Linda Colley has argued that it was George III, above all, who branded the monarchy's formula for nationhood, 'patriotic significance and a peculiar brand of subjugation'. The lesson of George III's reign had been to ride tribulation, ranging from revolution to a delinquent Prince of Wales, with this successful strategy: be seen to be splendid, but above all be seen; feminise the court, or rather display domesticity; engage the subjugated peoples by visiting the dominions. George's bequest to the Windsors was 'ritual splendour, an appearance of domesticity, and ubiquity'. (Colley, 1992, p236) This was the mantle bequeathed to Charles as he took his turn in the waiting game. Would he perform as a Prince of Wales or as a splendid, ubiquitous and domestic monarch?

2. The Domestication of Royalty

The reign of Queen Elizabeth II is a paradox: a woman presiding over a patriarchal order, organised by primogeniture, the most atavistic aristocratic mechanism to secure masculine power. That is the conundrum they, and we, have to sort out. Only after the death of Diana did Elizabeth embrace reform. In February 1998, in response to a massive public-relations operation on behalf of the monarchy, she declared herself in favour of the eldest child being the heir – whether male or female.

The crux of Charles' crisis as the heir to the throne lies in the monarchy's patriarchal tradition. Its culture produced a prince who behaved as a sovereign when his 'subjects' – including his wife – expected that he would want to behave like a modern man: someone who could take responsibility, take care of his loved ones and who could co-operate. The Prince emerged only as the modern incarnation of his dynasty's patriarchal mission.

Patriarchy has defined the European aristocracy for a thousand years. It is not eternal, it breached older networks of kinship in which women were not so bereft of property or esteem, and now it is a system under siege from women and children all over the world. The patriarchal system not only privileged men before women and children, it also institutionalised aristocratic men's distance from their children.

During their long tenures of the throne, neither Victoria nor Elizabeth disturbed the ancient rites of patriarchy embedded in the aristocracy. Without a care to their own fortuitous arrival on the throne, neither of these women seems to have been troubled by the system's oppression of their own mothers, daughters and sisters, the women of their kin or class. Indeed they seem to have quietly sanctioned the patriarchal practices of their sons. Elizabeth appears to have endorsed behaviour by her son which is scarcely sanctioned, in public at least, by any other class of white Anglo-Saxon Protestants.

Elizabeth and her family have perpetuated a sexual system that has lost its national mandate and now threatens the popularity, if not the stability, of the constitutional monarchy. She failed to feminise the monarchy. She failed to monitor monarchical rites, whether personal or public, with the egalitarian eye of her own gender; the gender which is pioneering great movements to reform relationships, to democratise the distribution of resources and respect between men, women and children. Instead Elizabeth gave her feminine authority to the rights of men fashioned in separatist and supremacist ideologies and institutions, in the militarisation of the royal household's administration and in the making of royal men. The cultural and political history of patriarchy is currently embodied to excess by the monarchy.

Phillip Hall's exhaustive study of the royal household and its finances, *Royal Fortune*, concludes that 'the supposedly modernized monarchy of Elizabeth II can be compared to her great-great-grandmother, Queen Victoria', for its conservative characteristics. At the beginning of the 1990s, after a reign spanning four decades, she had not made 'a significant black or Asian appointment'. Her record on gender was no better. 'That the queen discriminates on grounds of sex is obvious,' says Hall, 'there has never been a woman in the most influential of all the jobs at court.' Despite the existence of laws proscribing race and sex discrimination since the 1970s, the crown has remained exempt.

There is another sense in which Elizabeth failed to feminise the monarchy. Although her gender brought the fragrance of femininity to her reign, this new aura was no more than an appearance. It did not translate into effective change. She was always as estranged from everyday life – managed everywhere by women, the poorest people on the planet – as she was from her own gender. Her power made her exceptional. Like her contemporary Margaret Thatcher, she did not use that power to empower other women. With unprecedented élan and surgical skill, Thatcher improvised a regressive, patriarchal political project during the second wave of twentieth-century feminism. Like Elizabeth, she knew what she was doing. Of course, that did not make these women into men, nor even like men, but their reigns revealed that femininity, like masculinity, is not so much an identity as an idea, a production of culture. For both Margaret Thatcher and Elizabeth, femininity is what they wear and masculinity is what they admire. That made both of these women more than men: women who wear frocks and go to war.

Elizabeth was produced by, and then reproduced, a patriarchal system. She presided over encounters in which every act – the flick of a finger, eyes cast down or aside, who spoke, who sat, who was silent – enunciated the public power of the monarch. She emptied herself of the activities that evoked her own gender. Elizabeth began her reign resolving to reproduce her father's modus operandi. The Queen ruled like a king.

Her alienation from the world inhabited by other women was effected by her family's cult of sovereignty. The evidence lay in the little things. When she arrived from Kenya after the death of her father she was greeted by Queen

Mary, 'an expert on the niceties of royal protocol', who made formal obeisance to the new queen. For years, when the ladies left the men in the dining rooms of the palaces, Mary had always curtseyed to her son, the king. The dead king had left a grieving widow and two daughters. Elizabeth was the eldest daughter and heir. Her destiny was decided: 'I have a job,' she wrote at the time. But the future for her sister and her mother seemed empty, aimless and 'blank'. (Bradford, 1997, p169) Worse than blank – they were all Elizabeth's subordinates now. The widowed queen was bereft and furious: her daughter 'had suddenly become the focus of all the attention and the possessor of the power that had recently been hers'. (p170) The new queen was kind and accommodating towards her mother, but the interpersonal difficulties of royal decorum merely revealed their political importance. At this point in the twentieth century, her sister's prospects – in a profitable royal alliance – were diminished by the drastic decline in Europe's marriagable monarchies. Elizabeth dropped her children's duty to bow and curtsey when they met her; 'the relaxation did not extend, however, to Queen Mary or Princess Margaret, who formally curtseyed to their daughter and sister when they met her in company'. (Pimlott, 1997, p187)

A Poor Prince

With the accession of his nephew's wife, Louis Mountbatten proudly confided to friends that 'the House of Mountbatten now reigned'. (Bradford, 1996, p176) The ageing Mary, Winston Churchill and the cabinet thought otherwise and, provoked by Mountbatten's presumption, hastily urged that Elizabeth and her descendants should continue to bear *her* family name of Windsor. Philip was enraged. There were rows. But Elizabeth made a declaration to the Privy Council confirming that Windsor it would be. Philip 'felt robbed of his identity and he was, perhaps, disconcerted by Elizabeth's new-found ease and self-confidence'. (Bradford, 1997, p178) Now she had the power that only men possessed. Sovereignty saved her from the universal status of her sex.

Elizabeth's husband also became her subordinate subject. The royal couple struggled over his status – his personal power as a man was overwhelmed by her public power as a monarch. They fought over the space between them in their public perambulations, his name, their name, their children's names. To his chagrin he was not allowed to pass on his name to his children, not just because his wife was queen but more importantly because the reactionary affiliations of his Greek and German relatives made the government determined to erase his people's past from the royal family's future. Such was the compromise the postwar constitutional monarchy had to make with its people. Philip was not reconciled to the new name, the House of Windsor, and by the end of the decade appeared to have influenced, if not yet persuaded, Elizabeth. When their daughter married, Philip's name, Mountbatten, appeared with Windsor on her marriage certificate. (p286)

Philip was a poor prince; he brought neither land nor wealth to the union. But he had royal relatives, and he had his beautiful body, and in an era starved of royal candidates to marry the heir to the throne, that had been enough. Elizabeth would have his body but not his name. The poor prince felt unmanned. Now he knew what princesses felt like.

Philip, according to Elizabeth's biographer Sarah Bradford, was 'the first and principal casualty of Elizabeth's accession to her father's throne and to the traditions which he represented'. He and his children had to leave their home in Clarence House and move into Buckingham Palace. He had to quit his job in the Navy and he had to walk one pace behind his wife. The consort's throne, which had been used by his mother-in-law at the state opening of Parliament, was sent for storage in the belief that a male consort could only be given a 'chair of state' *below* the sovereign's canopy. (Bradford, 1997, p179) A family that lived by protocol died by it, too. Everyone around Elizabeth felt put out. What were they, after all, without their privileges? And what was Elizabeth's commitment to hierarchy, telling her family about who and what was important? These gestures were everything and nothing, too trivial and yet too important to revise.

Elizabeth also preserved her exclusive access to political power. Unlike Victoria, she did not defer to her husband in matters of state. 'Elizabeth had no intention of involving him in her official business as ruler.' (p176) She would operate just as her father had, with access to state papers and reports of Cabinet meetings and parliamentary proceedings supplemented by a weekly interview with the Prime Minister. This was an audacious assertion of authority, a determination that she would compromise her inherited integrity for no man. It was also a daughter's deference to her dead father's authoritarianism – she was only doing what her father had done. There is a view that Elizabeth compromised with her husband and, while reserving the work of sovereignty for herself, gave him the power within the family realm. Philip 'may have to walk a pace behind her in public, play a merely walk-on role on such occasions as the state opening of parliament, but in matters domestic Elizabeth has always acknowledged her husband as head of the family'. (Holden, 1989, p61)

But their family life was not concerned with the *labours* that produce affinity. Elizabeth's history in a secluded community of aristocrats hardly trained her in the art of imaginative interpersonal negotiation. She didn't perform the labours of love that routinely create domestic intimacy and responsibility. She was not schooled in the management of the inflammatory and unpredictable events of everyday domestic life. She was good at being dutiful and royal. She was nothing if not her father's daughter. Her domestic deference to Philip had more to do with her ignorance than a modern commitment to compromise and co-operation.

Philip was in a unique position; he was simultaneously powerful and powerless. A century earlier, Victoria's husband Albert had found himself in the same dilemma. Albert's formal status as Victoria's consort gave him access to her public power, and in their private life he reinterpreted the role of the patriarch by being a present and active parent, rather than being authoritative but absent. For both men, masculinity was at stake. No queen consort was caught in that matrix of impotence and authority, but for both these men masculinity could not be conceived outside the discourse of power. Both were cast in a contradictory and contingent relation to it. They gained access to public or political power by their proximity to the queen. Yet as spouses to the sovereign, their status was apparently subordinate. Both men redeemed their reputations as men in the *personal* realm of their relationships with their wives.

After complaining, 'I'm nothing but an amoeba', Philip invented himself in the image of countryman and corporate man, cleverly uniting the identity and interests of aristocratic thrill-seeker and industrious, middle-class innovator. The distinction between the two cultures is elegantly explained by Catherine Hall and Leonore Davidoff in their history of the middle class. Managerial skills, regarded as quintessentially masculine, were critical to 'the middle class challenge to the aristocratic male whose skills lay with gambling, duelling, sporting and sexual prowess. The accomplishments of middle class men were primarily sedentary and literate, the manipulation of the pen and the ruler rather than the sword or the gun.' (Davidoff and Hall, 1987, p205)

Philip became an ambassador for British business, a patron of science and sport, and of the countryside. His bad manners and saloon-bar racism became notorious, but only confirmed that he was a 'man's man' and therefore his own man. His reputation for being 'prickly and boorish' added an appropriate aura to his emergence as a prominent public figure in his own right. His public persona was 'a mark of unusual tenacity'. (Dimbleby, 1995, p62)

These traits were also characteristic of Philip the private 'family man'. Elizabeth gave him his place as the head of the family and if he was the boss of nothing else, he was the boss of his children. Since their mother was a distracted, defended person unschooled in domestic detail, unused to making relationships, and unpractised in the labours of love, Philip was perceived to be the more active parent. He changed the royal menus. He selected schools. He was neither an entrepreneur nor a land-owner but acquired responsibility for the royal estates and saw himself as custodian of family firm and field.

Gender mediated the supreme status of Elizabeth and Victoria as women, no less than their restless 'unmanned' consorts. As *married* women both abrogated intimate authority to their men. As sovereigns in the public domain their power was also contingent because they were *constitutional* monarchs. Members of Parliament might have to take an oath of obedience to these women, but as sovereigns their relationship to their prime ministers affirmed both the extent and the limits of their royal prerogative.

Ben Pimlott argues that Prime Minister Harold Macmillan's 'feline' intuition stretched these limits and mobilised the notion of a 'modernised monarchy' to support the renewal of popular conservatism in the 1950s: if the monarchy's *effective* power was declining, in the new age its subliminal *influence* flourished. (Pimlott, 1997, p273) He engineered with Elizabeth the enhancement of royal ceremony in popular culture. His parliamentary flattery and flirtation shielded the monarchy from the seismic shifts in civil society. Elizabeth's traditionalism and formality worked, too, to adorn the patrician politician with the sovereign's favour. Her gender brought not radicalism, but a conservative feminine endorsement to a patriarchal project.

3. Parenting by Proxy

Unlike the House of Spencer, whose dynasty stretched back to the sixteenth century, the House of Windsor was 'a fantasy. The figment of a courtier's imagination. The dynasty was created in 1917 to conceal the German roots of the King and Queen'. (Kelley, 1997, p5) The survival of the monarchy's reputation through the twentieth century's great wars depended not only on a plentiful supply of heirs but on a new name that would efface its German ancestry and rewrite its roots as indelibly English. The process began during World War I and was completed after World War II when the Windsors emerged, English, 'so English that by the end of World War II, the dynasty designed by dodgery was never more popular'. (p57)

Marriages, births and deaths were all mobilised to make the royal family as 'English' as possible, beginning with Elizabeth's marriage to a displaced prince who had some unfortunate relatives. The Windsors' popularity flowered again when Elizabeth gave birth to a boy in 1948. 'Our ancient monarchy renders inestimable services to our country and to all the British Empire and Commonwealth of Nations,' declared Winston Churchill to the House of Commons on 16 November when he welcomed the newborn 'little Prince' whose purpose was to support the future of the family that 'presides ancient, calm and supreme within its functions'. (Dimbleby, 1995, p4) According to Charles' biographer Anthony Holden, that purpose placed him in a paradox: how to find himself and yet honour his potential as 'heir to the loftiest position on earth still determined by heredity'. His was a 'claustrophobic, if comfortable life of inherited imprisonment'. (Holden, 1989, p11) Royal protocol, and the display of power that it prescribed, defined the priorities and possibilities not only of his public persona, but of the domestic details of his daily life.

The little boy began his day at 7.00 a.m. Two hours later he was taken to a 30-minute audience with his mother. His father was a naval officer and therefore absent. Charles didn't usually see his mother again until the end of his day. 'She liked to bath the children herself whenever her schedule permitted', which meant 'only sporadically, and unpredictably'. (Holden, 1989, p68) These bathtimes lived in the child's memory as virtual domesticity, approximations of affection rather than the real thing. Years later he said he could not remember one incident of maternal love from his childhood, except for an evening when his mother came to the nursery before his evening bath. She sat on a gilt chair with a footman behind her and watched his nanny bathe him. 'She didn't put her hands in the bathwater,' Charles recalled, 'but at least she watched.' (Dimbleby, 1994, p18)

The little boy bowed before kissing his great-grandmother Mary, and knew not to sit down unbidden by his grandfather, the king. Elizabeth abolished these ceremonies of subordination towards herself, although his grandmother's loss of power in her widowhood was scrupulously mitigated by her daughter, and under orders from his parents Charles continued to bow before leaving his grandmother's company.

Just before Charles' first birthday Philip was posted to Malta with the Mediterranean flotilla and a week after the birthday, Elizabeth joined Philip for a month of play and partying, surrounded by naval officers, other dukes and a social life orchestrated by Louis Mountbatten. The former Viceroy of India was with the Mediterranean fleet, which was then regarded as one of the most powerful afloat. (Bradford, 1997, p156) Mountbatten was later beloved by Charles, who treasured the man's attention as a surrogate grandfather, and Mountbatten, for his part, relished his role as a great-uncle and model of manliness. Mountbatten introduced Philip to the extravagant pleasures of polo and indulged in what might now be described as sexual harassment; 'he'd always rather do something under the table than above,' one of the ladies was warned by Mountbatten's former chief of staff. (Bradford, 1997, p158)

In Malta Elizabeth lived the life of a naval wife, though not a naval mother. 'She was happy and pregnant, apparently not missing her son.' (Bradford, 1997, p158) She returned briefly to Britain at the end of December – but even then she did not find it necessary to rush back to him. She spent a few days dealing with correspondence and then went to the races. (Pimlott, 1997, p162) From March until May she was back in Malta before returning to England to prepare for the birth of her second baby, Anne, who was born in August 1950. Charles' father and his baby sister arrived almost simultaneously. Suddenly the little boy's life was crowded with a family he hardly knew.

It wasn't crowded for long, however. A few weeks later Charles' father left for Malta, where he had been promoted to take command of his own ship. He was joined in December by Elizabeth, who enjoyed the sun, sea and perpetual parties, leaving behind her Charles, who again spent Christmas with his grandparents, cold weather, rationing and the frigid court. Elizabeth was accompanied by her maid, footman and detective, and 'her sports car, forty wardrobe trunks, and a new polo pony for her husband'. (Kelley, 1997, p91) Between dining and dancing, picnics and seaside jaunts, she visited an under-fives club for naval children, Malta's press reported, though without raising the question of why she, unlike other military mothers, had left her own children, under the age of five, in England'. (Kelley, 1997, p92) Malta was a redoubt where the living was easy and the partying excessive, hardly a reluctant posting for a long-suffering services wife coming from a society still struggling with postwar austerity and reconstruction.

In the spring Charles' parents visited Rome and returned to Britain in July, when Philip left Malta for good. King George VI was ailing and in October 1951 Charles' parents set off for an official tour of Canada. An apprentice monarch, his mother again missed her son's birthday. After a brief Christmas reunion, his parents undertook a long-postponed tour of the Commonwealth on behalf of the King. Elizabeth knew by then that her father was dying and that soon she would be queen. After the King died on 5 February 1952, when Elizabeth was in Kenya, 'the mother had even less time to spend with her children'. (Dimbleby, 1995, p21) Charles became heir apparent at three years old. 'Prince Charles was now the Duke of Cornwall, Duke of Rothesay, Earl of Carrick and Baron of Renfrew, Lord of the Isles and Great Steward of Scotland. "That's me, Mummy", he was heard to whisper when the Duke of Cornwall's name was mentioned in church among the prayers for the royal family.' (Holden, 1989, p70) For the first time since his son had been born four years earlier, Philip was present at Charles' birthday.

The coronation in June 1953 meant that the bewildered boy's 'parents would be going away yet again – this time for much longer than before'. (Holden, 1989, p74) Although his fifth birthday took place shortly before Philip and Elizabeth would be leaving for her first great Commonwealth journey as monarch, there was no special celebration; indeed, his parents weren't even present. They stayed at Sandringham, leaving 'the crestfallen boy' at Windsor. The tour was to last six months. It inaugurated a remarkable transition for a young woman who, until her marriage, had led a sequestered life in a closed and complacent community. With her new role as the head of the Commonwealth 'she was to be the most travelled British monarch in history and possibly the most travelled head of state in any age.' (Bradford, 1997, p217)

The eventual family reunion was a cruel lesson in royal protocol for Elizabeth's children. They were brought on to the newly commissioned royal yacht *Britannia* to meet their parents at Tobruk, Libya. This was their first adventure abroad. The media was bewitched by the spectacle of the royal children being reunited with their parents. As the Queen came aboard, according to the biographer Sarah Bradford, 'the family greetings in the true Windsor tradition were formal in public, a handshake from Charles for his mother and 'no hugs until they were in private'. (p217) Charles' biographer Anthony Holden gives more devastating detail; 'it was only with difficulty that Charles was restrained from joining the line of dignitaries waiting to shake hands with the Queen, as she was piped aboard. "No, not you, dear," were mother's first words to son after their six months apart.' (pp74–5)

Over the decades the royal parents have been excused as suffering from royal restraint and imperial duty. But what has been represented as reserve was something else: it was a *choice*. Their quarantined son was parented by other people; surrogates with whom the child enjoyed, according to his biographer Jonathan Dimbleby, 'bonds of affection' that were at least as powerful as those between the child and his parents. And between grandmother and grandson a fondness flowered which would later develop into the 'most intimate of the prince's relationships within the family'. (Dimbleby, 1995, p18) This might have been unusual for the time, but it was typical of the history of their class. The patriarchal system institutionalised the aristocracy's distance from their children. According to Lloyd de Mause, the historian of childhood subjectivity, until the eighteenth century the sons of wealthy Europeans were typically sent to wet nurses, cared for by servants, and later sent away again for their schooling. 'The amount of time parents of means actually spent raising their children was minimal. The effects of these and other institutionalised abandonments by parents on the child have rarely been discussed.' (Lloyd de Mause, 1991, p32) Unlike other classes in Britain, 'parents of means' and aristocratic parents perpetuated the practice of institutionalised abandonment right until the end of the twentieth century.

It was during the journey home from the great absence that Elizabeth decided *not* that it was time to get to know her son, but 'that it was time for her son's education to begin in earnest'. (Holden, 1989, p76) It began in his nursery, with a governess. Charles' early childhood was very like his mother's but unlike most of his contemporaries – for a boy to be taught 'by a governess instead of going to a nursery school was very unusual.' (Bradford, 1997, p278) But at least the governess, Catherine Peebles, *noticed* the little boy's presentation as a nervous, polite, often distracted child, 'a fragile ego whose confidence was easily shattered'. (Dimbleby, 1995, p25) A raised voice produced his humiliated retreat; 'he would draw back into his shell and for a time you would be able to do nothing with him,' recalled Peebles, one of the few adults to think that this child was in trouble. Already, one of the most privileged children in Britain was emerging as polite, frightened, subdued and sad. In another class, in another time, all of these signs would be read by child care professionals as worrying symptoms of confusion, appeasement and pessimism, signs of a defeated child.

Charles was already learning who was important to his parents: it was not the prince as a person, it was the prince as a function, a future for the royal family. His tragedy, as a child, was that he existed for his parents, rather than they for him. It was his purpose as a prince to service and sustain their interests. The prince was a projection of his parents and their primary interest: the preservation of the hereditary power of their friends and relations in the century of revolution and regicide, democracy and equality organised by the industrious working and middle classes.

At the end of this century it is still commonplace to hear politicians discuss children only as *potential* people, as subjects to be patrolled, trained and disciplined. But that rhetoric is a response to the reform of relations between adults and children. The reaction is evident in the distinction within debates about parenting between forms of parenthood which use children to project the drama of adults' ambitions and their own conscious and un-conscious, and parenthood which empathises with the child's needs and seeks to satisfy them.

In the 1990s it has become conventional wisdom to complain that the Windsors are a dysfunctional family ruled by absent parents. But these are not parents who didn't know any better. From the perspective of another class living through the same era, Charles' problem seemed *not* to be that of a child with a busy mother or absent father, but of a child whose passionate attachment was with a servant while his most precarious attachments were with his only social equals, his parents. The parental strategies of the royal family exemplified the politics of the patriarchal family.

Back in the 1950s Winston Churchill proclaimed a new 'Elizabethan age', crowning postwar propaganda about femininity and the reinstatement of domesticity as women's destiny. Elizabeth's marriage and mothering were, therefore, translated into the misty homilies of family life that were mobilised to reconstitute a national idiom of continuity and consensus. She was the mother of her own family and the 'family' of the Commonwealth.

This era has been represented as the great regression,

when women were dispatched back to the kitchen sink and the waged labour market was restored to its rightful owners: men. But feminist scholars have shown that something more complicated – and contested – characterised the 1950s. Women were not universally forced to withdraw from the world of waged work; indeed, they were being recruited to the new industries and services of the postwar economy. But the postwar Labour government was the agent of a modernised patriarchal settlement. If women were to enter the public economy, this was to happen with the minimum of disturbance to men's privileged place in both the public and the private sphere, and at no cost to the public purse.

Then, as now, Labour recoiled from any challenge to the patriarchal model of masculinity, or to the institutions or ideologies inscribed in its image. The two emblems of the Labour government's protection of a patriarchal political economy were its mass closure of public nurseries – child care was Labour's first target for privatisation – and its refusal to implement the 1944 Royal Commission on equal pay; a scandal that provoked a mutiny by the young Blackburn MP Barbara Castle, one of the great figures of postwar parliamentary politics. Women's relationship to their children, their men and their jobs, was the subject of a great debate within civil society, if not the state. Labour and then the Conservative government encouraged the employment of family women but they were only to be offered 'pin money' and no partnership in parenting. Like them, the head of state was a working woman. But her family was an ex-empire, an abstraction. There were no noses or bottoms to be wiped.

Precisely because the royal family is in no sense private, its intimate life is lived amidst a household comprising hundreds. Its performance as a family has always been an intensely political project secured by personal dominion and the public display of dynastic prowess. The politics of the monarchy pervade not only national institutions but the heir's intimate encounters with people in a 'home' the size of a factory. The other people in Charles' life were polarised between supreme beings and servants. The palaces, the corridors and kitchens, nurseries and ballrooms, were places which whispered the secrets of sovereignty, of hierarchy disciplined by curtseys, criticism, queues, clothes and strange sentences, as if people were speaking in tongues. Elizabeth, like Victoria, handed to her husband and other people the work of preparing their progeny for power.

So, how are *we* to see this troubled boy? There is barely a tradition of ethnographic scholarship that has put the private life of the contemporary aristocracy and the culture of their child care under scrutiny. There are sympathetic – and often craven – chronicles, which constitute the main body of work on the royal family, and there is radical indifference. In between there are testimonies by the small but growing body of privileged people who are beginning to come out of the closet of their class. But the rest of us can scarcely extend our own experience in order to understand Charles and his environment – our experience can only ever be a negative measure of a life none of us live. We are left with scraps – the tactical recollections of the men and women who serviced his family, the cautious and screened memories of the man himself, the texts of biographers who range from the sycophantic to the critically sympathetic, all of them constrained by the contingencies of power and reputation, and all of them dependent on the subject himself, struggling with his own flaky self-respect, his fury, disappointment and pride.

'Mummy, What Are Schoolboys?'

When he was eight Charles went to a pre-preparatory school, Hill House, just behind Harrods in Kensington, founded by Colonel Henry Townend, an Oxford blue and

an athlete who had represented England. Having been
schooled alone, at home, Charles asked Elizabeth:
'Mummy, what are schoolboys?' (Bradford, 1997, p279) He
was delivered daily by the royal chauffeur, and the boys'
swimming lessons took place not at a public pool but at the
Buckingham Palace pool because it was thought inap-
propriate for the 'heir of the throne to use the public baths'.
This seclusion was not normal but 'it was inevitable'.
(Dimbleby, 1995, p32)

From Hill House Charles moved to Cheam preparatory
school run by more military chaps and their wives. Philip's
grandfather had decreed that all male Battenbergs be
enrolled at this establishment. What was good enough for
one prince was good enough for another. The school was
the child's entry into society. 'Children may be indulged at
home,' said his father, in a more or less veiled critique of
the female company which hitherto had surrounded
Charles' childhood, 'but school is expected to be a spartan
and disciplined experience in the process of developing into
self-controlled, considerate and independent adults.'
Elizabeth remembered her son 'shaking with horror' when
he left Balmoral for his first day at Cheam. (Holden, 1989
p92) 'It was not so much leaving home he dreaded, but his
destination,' comments Dimbleby (1995, p41). It was the
first rung on the ladder which represented the beginning of
the 'brutal rite of passage from childhood to adolescence of
every British boy whose parents could afford it – the
boarding school'. (Bradford,1997, p280) It was hard and he
was lonely at this boys' school where his best friend was a
girl, the headmaster's daughter.

From Cheam Charles went to Gordonstoun, again his
father's choice. It was not only a spartan but a sadistic
regime. Kurt Hahn created the school near Elgin in the
northeast of Scotland after he – as a Jew – was compelled to
leave Nazi Germany. It was, however, organised on
Teutonic principles, a school which encouraged a cult of
suffering and strenuous exercise, cold showers and rituals

of humiliation and hardiness. Gordonstoun exemplified
the cult of militarism and masculinism which dominated,
and disgraced, the country Hahn had been forced to flee.
The school's tradition expressed the heroic 'tendency
toward the utopia of the body machine'. This tendency was
fetishised as drill and discipline, as the 'man of steel' and
the 'glorious predator'. The notion of equality only
appeared in uniform obedience to the rules and bonding
between those who already belonged to the elite. This
'conservative utopia' prized the muscular mentality of men
trained, through pain, to 'subjugate and repulse what is
specifically human within them' – the unruly and
disordered faculty for feeling. (Theweleit, 1989, p162)

All this 'character-building' was, of course, predicated on
the production of masculinity unencumbered by the
presence of women, who were dreaded, deemed dangerous.
Hahn's project was to police the 'awakening sexual
proclivities among the pubescent teenagers' under his
charge. (Dimbleby, 1995, p80) This manly management of
boys' 'dangerous years' could be interpreted as the miso-
gynistic management of young men who had to be
screened and safeguarded from contamination by
femininity. The macho body fetishism which characterised
the school's prospectus was, in time, magnified by the boys
and masters. When Charles was incarcerated there, he was
terrorised by its coarse, sexist, tyrannical culture.

Throughout Charles' childhood his parents *appeared* to
break with royal tradition – by sending him to school,
instead of employing tutors, for example – only to
consolidate its most grandiose, elitist and exclusive traits.
Charles may have been the first heir to the throne to be
sent to school, but his parents selected exclusive
institutions that would protect the boy from the people. At
Gordonstoun he didn't enjoy enlightenment and equality.
Despite the school's 'rigorous educational code founded in
pacifism' (Holden, 1989, p105), Charles was beaten,
harassed and humiliated daily, for years. Contemporaries

describe the school as tribal, disciplined by the 'casual brutality' of masters and predatory pupils who created an atmosphere of 'genuine terror'. (Dimbleby, 1995, p73) The prince hated it and described Gordonstoun in letters home as 'absolute hell'. His lament was to no avail. His parents did not rescue him.

Charles' childhood has come to be understood as an existence lived at the extremes of institutionalised privilege, power and powerlessness. But this insight into his upbringing comes only with the benefit of both hindsight and the social wisdom of classes who have moved away from elitism in favour of equality and empathy. What was regarded in his own infancy as 'exclusive' and 'elite', many of us reared in a more egalitarian and, therefore, more humane universe regard as institutionalised intimidation.

Charles' education exemplified the effort invested in the making of masculinity. Writing about similar movements erected to mould boys and men – the Scouts, public schools, the Hitler Youth and the cadets – the Australian sociologist, Robert Connell notes that 'the striking thing about these movements was not their success, always limited, but the persistence with which ideologists of patriarchy struggled to control and direct the reproduction of masculinity. It is clear that this had become a significant problem in gender politics.' (1995, p195) So, a gender identity that has been represented as a force of nature, a genetic drive to dominate, is unmasked as a character cultivated and chiselled into the desire for dominance.

From Gordonstoun, Charles went to Trinity College, Cambridge, 'always preferring the old to the new wherever possible'. (Holden, 1989, p128). Cambridge was his big chance, however. Although a privileged college, this was the closest he was going to get to being *in* the society whose sovereign he expected to become. He was there during high times – students were changing their world, regenerating the peace movement, mobilising against the

US war in Vietnam, and challenging the curricular orthodoxies of the canon. Even if he felt estranged from the politics, he had the opportunity to be a participant or at least an observer.

Charles has been represented again as a lonely, bemused boy, but he was only experiencing that heart-stopping moment in every student's life when they arrive at college, a stranger, no friends, worrying perhaps about how to avoid pregnancy, arrest, getting done for dope, or failure. Charles, like other students, just had to hold his breath and jump in. But he didn't. Oxbridge educated and entertained those who were 'born to rule'. Charles might have been expected to feel comfortable with enough of his contemporaries. But far from enjoying university as an emancipating encounter with his own generation – the revolutionary generation whose intellectual impieties hosted the greatest tumult since the 1930s – he had only superficial contact with other students. He did see – as a spectator – the Garden House Riot when students demonstrated against the Greek colonels' junta. (Dimbleby, 1995, p136) One of the demonstrators was Robert Rowthorn, later professor of economics at Cambridge, who appeared in the subsequent Garden House trial arguing that the students, in their confrontation with the police, had not treated them as fascists nor as personal enemies, but rather as 'coming between us and our objectives'. Rowthorn described Cambridge in the late 1960s as a place of 'great ferment, very exciting, full of self-confidence'.

There were other European and Scandinavian royals at Oxbridge during the 1960s whose student experience was less entombed, and there were young upper-class women and men whose privilege, by contrast, produced a positive engagement in their own societies. Tariq Ali was such a person, the iconic student revolutionary, whose radicalism had already been ignited among his relatives in Pakistan. His parents were privileged and progressive. 'I mingled with aristocrats, communists, peasants, leading left-wing

poets and poor women organising *as women* – all of these
people were passing through our house,' he recalls. So,
totally posh, but his people had the confidence to
accommodate 'a totally different world view', says Ali,
'unlike the Continental ruling families this lot here had no
self-confidence at all.'

The court rendered Charles a displaced person once he
was outside the royal laager, and he lacked the confidence
to make his own way among his contemporaries,
unprotected by the *cordon sanitaire* of his royal clique. Far
from breeding independence, the elite boot camps had
produced a person who didn't know how the world worked.
He was counselled against attending any of the political
societies which were buzzing at Cambridge in the 1960s.
Indeed a hit list of 'sensitive' societies, including Amnesty
International and the Buddhist Society, was drawn up by
his college. Thus the Prince of Wales was exiled from the
cultural revolution created by his own generation. He was
often – to the irritation of Trinity Master R. A. Butler, one
of the great Conservative architects of the postwar
consensus – hauled away by the family for what Butler
irascibly described as 'balcony jobs': state ceremonies.
(Holden, 1989, p134)

Clearly, Charles was not being helped to enter the real
world, but he too fled from opportunities to engage as an
equal with his contemporaries. Charles preferred the
security of his hunting and shooting cronies to the
heterogenous college community. In a letter from Charles
to a land-owner friend with whom he went shooting, he
wrote that any excuse to escape from Cambridge and plod
across ploughed fields 'instead of stagnating in lecture
rooms is enormously welcome.' (Dimbleby, 1995, p135) He
got away at weekends to the reassuringly elite pastimes of
his class. The royal undergraduate found it exceptionally
difficult, comments Dimbleby, to reach out beyond the
safety of his own circle. During the winters of 1968 and
1969 the Prince regularly invited friends to join him at

Sandringham, where they could take part in impeccably
organised shoots. Charles 'was keener on the sport than
ever' and demonstrated 'the timing, grace and co-
ordination which – for the committed – can transform a
slaughter into a sport'. (Dimbleby, 1995 p135) Dimbleby's
biography, well written and well informed, ruminates
sympathetically on the apparent contradiction between the
'big shot' and the sensitive, shy boy, humbled by his
truculent father. Had Charles' passion been for the ball
games enjoyed by most men, the apparent contradiction
might have faded; it was the fact that his passions involved
death – death for the bird, for the fox, for the stag and for
the fish – which 'brought the apparent contradiction so
sharply into focus'. (Dimbleby, 1995, p135)

Training by Shooting

Hunting and shooting became the *mise en scène* of
Charles' making as a man. While connecting the royal
family to rusticity, land and the anti-urban fantasies
embedded in Englishness, the country estates became the
terrain of the royal seasons at precisely the time when the
landed aristocracy were losing land, when their wealth,
power and status were no longer based on territory, and the
'labour-intensive theatricality of aristocratic life has
virtually come to an end'. (Cannadine, 1990, p638)

Like Balmoral, another rustic folly built in the north of
Scotland by Victoria's consort Albert, Sandringham became
one of the theme parks where for a century monarchs
scored unseen by the prying masses. Here, too, royal
identities were shaped, genders and generations were made
– men striding with dogs and guns, women watching men,
and children waiting for adults.

When Charles was a boy, Sandringham was still a fixture
in the royal seasons. Men breakfasted in the dining room
while the women lay longer in bed, the shooters

assembling in the saloon waiting for their vehicles to take them around the secluded acres. Elizabeth would work on her papers or take her horse out for a ride while the other women lingered aimlessly until lunchtime when she emerged, ready to receive them. Then the women were driven off together to meet the men for lunch. After they had eaten, the heated silver containers were closed by the royal footmen and the women joined the men for the afternoon's sport, 'to watch and admire' before turning in from the cold to tea, 'a ritual from which the children were excluded'. (Dimbleby, 1995, p57) After tea the children were enlisted for jolly games before they were banished once again while the adults dressed for dinner.

These shooting parties were opportunities for the aristocratic community favoured by the House of Windsor to witness and indeed participate in the training of the heir to the throne.

Public pleasures, whether on the terraces peopled by working-class men, on John Major's village greens lubricated by warm beer, or in the royal killing fields, are never neutral. Sport, no less than sex or work or politics, maketh the man. The culture of sport is always a culture of class. The camaraderie of blood sports, and of Charles' other passion, polo, a wild and wildly expensive game of hockey on horses, played by toffs, completed the closure of his world. The economic resources required to sponsor the spectacles, their significance in the seasons of 'society', the performance of the players and the attendance of their audience, all wrapped the Prince in a shrinking community.

It was also a sexist culture of masculine performance and female spectatorship. Polo was as butch as boxing, but without the terrible tension of visceral, plebeian suffering and redemption. The contradiction to which Dimbleby alludes was, in the end, resolved by Charles himself – the shy boy became an excited participant in bloody sports which, towards the end of the century, became increasingly besieged by popular dissent. Despite his later rhetoric advocating spiritual reconciliation with 'nature', Charles located himself finally in the elite tradition of murderous manliness deemed by his forefathers to be the proper pursuit of kings.

4. The Mentors

Three old men wearing their brittle vanity on their ludicrously lovely uniforms, Philip, Louis Mountbatten and Laurens van der Post: these were the martinets whose mission was to model the masculinity of the heir to the throne.

Their intrusive intimacy presumed to frame Charles' identity as a lover, a thinker and a sovereign. They badgered, bullied, flattered and interfered in his sexual life, his grammar, his ideas, his manners. Truly, they were pedagogues in the classical sense of men who monitor youth; pedants who discipline and train. The manner of their pedagogy encouraged in Charles fear, awe and an abject subjectivity attracted to authority. The mentors' mission was narcissistic in so far as it constituted the troika themselves as *great men*. Their presence in Charles' life led him away from his own generation, leaving him a stranger to his own time. His own generation assailed authority *as authority*, as the power to enforce obedience, and in its wake it challenged the sovereignty of white men, as well as monarchs.

In the anti-feminist counter-revolution of the 1980s and 1990s, it became commonplace to invoke the ghost of the 'masculine role model'. This implied that young men could not discover how to be human without a praetorian phalanx to patrol their growing pains. It also proposed a single template of masculinity, as if to reassert its authority against the proliferation of masculinities burgeoning in the late twentieth century. So, the troika were self-proclaimed role models. They were dedicated misogynists. They loved women, they'd say, and they loved lording it.

Hello, Sailor

Friends of Philip were appalled by his 'very bullying' behaviour and rough reproaches which often brought the boy to tears. There was no one to protect him. Family friends were also frustrated by the failure of the child's mother to intervene by 'protective word or gesture'. She was not indifferent so much as 'detached', deciding that in domestic matters she would 'submit entirely to the father's will.' (Dimbleby, 1995, p59) Philip would regularly rebuke his subdued son and reproach him, belittle and terrify him. Prince Charles' biographer Jonathan Dimbleby notes that Charles balanced these horrors, often endured in public, watched by the family's aristocratic friends and his disconnected mother, with fond memories of his family shooting and fishing together, his parents showing 'a deep if inarticulate love for their son' and father teaching him to swim or make models. This, then, was father doing his best in the only way he knew 'to achieve his supreme objective – to mould a prince for kingship'. (p60) Whether or not he made the Prince fit to be a king – or indeed a man – he locked his tearful son into the traditions of the Prince of Wales, disastrous traditions to which Charles would cling as an adult.

Philip was a 'man's man', frightening, sporty, given to gadgetry and widgets, a man who loved a rollick and a good laugh with the lads. A man with a reputation. Unlike a

woman, a man must have a reputation; a real man doesn't
have to like women, but he does have to like *having* women.
When Elizabeth fell in love with Philip, her father was
worried by his reputation as a lover-boy, and he fretted about
Philip's fidelity. Philip and Elizabeth, according to Sarah
Bradford, have a long and active love life, in which he was
not expected to be faithful, only loyal. Philip and a couple of
his pals, known as the Three Cocketeers, were reputed to
take women to regular parties at his equerry's flat in London.
He was also a member of the Thursday Club which met at
Wheeler's in Soho's Old Compton Street, and which
included the *Daily Express* editor Arthur Christiansen, the
actor David Niven and the musician Larry Adler. Their
guests included the clever Tory politician Iain Macleod, the
spy Kim Philby and the society pimp Stephen Ward, whose
life was ruined in the aftermath of the Profumo sex-and-
state-secrets scandal. (Bradford, 1997, pp265–6)

Newspapers across the world reported a rift in the royal
marriage when Philip journeyed to the other end of the
world to open the 1956 Olympics, and stayed away from
Britain for four months, playing on the royal yacht
Britannia at public expense. 'Philip was escaping from the
Palace.' (p264) The trip had been planned with his old
shipmate Michael Parker, who was going through a
divorce at the time. The international press, unconstrained by the palace's successful censorship of the
British media, relished the rift story and reports of Philip's
romances en route. Landing at Gibraltar on their way
back, Parker was bounced out of the partnership – the
royal family could not countenance divorced men on its
payroll or in its company. (p265)

Philip's affairs abroad and the stag nights and days (with
exceptions made for 'actresses') could be kept in the closet,
but Philip's associations with women within the
aristocratic and upper-class communities, such women as
Princess Alexandra and half a dozen other intimates, were
part of the eiderdown of everyday life. They were known

because they were *in* the prince's life, facilitated by spouses, courtiers and servants. The Queen's biographer Sarah Bradford suggests that Philip's fidelity is, like the real extent of Elizabeth's personal fortune, the last bastion which 'courtiers will defend – metaphorically – to the death.' (p400) Money and sex, subjects which interest readers most, are the least exposed by the courtiers. Phillip Hall has exposed the money and Kitty Kelley has penetrated the courtier *cordon sanitaire*. Bradford suggests that Kelley's ability to bankroll her investigation into Philip's affairs by consulting a great many contacts at court has ruffled the royal dovecotes. Philip's enduring alibi – that the presence of his detectives would deter any dalliance – was finally blown, she suggests, by the evidence of Charles' long love affair with Camilla Parker-Bowles.

It is widely believed that if Philip wanted a woman – an aristocrat's wife, a businessman's wife or an officer's wife – then he could have her, often with dire consequences for the wellbeing of the woman. By the account of princely philandering reported both in Kitty Kelley's book and repeated in Sarah Bradford's biography of Elizabeth, it could be inferred that the women suffered sexual harassment, the men humiliation; to say no was to say no to royal patronage.

If Philip felt constrained by the marriage, then he also gained access to his wife's great wealth and worldly goods, and he worked the system to maximise his access to whatever goods or women he wanted. The moral of the story and this model of manliness is that princes can use proximity to the monarch to seduce women and to protect themselves. If Philip was discredited as a 'role model' for the heir, it was more for his intimidating parenting – the Murdstone mode – than for his way with women.

Fairy Godfather

Philip's uncle, Louis Mountbatten adopted seduction rather than sadism as his approach to kingmaking. Charles became the object of his charming megalomania. He was encouraged by the alliance between Charles' parents. He tried patrician sexual management on his own children, with and without success. And later he became excited and engaged when Prince Charles, alienated from his parents, became available for intellectual and sexual mentoring. Charles, in turn, loved Mountbatten's gossip, his grandiosity – and his attention.

Mountbatten was notorious for extravagent self-promotion and fastidious royalism, bankrolled by an awesomely rich wife – these Mountbatten men were lucky with their moneyed wives. Mountbatten specialised in royal matchmaking and a kind of kingmaking.

Mountbatten's life was shadowed by his German genes. In postwar England the royal family's German origins had to be purged – English xenophobia and German expansionism, and later fascism, rendered the transnational networks of ruling families an embarrassment in a world at war. When World War I began Mountbatten's father was sacked as First Sea Lord and his name, Battenberg, was anglicised to Mountbatten. So, Mountbatten was a man with a mission: to exorcise this shame, to stabilise his dynasty, to redeem its reputation. Whether as redemption or revenge, he was, according to Anthony Holden, 'a man of devout dynastic ambitions', a man who wanted his own people on the throne.

Elizabeth was 13 years old when she first laid eyes on Philip and fell in love with him during a royal visit to Dartmouth College. During the war, when Elizabeth was a teenager, Philip was sponsored by his cousin Princess Marina and by Mountbatten, who played the courier between Elizabeth's father, King George VI, and Philip's father, King George of Greece. The Greek king's weak and compromised family were, of course, thrilled at the prospect of a union with the Windsors.

It was Mountbatten who encouraged Philip to join the Navy and it was he who insisted that Charles too should become a naval officer after Cambridge, on the grounds that it was the senior service and that in any case his great grandfathers and grandfather had also served there. Mountbatten exemplified a passion for precedent and protocol as patriarchal lore. The authority of his class, his gender and his generation was recognised by *repetition*, by uniforms, procedures, traditions, all of which were codified gestures of personal and public power. All that Charles had to do to be a man, and then to be a king, was to do what the men of his family had already done, in the way that they did it.

The armed services were more important than the academy, they were, par excellence, the apparatus of authority, discipline, hierarchy, conquest and, crucially, sexual separatism. They were also part of the apparatus of royal masculinity. The Windsor-Mountbatten men loved dressing up and the great mentor wore his identity as a man in his medals and his uniforms. It didn't matter what was hidden – an aristocratic man could do anything with his body, with anybody – appearances were what mattered. They were not surface or artifice, but a symbol system which operated as a material force in social relations. Appearances affirmed authority: all those medals, the uniforms, the womanising, the anecdotes which represented themselves as the *real* story, and the authority over other men.

If Charles had been bored at Cambridge and semidetached from its intellectual challenges, his experiences in the institutions advocated by the Mountbatten men in his life left him distressed and defeated. The Navy was disastrous. Like Mountbatten, Charles was liked by his men, but he couldn't navigate. Mountbatten had been heavily criticised during his own naval career for some 'mad' débâcles – including the capricious and cavalier daytime attack on Dieppe during World War II. (Ziegler, 1985, p190) Again, however, it did not matter whether either man had actually *liked* the experience. Appearance, rank and precedent were what mattered in the making of the royal male.

Above all, Mountbatten took it upon himself to tutor the heir in what it meant to be a man. He was enthusiastic, but his project was also self-interested. Mountbatten's megalomania was expressed in his eternal meddling; he was 'the greatest fixer of all time,' commented the Singapore premier Lee Kuan Yew. (p701) His reputation as a naval officer and as the man who successfully managed Britain's dignified, if disastrously rushed, exit from colonial India, was that of an obsessive, though often careless, grandiose organiser, whose membership of the Establishment masked mistakes and a penchant for self-promotion.

By the time Charles was in his early twenties, when he was already alienated from his parents and estranged from his own generation, 'Mountbatten had become his closest confidant and the greatest single influence on his life'. (Bradford, 1997, p397) Elizabeth, self-absorbed and emotionally numbed, was fond of the old Sea Lord and 'did not mind Mountbatten's influence on her son's life'. (p398)

Mountbatten's privileged position protected his reputation from popular scrutiny, and he used his power to make sure it was so. He was by now shameless in his scheming interference in the sexual independence of others. He admitted to his favourite daughter Patricia that in the 1940s he had 'done so much to induce you to marry John [the seventh earl of Brabourne, John Knatchbull] when you were wavering'. (Ziegler, 1985, p575) This was the daughter for whom he proclaimed a creepy kind of love; 'You know how basically fond I am and always have been of Mummy, you know pretty well about my girlfriends, but none of them have had that magic something which you have,' he wrote in 1953. He loved her sister, too, he said, but because 'she is *your* sister and *you* love her'. (p574) Mountbatten's relationship to his wife and daughters engineered envy: he adored his daughter above *all*, and they all knew it.

Mountbatten was an old man when he took on the

affectionate tutoring of Charles. Only with Mountbatten could the prince talk 'man to man' about sex, love and passion. 'His great-uncle combined a traditional view of women with a worldly attitude to sex,' comments Dimbleby (1995, p220), who concedes that 'from the perspective of a later generation Mountbatten's advice on matters of the heart may seem trapped in the values of another age'. (p248) Had he been closer to his parents or 'any other mature adviser', or had he been more self-assured and independent, Charles 'might have weighed the old man's words more carefully. As it was, they seemed to be models of acuity and wisdom.' But the misty chronicles of Charles' insecure and infantilising infatuation with charismatic old men imply that counsel from old codgers was the only conversation in town. What their dialogue did, however, was to beam him up, up and away from the planet on which he was living. But this was Charles' *choice*. When it came to mentors, he was the one who selected sexist martinets.

In the 1950s men and women's expectations of each other, though still occluded by the rhetoric of respectability which suffocated women's sexuality, were already disturbed by the quest for pleasure. The companionate marriage was an aspiration if not an actuality. Young men were still messing up women, but they weren't turning to 'mature advisers' for permission. Cultural revolution was ricocheting across the landscape of sex and class, and young people were already asserting their generational autonomy by the time Charles was into his adolescence. This was the heaven and hell of the blues, rock and roll and then soul, the mass music that Charles hardly heard. The sexual revolution of the 1960s both encouraged the sexual exploitation of women and also exposed it: the contradiction combusted and women's dissent created the conditions for a new sexual revolution sponsored by the women's liberation movement. While the new feminism was confronting the pleasure deficit and, with wild optimism, changing the sexual contract between men and women, Charles turned away from his own generation and poured out his heart to his great-uncle.

Great-uncle's counsel was consistent with the sexual contract which seems to have operated as an open secret between privileged, polygamous men for a millennium. In Charles' Britain it was only within the working and middle classes that this ancient sexual settlement was queasy, under pressure and, indeed, losing its mandate. Not among royalty, however. The aristocratic emotional economy remained peculiarly patriarchal. Mountbatten's advice and action were founded on the 'wild oats' principle and consisted of providing the premises, privacy and protection for Charles to sow the seed. The premises were his grand Hampshire home, Broadlands. This was also the place where Charles honeymooned with his new wife almost a decade later.

A much-quoted memorandum from the Mountbatten archive, written to Charles in 1974, contained 'unequivocal' counsel frequently repeated in a 'whirl of correspondence' flying between the great-uncle and the Prince in the early 1970s: 'I believe in a case like yours, that a man should sow his wild oats and have as many affairs as possible before settling down. But for a wife he should chose a suitable and sweet-hearted girl before she meets anyone else she might fall for.'

He might have been ruminating on the challenges of not marrying a sweet and suitable girl himself: his wife Edwina brought social power and a fortune to the marriage. She was the favourite granddaughter of Sir Ernest Cassell, one of the most influential financiers in Europe, who left her £2.3 million when he died in 1920. He had the royal connections and she had the money, and her relatives were also deeply rooted in the English aristocracy – Cassell had managed Edward VII's finances. Edwina was known for her glamour, her fast, shattering wit, her radicalism, and her independence of mind and body – one of her enduring romances was with the great Indian independence leader Jawaharlal Nehru, who worked with Mountbatten on the closure of colonial rule. (Ali, 1985, p76)

Mountbatten's note to Charles ostensibly concerned his own dynastic plan – to marry the Prince to his great-granddaughter Amanda Knatchbull, his favourite daughter's daughter. She was then 15 years old. The younger, the better, it seemed. After all, he reminded the heir, his mother was only 13 years old when she fell for Prince Philip at Dartmouth College. To be betrothed so young was all part of the patriarchal plot: 'I think it is disturbing for women to have experiences if they have to remain on a pedestal after marriage,' wrote the great-uncle. This was not the insouciance of an ignorant and old-fashioned man. Had this been a memo to a young *woman* at the time, the great-uncle might have been seen as a sicko. These men knew what we all know: that experience produces excitement and expectations; that experience gives women judgement. A woman with judgement was not the woman for a prince.

The great-uncle's princely project has been discussed by biographers as if it were the bungling sport of a benign old buffer. It was not; it was malign. Mountbatten and the royal relatives, from Diana's parents to his, were all implicated in a machiavellian ordinance to the Prince:

- Thou shalt be married to a WASP virgin
- Thy wife shalt know no better

The great-uncle's plan for his granddaughter was to encourage her feelings for the Prince at assignations organised by the great man himself. Rendezvous and holidays were arranged for them while she was still only a teenager, presumably on the calculation that she would understand her duty, preserve herself for life on a pedestal, while the Prince tried both to secure her affection and to carry out his own secret life.

The Prince was already beginning to live the parallel

lives urged upon him by the royal community, which ultimately ruined his reputation. It was not falling in and out of love that was the Prince's problem; it was the misogyny of the martinets to whom he entrusted his intimate future, who proposed a double life of serial relationships and one-night stands while holding a suitable girl in reserve for matrimony. Mountbatten was 'his linchpin, trusted above all others' (Dimbleby, 1995, p322), the 'royal procurer' as well as the prince's propagandist. He told *Time* magazine that Charles was always 'popping in and out of bed with girls'. (Holden, 1989, p152) Charles' biographers report that he had 'innumerable romances' in the 1970s. (p152) Meanwhile a 'suitable' girl was being cooked in royal fantasies as a prospective spouse. The Prince wrote to his great-uncle in 1974 that his mind was on marriage – though not yet – and Amanda, a fun-loving, loyal companion and 'a country girl as well, which is even more important', was an 'ideal' choice because she would 'intuitively understand the role required of her'. (Dimbleby, 1995, p249) He was not in love and she was only sweet 16, but already Charles was discussing her destiny with everyone but the girl herself. He had even consulted her mother, who counselled caution because the girl was too young.

The Prince had rehearsed his proposal in his own mind, and told his confidant that marrying him meant 'an immense sacrifice and a great loss of freedom'. Still, for several years he hoped that the girl would consent to her own martyrdom. The great-uncle did not recoil from letting his granddaughter in for such a fate, nor did this insight help the Prince review either the relevance of the role prescribed for a Princess of Wales, or the nature of a man who would want to subject a woman to it.

Towards the end of the decade the Mountbatten men, Philip and his uncle, were beginning to reproach the Prince for the visibility of the women in his life. It was one thing to have secret affairs, it was quite another to let the women be seen. In the mid-1970s Charles' father rebuked him for having 'paraded' a woman in public, and by the late 1970s the behaviour of the playboy prince worried courtiers and the great-uncle alike that the Prince of Wales was living like ... a typical Prince of Wales. Mountbatten warned him that he was going the way of the Duke of Windsor. Early warnings were to little or no effect. By the end of the decade Charles' habits were confirmed. Worried by his protégé's public persona, Mountbatten intervened again.

The Mountbatten archive trawled by Clare Hargreaves and Jonathan Dimbleby offers fascinating details from the busy correspondence between the two men. In Mountbatten's last great manoeuvre to advance his patriarchal project, he proposed that he, the last Viceroy of India, should accompany Charles on his forthcoming tour of India, and that they should take the suitable girl too. Their family connections would provide camouflage, he said, and Charles agreed. But Philip protested – the old man's presence would overshadow his son. Elizabeth was worried that whatever the pretext, Amanda would be under the spotlight for the first time, the press, so far, had been indifferent to their assignations at Broadlands. (Bradford, 1997, p426)

The response of the suitable girl's parents was also suggestive of the aristocracy's atavistic attitude to women: her father, John Brabourne, thought that the young pair were probably drifting in the direction of marriage. But if Amanda attracted the media's attention, this might wreck her chances with the Prince. She would be hurt and Mountbatten would be to blame. The old man turned to the girl's mother, who insisted that the India tour would bounce the pair into an announcement or a denial, and that would wound her daughter. Dimbleby concludes that this 'inter-family council of state' revealed the media's power over royal lives. But it also revealed the intrusive manoeuvres of aristocratic parents. It was all in vain anyway. Amanda had a life and a mind of her own. When the Prince proposed, she turned him down. Her rejection should have alerted him to the urgent need to review the royal lifestyle and its requirements of a daughter-in-law. It confirmed Charles' strong suspicion that to marry into the House of Windsor was a 'sacrifice that no one should be expected to make'. (Dimbleby, 1995, p322) However, he would not give in; it was not a sacrifice that he was candid or kind enough to rescind.

Back-to-Basics Bushman

Laurens van der Post, a white South African who had served under Mountbatten after World War II, had acquired a spectacular reputation as a savant and storyteller. He was a prolific writer and propagandist for the disappearing 'natural' way of life of the black Bushmen of southern Africa. When he died in 1996, a few days after celebrating his ninetieth birthday, he was memorialised as having 'the spiritual presence of a saint'.

The feminist travel writer Dea Birkett met the old man in his Chelsea penthouse flat in the last year of his life and noticed an old Christmas card from Prince Charles and photographs of his sons on the shelves. The Prince, like millions of other admirers, had been enthralled by van der Post's messianic, mystical advocacy of 'natural man'.

Van der Post was on the conservative end of the New Age ideologies which flourished in the last decades of the century, a time when the relationship between subjectivity and society reached a radical clarity, first in black liberation politics and later in feminism. These liberation movements created the conditions for a *politics* of subjectivity, exemplified by feminism's mantra, 'the personal is political'; bearing witness to the pain of oppression and trying to create the conditions for testimony and recovery, challenge and celebration. Van der Post's notion of 'natural man', however, celebrated an exotic, elusive *other*, as far away from Chelsea as it was from the future. His notion of 'natural man' did not locate itself in the drama of self-discovery which created the liberation movements that steadily ousted the white terror in southern Africa. He proposed spiritual redemption through the Bushmen's mindset and supposedly simple life rather than active citizenship and participation in social change. The great white Bushman hated the women's liberation movement (he called it Amazonian gang warfare) and was conveniently contemptuous of the black anti-apartheid movement and its emblematic figures, the 'miserable' Nelson Mandela who 'speaks with double tongue' and 'wretched' Bishop Tutu. (Birkett, 1997)

Van der Post's acrid response to Mandela's momentous exit from Robben Island prison provoked a reaction from Alex Callinicos, professor of politics at York University, who felt that if it wasn't clear before, it was now crystal clear that van der Post was aligned to the conservative axis in southern Africa. 'I had just seen him as purveying a mystified vision of Africa. But he was providing a sympathetic voice to southern African regimes.' He lent his authority to a familiar settler apologia, 'We have an intuitive relationship to black people.' Callinicos and other critics recognised the tone; 'this is an old story among defenders of the old regimes in southern Africa. They say "we understand black people, not like those urban metropolitan people who don't understand our intuitive relationship."'

It was also as if van der Post felt usurped by a black consciousness that was beyond his interpretive *power* and, therefore, beyond his control. It was as if he was jealous of Mandela and Tutu and their global resonance as great liberators. Their radicalism, stamina, political finesse and, of course, their blackness produced a politics alert to the needy, greedy *otherness* of white power. In the end *black* responsibility – to paraphrase white South Africa's transitional leader de Klerk – relieved *white* power of the burden of its own history.

The great white Bushman, then, was neither impressed by, nor part of, that struggle. His black people, 'my Bushmen', as he called them, were part of nature, beyond the pale of politics. During the apartheid era he preferred the more accommodating homeland strategy of the Zulu chief Buthelezi to the anti-racialised landscape of the African National Congress. He was vigorously opposed to economic sanctions against apartheid. The *Observer*'s Commonwealth correspondent Colin Legum recalled his early opposition to anti-apartheid activists, 'We called him Laurens van der Posture. He was a real poseur.' And Margaret Thatcher appreciated his support in the mid-1980s. Her 'good friend' talked 'good sense about South Africa'. (Thatcher, 1993, p521)

Nonetheless the great white Bushman was adamant about his own anti-apartheid credentials, boasting that his 1934 book *In a Province* was 'the first book by an indigenous South African against racial prejudice'. But Alex Callinicos reminded *Guardian* readers after his death that there were several challenges to the great white man's claim, notably Sol Plaatje's *Native Life in South Africa*, written in 1916, 'but Plaatje was only a black, so presumably didn't count'. (Birkett, 1997)

During van der Post's long career as a vivid storyteller, several knowing readers noticed fictions in his travelogues and saw his representation of the Kalahari Bushmen as the last living 'original people' as a sentimental phantom. Anthropologists had for 40 years been recording the precarious, poor life of bush people – hunting and gathering, scavenging, trading, getting by. In the 1960s the campaign to 'preserve' them, to protect them from modernity, produced a game reservation – a kind of containment that assumed these humans were *different*, when they were actually *deprived*. According to the anthropologist Edwin Wilmsen, 'you only have to spend 30 minutes with them to see their abject poverty. If that's how humans lived 10,000 years ago, you wouldn't want to be one of them.' (Birkett, 1997) Van der Post didn't want to be one of them either. Though he proclaimed spiritual redemption through them, he also spurned other travellers' connections: when Dea Birkett tried to discuss her time with Namibian bush people, he protested, 'But they're not like my Bushmen ... they're touched, they're not natural.'

None of these political controversies engaged Charles' curiosity. What entranced him was 'the magic in van der Post's cosmology'. (Dimbleby, 1995, p302) 'He purveyed a very mystified view to a Western audience in search of the exotic,' said Callinicos. 'People saw him as a slightly fraudulent figure.' Callinicos could see his attraction, however, as an adventurer – rather like Mountbatten, an Establishment traveller with a 'slightly raffish air'. His mystification of nature, too, encouraged admirers like Charles 'to think he was responding to an ecological critique'.

Charles proclaimed the great white Bushman, together with the great-uncle, as his mentor. In the late 1970s van der Post presented Charles with his Jungian hypothesis that by taking 'sophisticated people' into the bush 'we have produced the most startling re-educative and therapeutic effects upon their divided personalities'. According to Dimbleby, Charles' intuition at once responded "Amen"'. (1995, p303)

Charles' isolation from progressive popular culture and his mesmeric dependence on grandiose old fogeys was again exposed years later when he called upon van der Post during his honeymoon at Balmoral to do something with his wife. The woman had married a man who wasn't sure he wanted *her*; he took her on a honeymoon to his territory, snared by his family, who didn't really want *her* either. The great white Bushman had several sessions with the young woman and, not surprisingly, discovered that her troubles were beyond him. Of course, the wife's problem was the Prince and the patriarchal project that, madly, she had married into. How could she be understood by an old patrician who loved the Prince's patronage, who was greedy for exaltation and a stranger to challenge?

Early in the friendship the Prince was excited by van der Post's proposal that together they go into the Kalahari, with a BBC television camera, an offer that action man – whose passion for guns and cars, for horses, hunting, shooting, nightclubbing and polo playing exasperated courtiers – could not refuse. But the Foreign Office was unhappy. Southern Africa was not safe, said the diplomats, while it was struggling for release from white regimes. It took a decade for Charles to make it to the Kalahari with his mentor, and then they managed only a few days under the desert skies. Dimbleby notes that in his brisk and brief record of the experience the Prince was 'unaccountably prosaic'. But this was 1987 and his life was a mess. He was an often absent father and this was the year when the *Sun* asked, 'WHAT KIND OF DAD ARE YOU? He was miserably married and having an affair that seemed to be accepted at Buckingham Palace but was an agony to his wife. Neither the Kalahari nor the great white Bushman could heal his 'divided personality'.

5. Field Sports

Charles' problem in the 1970s was that he behaved like a Prince of Wales. Having put himself in the hands of the patrician defenders of the monarchy's sexual status quo, he learned secrecy, duplicity and the macho manners of the court. The patricians did not, however, help the Prince conceive of a sexual life at ease with the secular temper of contemporary Britain.

Towards the end of the decade, Charles' career as a playboy was approaching its end. He had set himself a deadline to terminate the pleasures of princely wild oats. Thirty was the age to get wed, he'd said, confident that there would be a woman who'd wed him. It was as if he were describing a mortgage rather than a reciprocal relationship that might move in its own seasons. Having determined to find a wife, Charles reproduced the stereotypical schisms between courtesan and companion on one hand, and wife and mother on the other. But he did not learn how to have a *modern* life from the people who could have helped him – women.

What the women with whom he fell in love revealed to

him was that whether or not they wanted *him*, they didn't want the scrutiny and emptiness that defined life as the virgin wife of the Prince of Wales. Nor did they necessarily want to put up with the Prince of Wales' historic prerogative – mistresses. Camilla's ubiquitous presence had been noticed. Lady Jane Wellesley was one of his early companions, a woman who, whether or not she had a history, certainly expected to have future. And what meant *not* being a Princess of Wales. In any case Charles was young and, by all accounts, behaved like a bit of a boy. She was fond enough, however, to remain his friend for many years.

Among his other early lovers were Sarah Spencer and Davina Sheffield. When he dated Sarah Spencer she was suffering severely from anorexia nervosa. Charles had invited her to join his party for the Ascot races and immediately noticed the skeletal signs. They discussed the possibility of marriage and when she joined him on a skiing holiday, a bodyguard slept in the corridor of their chalet to police their privacy from the press. But Charles was also involved with several other women. And anyway Sarah confided to a journalist that, although she liked the Prince, she was not in love with him. That was the end of that.

He met Davina Sheffied in 1976 and fell in love with her. She was working with refugees in Vietnam and returned to Britain after her mother was murdered. But she was deemed an impossible partner because some of the men in her life did the indecent thing and revealed to the press that she had a history. She had lived with a man she once loved, and she was *experienced*.

Next, Charles proposed to Amanda Knatchbull, the great-uncle's candidate. She turned him down. He fell for Anna Wallace, the daughter of rich Scots land-owners, whose reputation was that of a strong and sexy, independent and uninhibited woman. 'There had been a sharp intake of breath among his friends when Charles started escorting Anna,' recalled the royal reporter James Whitaker; 'she was not in the slightest bit overawed by having the Prince of Wales pay court to her.' The Prince of Wales did not not know how to behave himself, however. Whitaker didn't publish what he had seen when the Prince took Ms Wallace to Balmoral. He was watching from the bushes while the lovers were on the beach of the River Dee. 'He spotted us crawling on our bellies with binoculars. He jumped up and hid in the bushes.' The Prince hid and 'left the young woman unprotected. He shouldn't have done that – I was ashamed for him – but, of course, I didn't print the story. He is, after all, my future King.'

At the eightieth birthday ball for Elizabeth, the Queen Mother, in the summer of 1980, Charles danced with everyone but Ms Wallace. When she rebuked him, 'No one treats me like that, not even you', he was apparently astonished. Showing who was master, at a polo ball a little later, he ignored both the hostess, Lady Vestey, and Ms Wallace. She 'looked on with a mixture of anger, disbelief and horror as the prince, who was clearly besotted, spent the evening holding Camilla Parker-Bowles close.' No surprise, then, that 'whatever actually transpired, it looked as though *she* dumped *him*'. (Whitaker,1993, pp105–7)

She would have been aware of Camilla's place in his life, and would have known, suggests Andrew Morton, 'as Diana discovered too late', that Camilla's practice of vetting her lover's women 'was not so much to assess their potential as a royal bride but to see how much of a threat they posed'. It might, of course, have been both.

Charles' young women friends were presented with his princely code at a time when, encouraged by feminism, women were facing men with their own sexual self-confidence.

Patriarchal Vigilante

By the end of the decade, and with the Prince's own deadline approaching, his relationships with women were under intense scrutiny. The world in which he lived was in no sense private. The Prince's liaisons were always conducted under the intensely interested eye of his own public – that is, the exclusive community in which he moved, his family, courtiers and servants. But Charles had personally devised no strategy to protect either himself or the women he courted from the lens of the mass media or the beady eyes of the patrician guardians of royal reputation.

His father had an investment in Charles' women because Charles' wife represented the future of the Firm. Philip had invested his life in the monarchy and intended to protect his investment. The patriarchal vigilante intervened when Charles became involved with a woman of whom he disapproved. Charles and his friends would be complicit in the evicted woman's humiliation.

Charles fell in love again in the wake of his great-uncle's assassination on the coast of Ireland in 1979. The woman was Zoë Sallis, a Buddhist whose religion was embraced with enthusiasm by the grieving prince. The discipline of a pacific and contemplative life, together with transcendental meditation that promised trans-terrestrial communication, was attractive to someone who was quarrying superstitious and supernatural ideologies for the meaning of life. But palace prejudice swiftly saw off Zoë Sallis. She had to be purged, not only because she was a mature woman who had experience of passionate relationships, but also because her faith was an affront to the Anglican settlement which prescribed the belief system of the man who was destined to become the Defender of the Faith.

Charles' prospects as a monarch were knotted to his embrace of a single divinity and institutionalised Protestantism. He couldn't marry a Catholic, still less a Buddhist. The protocols surrounding kingship and religion were 300 years old and the Prince was not prepared to renounce the legal impediment to his own feelings and faiths. The 1701 Act of Settlement, which banned marriage to a Catholic, had never been rescinded. It remained as more than a relic of another era of Protestant dominance; it was an active measure of the misogyny and repressive religious prejudice of the English Establishment.

By prescribing the monarch's role as the supreme governor of the Church of England and confirming the royal family's exclusive attachment to Anglicanism, it was also an insult to the many faiths which flourished amidst prevailing atheism in late twentieth-century British culture.

Another aspect of the Act meant that as supreme governor, the future monarch was banned from marrying a divorced woman or 'any girl with what the British like to euphemize as "a past"'. (Holden, 1993, p147). The royal family's relationship to the established religion, therefore, immunised it from the consciousness of sexism which found limited expression in the equality legislation of the mid-1970s. A woman with 'a past' was proscribed by Protestant, patrician ideology which simultaneously celebrated 'a past' as a precondition of a manly monarch. Charles could have rejected this ideology, but instead he chose to put his ambition before the women he adored. He had learned nothing.

Everyone except the Prince was in a hurry. It was Charles' duty, he'd been told, to find a wife, quick. Which meant that it was his duty to sacrifice a woman. That's what wedlock would be, he already knew that, he'd said it himself. In order to be king, he *had* to have a wife. When he wrote to his great-uncle about the monarch's spouse as a 'sacrifice', he was perversely constituting himself as a victim too. In fact, she was to be sacrificed to *him*, to his ambition and his advantage. He didn't need love. Some women loved him, indeed they'd loved him for years. He didn't need sex, he already had that. He just needed a wife. Why couldn't he wed one of the woman he really wanted? Well, he tried. But they didn't want to marry him; the women he'd wanted knew that they would be martyrs to the monarchy and a surprisingly misanthropic man who managed all of his relationships exclusively on his own terms. Sir, they had to call him. A man who wants to take a woman into his arms doesn't need to hear her say 'Sir' unless he wants to witness her subordination.

The women went to his homes, admired his hobbies, paid attention while he was playing polo, fishing, riding. His office organised their rendezvous, their tickets, her flowers. They refused him, these women. They already had privilege and a place in the sun, they had riches, freedom of movement and freedom of thought within, of course, the constraints of their class.

The lessons of Charles' lovers were clear: to have the women he wanted he would have to engineer a new reformation, he would have to modernise the monarchy. A secular state and sovereign, released from religious and patriarchal principles, was an idea whose time had come. Without a new reformation the Prince was mired in a self-pitying sense of victimisation by the very system that paradoxically gave him power and yet left him feeling powerless. A new reformation was the only route to self-respect and respect for the women who had rejected him. Unfortunately for the state, for Diana and for Charles himself, that reformation never happened.

Part II
Making a Marriage

6. Born to be Queen

All that mattered on 1 July 1961 was whether Frances had given a son and heir to Johnnie, Viscount Althorp, later the eighth Earl Spencer. He was about to light bonfires on the Sandringham estate to celebrate – so certain was he that his name was secure and his wife would deliver a monument to his manhood, a baby· boy. (Morton, 1997, p77) But Frances had given him a girl. She was so unexpected that no name had been chosen. When she was a week old she became Diana.

Frances was not forgiven. Johnnie was an aristocrat, Viscount Althorp, whose destiny left him life loitering with intent, 'waiting for dead men's shoes'. The meaning of his life was that he should become what his father already was and then guarantee the line of succession to the ancient dynasty by siring a son. These people are represented as the essence of Englishness. The Spencers founded their dynasty in the sixteenth century. Their wealth came from sheep and their strategic marriages within aristocratic and royal circles. At their wedding in

Westminster Abbey in 1954, Johnnie and the Honourable
Frances Roche were reminded of their place and purpose in
the national firmament when the bishop announced, 'You
are making an addition to the home life of your country on
which, above all others, our national life depends.'
Johnnie's *raison d'être* was rooted in his body: he had to do
no more than reproduce himself.

But he kept harvesting girls. Or rather, he fancied that
Frances suffered from genetic delinquency that reaped the
wrong gender. With two girls in the family he was already
disappointed. When Frances gave birth to Diana, he
became desperate. And so he dispatched her to the 'top
man' in Harley Street to uncover the secret of her supposed
genetic deficiency. Patriarchy and primogeniture prevailed
in the English aristocracy. It is one of the great ironies of its
history that some of the most successful monarchs have
been women, though this fact may have been lost on the
Spencers and the rest of their class. During the twentieth
century, when the rest of society was approaching a new
settlement between men, women and children, they had
made no move to revise the primitive, patriarchal priorities
that rendered the aristocracy the most regressive, racist
and sexist clique in British society.

Johnnie Spencer's monarch was a woman who sojourned
at the Sandringham estate with her progeny. His daughters
were reared to consider her sons as potential partners. But
to Johnnie Spencer and his relatives the birth of a boy was
more important than anything, more important even than
the wellbeing of his 23-year-old wife. 'For Diana's mother,
fiercely proud, combative and tough-minded, it was a
humiliating and unjust experience, all the more so in
retrospect as nowadays it is known that the sex of the baby
is determined by the man,' comments Andrew Morton.

Diana had in fact been preceded by the birth of a boy,
John, a severely disabled child who died after only ten
hours. Frances never saw or held this baby. It was not until
the 1980s that the mothers of infants who were dead before

or soon after birth challenged the paternalistic practice that separated them from their parents. The masculinised culture of obstetrics anaesthetised the tragedy by erasing the evidence – in those days parents were routinely deprived of the sight and touch of their child, leaving them without any memory of its being, their empty arms almost aching from its absence. How could they grieve, these parents, for someone they had never met?

Three years after Diana's birth, her brother Charles was born. Johnnie Spencer had proved himself. His triumph was rewarded by the Queen herself, who became godmother to the son and heir.

But Johnnie's patriarchal imperative destroyed his marriage, produced a divorce – rare in this class – and blighted his children. The legacy bequeathed by the death of baby John and the obsession of his father, withered this generation. 'Charles feels that his parents would have completed their family with Diana while the Princess herself feels that she would not have been born.' The pressure, the disappointment, the blame and the bullying bled over the mother and the rest of the children. 'It was a dreadful time for my parents,' Diana's brother Charles told Morton, 'and probably the root of their divorce because I don't think they ever got over it.'

The break-up of the marriage is usually described in swift asides which are mobilised to explain Diana's commitment to marriage. But what the children endured was much worse than the social stigma of divorce, they were witnesses to drinking and domestic violence. (Whitaker, 1993, p179) Andrew Morton notes that Diana witnessed from behind the drawing-room door 'a particularly violent argument between her mother and father'.

Brutality

The biographies of the royal family written during Diana's era rarely and barely mention Johnnie's brutality, nor the

scandal of an equerry's sordid treatment of his wife. These
textual omissions (most dramatic in Dimbleby's
representation of the Spencers), together with Diana's
ambivalence as an abandoned but adhesive daughter,
contributed to representations of Johnnie as a benign old
buffer who had himself been abandoned to bring up his
babies alone. But Anthony Holden alludes to the Earl's
dangerousness when he comments that Frances abruptly
disappeared from her home, although she tried and failed to
get custody of the children and then sued for divorce on
grounds of physical and mental cruelty. Johnnie parried
with a counter-suit and recruited a posse of witnesses to
discredit his wife, ranging from his children's head teacher
at Silfield school, Jean Lowe (Morton, 1992, p20) to his
aristocratic mother-in-law. 'So wretched was Frances'
marriage,' says Holden, that 'she was prepared to lose
custody of her children to escape him.' What does it take,
he wonders, for a woman to forfeit her title, her home, her
reputation and her children to get away from a man?
'Spencer beat up Frances,' says Holden. 'That divorce case
when Diana was six years old was bizarre then, it would be
now, but then! She sues him for cruelty. He counter-sues
and gets all these toffs to support him. He wins and he gets
the kids.'

James Whitaker, the royal correspondent regarded as the
doyen of the 'ratpack', notes that Frances, who was by then
having a relationship with a rich Australian, Peter Shand
Kydd, was regarded by 'high society' as 'a bolter'. But he
gives her version of events in his book *Charles v Diana*.
When the Spencers agreed to a trial separation in the
summer of 1967 she enrolled her younger children in
London schools – Johnnie had seen the schools and
approved them. The older sisters, Sarah and Jane, were
already at boarding school. For the first term Diana,
Charles and their nanny lived with Frances in a London
flat. Sometimes Johnnie came to visit during his London
trips and the children spent most weekends with their

father at the family home, Park House, on the
Sandringham estate. But by Christmas, when it was clear
that the marriage was irretrievable, 'Johnnie now insisted
that Diana and Charles should be sent to school in King's
Lynn, not far from Park House, and that they should
thenceforth stay at the house with him.' He refused to
resume the agreed arrangements. 'I strongly objected to
this, and in a court action in June 1968 sought that the
children be allowed to live with and be cared for by their
mother. I lost the case and the custody of the children,' she
told Whitaker. She began divorce proceedings. 'Shattered
by the fact that she had left him, and fearful that the details
of his cruelty to her would become public, Johnnie
launched a massive counter-attack designed to squash his
wife at all costs.' Spencer cited his wife's relationship with
Peter Shand Kydd. 'She didn't stand a chance,' says
Whitaker, 'bruises disappear but adultery does not.' (1993,
p179) She was persuaded not to make a fuss, and so she got
her day in court. She lost her home and her children and
she had to pay the Viscount, the heir to an earldom and a
small fortune, £3000 towards his costs.

One of the witnesses to give evidence against Frances
was her own mother, Ruth, Lady Fermoy, one of the Queen
Mother's best friends, who lived within 'royal circles all
her life'. Class, power and privilege ran thicker than
solidarity with her own daughter and grandchildren. 'She
really could not believe that her daughter would leave a
belted earl for a man in trade,' says Penny Junor, a
journalist who became an advocate for Prince Charles. Her
defeat was 'hardly surprising,' wrote Whitaker, after 'a host
of Johnnie's high-powered aristocratic friends' turned
against her'. (1993, p178)

Whitaker says that Frances would not have been able to
describe her husband as a wife-beater, it wasn't done, 'but
there was little doubt in the minds of Norfolk society – and
in the wider world – that it was so.' Earl Spencer's brutality
is the raw material for Erin Pizzey's novel *In the Shadow of*

the Castle. Pizzey was active in the early women's liberation movement and a founder of Chiswick refuge, the first sanctuary for women being battered by the men they live with. The refuge movement became one of the enduring monuments of modern feminism, challenging and changing the way the statutory services respond to domestic tyranny and men's crimes against women. It was not until the 1980s that the impact of men's violence towards women was recognised as having a devastating effect on children – confirming girls' fear and facing boys with wrenching dilemmas about their own gender, as witnesses to the most important person in their lives being defeated by the most powerful.

Domestic violence is massively underreported but the British Crime Survey estimates that there are more than half a million assaults on women by the men they live with every year and in more than 90 per cent of these incidents children are in the same room or nearby. Diana Spencer witnessed her father's violence towards her mother from behind the drawing-room door. (Morton, 1997, p77) Exiled from their mother who was living in London, the children also, in effect, lost their father. He retreated from everyone at home, including his children, and the only person to whom he spoke was his butler. As a little boy Charles Spencer would lie in bed – in a separate wing from his sister – wailing 'I want my mummy!'

Like many men who fight for custody, what Johnnie seemed to want was to hurt his wife, rather than to have the care of his children. He was cold and sometimes cruel; according to Holden, a traditionalist and a disciplinarian who physically punished the children. Holden records a nanny's testimony that they were 'very strictly brought up, in a very old-fashioned way, as if they were still living at the beginning of the century'. Every weekend the children and their nanny took the train from Norfolk to London to see their mother, who would soon start weeping at the prospect of their imminent departure.

Their father's reputation was protected by the public defeat of their mother. He had recruited his friends and relations to his campaign to discredit and defeat this woman, he had enlisted witnesses from the children's everyday life. Thus their world was peopled by their mother's enemies, people who had signed affidavits and affirmed in public the honour of a man who assaulted their mother in private.

They were traumatised. They were neglected and needy. They kept his secrets. He wielded absolute power, cemented in the coupling of authority and absence. As children they were both privileged and powerless. Cared for by nannies, some of whom were kind, some of whom were cruel, they were sent off to boarding schools, children's homes for the upper classes. Shame and fear infused the childhood of Charles and Diana Spencer, manifest in their public politeness and private tremors. Later it was to show itself in Charles Spencer's inflammatory quests for love, his own brutality towards women, and in Diana's presentation of herself as kind, helpful and good, very good.

Cheap Labour

Charles went to Eton and then to Oxford. Diana went to a posh girls' school, West Heath, where she sat five O levels and failed all of them. West Heath, despite being expensive and fashionable, managed only average results among those girls admitted for public examinations. But Diana's results prompt the question: why didn't her privileged school and parents care that she was failing? Why didn't they do something about it? What seems amazing to any other class is that aristocrats with access to anything money could buy didn't think it was worth buying their daughter whatever she needed to help her acquire the intellectual capital to make a living and secure her own place in the world. This privileged school didn't seem to care, or contemplate the possibility that the child was having problems.

When she was dispatched to a Swiss finishing school to study cookery, she begged to be released back to England. With enough inherited money to buy a flat in west London, she emerged into the society of the Sloane Ranger. She became a Sloane cleaner, a Sloane baby-minder and kindergarten helper, and a Sloane skivvy. David Cannadine notes that aristocrats, having seen the endless supply of cheap labour vanish, turned instead to their own daughters: 'Instead of employing servants, many young patricians are themselves thus occupied: cooks hired for the weekend, or nannies, for instance, are now more likely to be "Sloane Ranger" girls than traditional domestics.' (1990, p688)

Diana could dance, play the piano, swim and dive with élan. But something had stolen her confidence and concentration. With all the resources in the world, the Earl didn't make sure that his daughter acquired the means of earning a living. Marriage was to be her career. Somebody would wed her. Diana Spencer was one of the few girls of her generation for whom biology was destiny – a fate to befall the daughters of only the very rich and the very poor.

The Reign of Raine

When Johnnie introduced a new woman into his children's life, he didn't tell them who she was and what she was for. She was a stranger. Raine was a Tory local government politician in London, the former wife of the 16th Earl of Dartmouth, who also lost her children when she left her husband for Johnnie. This class learned nothing – they'd bid for and bargain over their children, they'd lose their own and gain others. What they didn't do was take care of them. In any case that was not what this class expected of parenthood. Johnnie's mission was not so much to care for his children as keep them.

When Johnnie married Raine in 1976 his children weren't invited to the wedding. Charles was given the news by his prep-school headmaster. This was an emblematic moment in a new era dominated by a father who exercised power but not responsibility. The children resented his new wife, they tripped and tormented, blamed and cursed her.

Her mission was to marry their father and to modernise the Spencer estate. She marched into their lives and provoked a restless, resentful mutiny. When pictures from the Earl's great collection of paintings and *objets d'art* disappeared, either to bankroll refurbishment or be restored, the Earl's children felt as if there was a thief was at work. *She* was touching their stuff. As if the stuff was the soul of the Spencers. In a sense, of course, it was: the aristocratic family was, above all, about ownership – of *objects*, land, property and people. For a thousand years the people of this class were subordinated to the interests of their 'possessions'. It was not so much that they mattered less, but that their lives were instruments in a greater project, the acquisition and protection of property.

Earl Spencer neither soothed nor sorted matters out. He left his new wife and his children to slug it out, while he enjoyed the success of her triumphant and energetic entrepreneurship around the estate. Commodity fetishism became the children's emotional currency. While the Earl and the Countess spent their weekdays in London, the son and heir stalked the family house 'with a briefcase full of papers, checking to see if anything had disappeared'. (Whitaker, 1993, p198)

After his daughter married the heir to the throne, Johnnie Spencer cashed in on the wedding of the century by marketing mock-ups of his daughter's wedding dress to the Japanese – without telling her – and lending the R-word 'royal' to a merchandising scheme, a proposed Royal Spencer Golf Club. 'He even boasted to me that Raine had learned Japanese so she could further her commercial ambitions,' reported James Whitaker; 'in late 1991 it emerged that Spencer had effectively flogged the family name, title, crest and arms to the Japanese.' (p200) Spencer himself, though an aristocrat, was not royal. 'I learned that Buckingham Palace officials were beside themselves with rage because of Johnnie's blatant breach of protocol – he'd been an equerry, after all. He knew the ropes, and should have known better,' wrote Whitaker. Spencer alienated his children and then his greatest asset, his connection to the Queen. Thereafter he was *persona non grata*, becoming 'not so much royal in-laws as out-laws'. (p201)

Raine's investment in Johnnie was gilt-edged, however. Everyone agreed that it was she who managed to keep him alive and more or less well. She nursed him through the illnesses of old age with redoubtable dedication. He became ill with pneumonia in 1992, and again Raine was stalwart in the face of his notoriously bad behaviour – only to be rewarded by incoherent, ranting rebuffs. On the day of his death from a massive heart attack, hospital staff heard a terrible row and Spencer roaring, 'Get out!' These were his last words to her. (p185) His children had barely communicated with him during the last years of his life, still less with his loyal wife, and yet his distraught daughter Diana's message on her wreath said, 'I miss you dreadfully.' She had, of course, been missing a father for most of her life.

The Sins of the Fathers

The Earl's death had a centrifugal effect on his family. Raine had lost her husband and now she lost her home. Although Johnnie had specified in his will that she should be given six months to move out of Althorp, Charles wanted her out immediately. The new earl ordered her to provide proof of purchase before she removed any of her property from the manor that was now his. He didn't even like it: 'It was like an old man's club with lots of clocks ticking away. For an impressionable child it was a night-marish place.' (Morton, 1997, p72) The impressionable child was, however, wrought in his father's image. He had been trained well, he went to the most privileged and patriarchal educational establishments – Eton and Oxford – where rich boys learned how to be: insecure, autocratic, unencumbered by empathy or equality. His behaviour as an irascible playboy during the 'new lad' era prompted his critics to wonder whether the Spencer genes were jinxed. However, his priorities were only those valorised by his class for over a millennium. 'Harshness bred harshness.' (*Independent on Sunday*, 30 November 1997) He was, after all, his father's apprentice and those priorities were what produced him as a man, an aristocratic model for William McIlvanney's lament in *Docherty*: 'the sins of the fathers *are* the sons'.

While at Oxford in the 1980s he was known as Champagne Charlie, a boorish party-goer who was to be seen clubbing around London in a black Mercedes with his friend Darius Guppy, another old Etonian who became best man at his wedding before being sent to prison for fraud. Spencer remained loyal to his buddy. But there seemed to be more to him than a taste for champagne and sex. 'Spencer was sophisticated, well read, intelligent.' This was a rarity and 'among his own set he was treated reverentially'. (*Independent on Sunday*, 30 November 1997)

His own career followed the same trail as his father's. While waiting in his father's shadow for his inheritance, he had managed the Althorp estate, quarrelled fiercely with his father and they, like father and son before them, stopped speaking to each other. It was inevitable. And it didn't matter. Inevitable because Spencer senior had barely parented this child. Why should they love or even like each other? It didn't matter because Spencer senior's estate was destined for Spencer junior – he didn't have to do anything but wait.

In 1989, when his sister's marriage was all over bar the shouting and his brother-in-law's long-standing love affair with Camilla Parker-Bowles was well known in aristocratic circles, Charles Spencer married Victoria Lockwood, a successful model who suffered from anorexia nervosa. Within six months he began a love affair with another woman. However, Victoria and Charles delivered four children to his dynasty, including, in 1994, a boy. Nothing had changed in this dynasty. 'Securing the male succession' was an obsession.

The traumatised child who had cried for his mother in the night had learned everything about power and love from the most powerful people in his family. Like many boys, and apparently like abandoned aristocrats, he was destined to repeat the brutalities he had witnessed in his youth. Thirty years after his own birth completed and simultaneously exhausted his parents' marriage, Charles Spencer telephoned his wife while she was in the bath to tell her that he no longer loved her. During her pregnancies and illnesses he had been involved in many love affairs with other women. Just as his own father had gone to war against his first wife, so Charles Spencer conducted a bitter and belligerent struggle against his troubled wife in 1997 by launching a legal campaign to minimise Victoria's financial settlement.

According to his wife's divorce affidavit, 'He is an extremely domineering man and I was never allowed an opinion or a voice.' He humiliated her in public and notoriously entertained his Hooray Henry amigos with a merry quip prompted by his father's counsel that he needed a wife who would stick by him through thick and thin: 'Those of you who know Victoria know that she's thick and she certainly is thin.'

According to the matrimonial lawyer Jeremy Posnansky QC, who represented Victoria in the divorce case, the Earl's inheritance gave him an estate believed to be worth more than £100 million, a personal fortune of £6 million and an annual income of more than £1 million. He had resolved to resist his wife's bid for a £3.75 million divorce settlement. He offered her £300,000. One of Victoria's friends insisted that her claim was modest since 'he is a rich man with rich children who need to be brought up a certain way'. Revealing the persistence of patriarchal values, her friend added, 'Victoria cannot believe that Spencer would want his son and heir to spend five days a week in a small home, which is all she will be able to afford with the money he is offering.' (*Sunday Times*, 30 November 1997)

But unlike his mother's generation, the women of *fin de siècle* Britain weren't going quietly. An audacious alliance was formed between Victoria Spencer and Chantal Collopy, the former lover for whom the Earl moved himself, his wife and children to South Africa. They appeared together to challenge his divorce court action in Cape Town, where he had hoped to preserve his privacy from the British press. He failed. 'Three decades of feminist empowerment later, Charles Spencer faces a united enemy.' (*Sunday Times*, 30 November 1997)

If he couldn't empathise with his wife, he might have been expected to sympathise with his sister. With aristocratic riches went responsibilities, and etiquette obliged the heir to perform as both patron and protector to his relatives. But Diana's divorce exposed his contradictory and capricious concern. During the interminable negotiations over her separation from Prince Charles, Spencer grandly proposed that she move to a house on the Althorp estate where she could live with her children – an exciting offer of easy escape from Kensington Palace. A few months later he withdrew the offer. He didn't want the press around his property and, presumably, prying into *his* private affairs.

The Spencer story is a paradigm of patriarchy. The family's fissured and fragile attachments were sometimes interpreted as the Spencer genes, the consequences of a dysfunctional family and their dynastic pathology. The great expectations of Spencer's son were expressed in excess and – to paraphrase Lenin – in the infantile disorder of toff laddism, facilitated by the mighty financial legacy that gave him licence to do what he pleased with mind and body. What he did with his power was to refine the art of domination.

Diana was the last child listed under Johnnie Spencer in *Burke's Peerage* – whatever their running order in real life, the boys come first. Neither the best schools nor the best families thought it mattered that she left school without any qualifications. She was a good swimmer, diver, dancer, and she was a good enough piano player to best her husband many years later by bashing out a bit of Rachmaninov. So, what was happening to her mind? Perhaps life was already too difficult, too chaotic for concentration. Perhaps she did what many distressed, neglected and frightened children do: decide not to know, not to think because it was just too difficult to live *in* her mind, and it was better to busy the body.

The expectations, of the old earl's most famous daughter were both ambitious and abject: she was to enter the elite marriage market, to which she was required to bring only her body and the aching art of subordination.

7. The Prince Goes a-Courtin'

By the end of the decade the premier family's patriarchal problem had been unmasked by the women who had been offered its only prize – the Prince. The problem became both simple and insoluble: he had to find a woman who would be sacrificed so the Prince could have his prize – the crown. The man was ready to ruin a woman in the interests of his own advantage and ambition for he already knew that this was the only meaning of marriage to the future monarch.

His friends had drawn up a list of suitable and sweet virgins. His community was complicit in a great conspiracy. Women who in the olden days would have been deemed courtesans, concubines or official mistresses, presided over the game. His great confidantes were Camilla Parker-Bowles and Dale Tryon, 'Kanga'; the *married* women with whom the Prince had been enjoying long love affairs, women who moved in court circles and who constituted a sexual ménage for the Prince. Camilla prefigured her stalwart relationship with Charles when they met at a London club and she introduced herself as the great-granddaughter of Alice Keppel, George VII's paramour, 'so ... ' He would never have married them, of course – they were already too *experienced* – but their expertise was enlisted in the hunt for the suitable girl.

But these closeted amours exposed the deceit and *danger* of the Prince's patriarchal project: some woman would be destroyed by it. This was certain. The innocente would be the sacrifice. That was why the secret had to be kept from her and from us.

So the Prince scoured the shires to find a suitable girl who knew no better, a girl who'd been nowhere and done nothing. Only aristocrats harvest girls who go to the best schools and get no qualifications. Only aristocrats and religious maniacs make girls 'save' themselves for marriage. Only aristocrats set up their 16-year-old siblings for princes mad about sport, sex and older women.

When Sarah Spencer's liaison with the Prince faded, she confided, 'I'm not the one for him but I know who is.' Though her sister was only 16, 'she would be perfect for him'.

Courtly Love

So, the ancient House of Spencer offered the House of Windsor just such a suitable girl. When Lady Diana Spencer thought she was having a romance with the Prince, she was wrong. But then how could she have known?

The royal family is famous for frozen feelings, callous courtliness, custom and practice. When the Prince went a-courtin', commoners could have been forgiven for confusing cultivated coldness and family frigidity with 'courtly' courtship. The idiom of temperature doesn't help: hot and cold can't help us assess their conduct. Partly this is because *we* don't live with *them*. We see representations of their relationships and infer, therefore, that these *are* their relationships. But even by the standards of the court, what was to come did not bear any resemblance to the decorum of courtly love, a code which emerged as a reaction against the absence of love in the medieval marriage system, and against the Christian contempt for eroticism. The lore of courtly love, enunciated in the syntax of the lover's subservience, implying the lover's ennoblement by homage to the loved one, and expressed in the poetry of romance and the frisson of denial, did not infuse Charles courtship of Diana.

The manners of the court may have masked inflammatory spasms of love, sex and passion, but they could not douse them. There is no evidence that the House of Windsor is any more cleansed of the sticky business than the institutions with which they enjoy a symbiotic relationship: Parliament, the church and public schools. Unforgiving rage and a passion for four-legged furries are well within the range of its emotional repertoire. They shout at photographers, they shoot birds, they run foxes to their exhausted limits and then watch them being eviscerated. They like the cold sweat and blush of sport. These people like excitement. They have their ways of doing things – they've spent generations practising, and they have their ways of *having* things – called gratification. These people have got 'love' and 'hate' tattooed on their tiaras.

Nor did Charles' cold courtship of Diana have anything to do with the fabled Hanoverian *hautfroid* (even though commoners could be forgiven for fantasising that Diana would defrost him). Diana Spencer – designated Lady Di in the mass media – was not being wooed, she was being displayed, put on parade, and informally interviewed for a job with the Firm.

The crisis of the court was that it could no longer entirely control the size of the stage upon which its community performed, and when the royal family spied on the girl, they couldn't control the size of the audience either. She began appearing in the Windsor houses in 1980. At the beginning of the year she was attached to Amanda Knatchbull, 'keeping her company' at Balmoral during Amanda's purported relationship with the prince. In July the Prince was noticed noticing her. He had just finished his wretched affair with Anna Wallace and had been invited to a summer-house party organised by a couple close to the court, Robert and Philippa de Pass, lifelong friends of the Prince's parents. Their son had invited Lady Diana Spencer, saying, 'You're a young blood, you might amuse him.' They sat together on a hay bale during a barbecue. He was 'all over' her, she told Andrew Morton, and 'I thought this was very odd'. She flattered Charles' self-pity when she remembered his sadness at Lord Mountbatten's funeral, saying, 'You should be with someone to look after you.' That was something Diana Spencer knew how to do: she had taken care of her parents in the aftermath of their divorce; she was empathic, supportive and sweet. She'd caught his attention. 'The next minute he leapt on me practically and I thought this was very strange, too, and I wasn't sure how to cope with all this.' He asked her to drive back to London with him the next day. 'I've got to work at Buckingham Palace, you must come to work with me,' he told her. She refused. It would be rude to their hosts, she said. (Morton, 1997, p32)

A Teenager

The *Sun*'s photographer Arthur Edwards spotted the girl that weekend when the Prince was playing polo with his father in the Blue Devils near Midhurst in Sussex. 'I hate polo,' says Edwards. He started mooching around and discovered that Diana was the new girl, took some pictures and called the *Sun* in London to get details. 'I discovered that she had just celebrated her nineteenth birthday. It made me wonder what the prince was doing with a teenager.' (1993, p72)

Not much later Diana's flatmate Carolyn Bartholomew walked into their west London flat to find that Diana had been asked to meet the Prince in 20 minutes. They were going to hear a performance of Verdi's *Requiem* at the Royal Albert Hall. She had to get dressed. Where was that dress? Bartholomew was outraged: 'How dare he ask her so late?'

Although she had been asked at the last minute, this was hardly a spur-of-the-moment surprise. There was a plan. Charles' memorandum to his staff ordered elaborate arrangements for supper and for the chaperone – the girl's grandmother. It was not courtship, exactly, but it was courtly. Prince Charles was not courting her, he was checking her out. Could he be seen with her at the opera? Would she wear jeans, snore, expect a chat?

August

Prince Charles sped from his polo weekend to the Solent for Cowes week, a regular fixture in the royal calendar where Prince Philip always presided over a party including his friend Princess Alexandra (and, of course, her husband) and his German relatives aboard the *Britannia*. Charles invited Diana. She was spirited aboard, unseen by the public spies. But she sensed the gimlet eyes of his friends, all of them belonging to an older generation, watching, as if they knew what was going on. Charles confided to a friend that he'd got the girl he thought he was going to marry. (Bradford, 1997, p434) 'I felt very strange about the whole thing, obviously somebody was talking,' Diana later told Morton.

September

Balmoral and the Braemar Games. Diana had been booked by Charles and stayed with her sister Jane and her husband Robert Fellowes in a grace and favour cottage on the Balmoral estate. As the Queen's assistant private secretary and son of her Balmoral land agent, Fellowes was a member of the royal household. The party included Charles' great friend the Tory politician Nicholas Soames, Charles' long-time lover

Camilla Parker-Bowles and her husband. The Parker-Bowleses shadowed the entire process. 'Mr and Mrs Parker-Bowles were there at all my visits,' Diana told Morton.

The games weekend was always in the press calendar and a posse of journalists were prowling around Deeside. Arthur Edwards was driving by the banks of the River Dee bordering Balmoral with James Whitaker and Ken Lennox, who were working for the *Daily Star*, when they noticed Charles' Land-Rover parked by one of his favoured pools. There they saw Charles fishing while a figure in an old green Barbour waited and watched him. She hid behind a tree hoping they would disappear. They didn't. So she did. When the pressmen ran towards her, a local landowner appeared and, roaring, evicted them from his land while the couple sped off. But, being experts on royal habits, they tracked the Prince to another bank. 'He was so predictable,' recalled Edwards. Again the Prince was fishing while his partner watched. A slash of light from binoculars revealed that she too was being watched – not by the Prince but by the press. While the Prince continued fishing, she retreated behind a tree and, through the mirror of her compact, watched the watchers. 'This meant that she could see us but we could not get a clear look at her,' said Edwards. In one adroit manoeuvre she swept up through the trees away from the river bank and, without ever looking back, disappeared. Two top freelances who had been hiding in the bushes, too, erupted when they saw the tabloid trespassers. Fleet of foot and mind, Diana had rescued herself and the Prince. They had been hoping for a scoop. Everybody was scuppered. 'In fact,' said Edwards, 'nobody pictured them together until the day of their engagement, nearly six months later.'

Though they didn't have the pictures, they had the story, which soon flooded the press. The relationship had been reconnoitred by the mass media the moment it began.

Although the tabloids' prying presence has been blamed for the decline and fall of the royal romance, little did they know that they were recording not so much a courtship but a *conspiracy* – under the eyes of everyone. Prince Charles had arranged for Diana to leave Balmoral escorted by his boys, Soames and Parker-Bowles. The press were on the same flight from Aberdeen. There was no sign of Camilla. She had been invited to stay on at Balmoral with the Prince and the royal family. 'Only in the light of recent discoveries have I understood the significance of this,' said James Whitaker.

For a month the couple eluded the mass media, although Arthur Edwards reports that bit by bit these intrepid investigators learned a little more about the listening and eating habits of the woman he described as their 'quarry'. Somehow, the *Daily Mail*'s gossip columnist Nigel Dempster was privy to the crucial credential for the royals, which he then shared with the rest of the world: 'She has been pronounced physically sound to produce children.'

When I asked Buckingham Palace whether, why and how this test had been performed, the reply was: 'We would never confirm anything of that sort. It's personal detail. I'm afraid we can't enlighten you on that.' Except, of course, that it has always been a profoundly political concern to the court.

October

Diana went to the Ludlow races to see Charles ride his horse Allibar while they stayed at the Parker-Bowleses' home, Bolehyde Manor, in Wiltshire. The following morning, while Charles and Camilla's husband went out riding with the Beaufort Hunt, Diana was assigned to Camilla. Again Charles' confidante was at work assessing the suitable girl. During that weekend Charles took Diana to his new home nearby, Highgrove. Would she organise the interior decoration? he asked the astonished 19-year-old; a suggestion that seemed improper since he had not yet proposed. They were back at Camilla's home the following weekend.

Diana's mother, Frances Shand Kydd, was aware of the talk and confided fatalistically at the time that since Diana had been invited to Balmoral and Sandringham for a fourth time, 'she obviously hasn't blotted her copy book.' (Whitaker, 1993, p110)

November

Diana joined Charles at the Ritz for Princess Margaret's fiftieth birthday bash. In the middle of that month the *Sunday Mirror* ran a story, based on strong sources, that Diana had joined Charles for a late-night tryst on board the royal train, stationed overnight in Wiltshire, the day after the party. Diana was robust in her repudiation of the report. So, too, was the palace. There was a woman with blonde hair on board that train. But it was not Diana.

There was still no announcement. Even the *Guardian*, which should have known better, was pleading for a royal wedding to induce a happy, clappy mood in the midst of the alarming economic crisis – 'if it isn't hurting, it isn't working' – created by Thatcherism's new political economy. The only mainstream broadsheet on the centre-left complained that the failure to announce a wedding was 'profoundly disappointing for a nation which, beset by economic and political dissent, had briefly believed that the sound of distant tumbrels was to be drowned by the peal of royal wedding bells'.

December

The episode of the royal train did not, of course, engage the broadsheets. But it had locked Diana into Charles' precarious personal life, unbidden, exposing the royal representations of family and fidelity to the risky discourses of princely impropriety. Diana herself was not yet privy to the Prince's intentions. Charles went off to his long-planned tour of India in December, having initiated a conversation about marriage. Whitaker had asked her whether she was going to marry the Prince and her answer, 'I really don't know', was bewildering. He came to the view that her confidence was ebbing. The problem was the

Prince's relationship with Camilla; 'she knew that the prince was involved both mentally and physically with her, and Diana's nerve was failing.'

When the Prince returned from India it was a week before he saw Diana again. He told her that he had been busy. But it wasn't with work, it was with a woman. Many years later Whitaker learned from the Prince's valet Stephen Barry that he was with Camilla.

During the Christmas holiday with his family, the Prince was put under intense pressure by his irascible parents. He told his mother that he might marry Diana, but he hadn't yet popped the question. Get on with it, they grumbled. He felt 'ill-used and impotent'.

January

He still couldn't make up his mind. His correspondence at the time reveals that he was not worried about making a mistake for *her*. 'I expect it will be the right thing in the end. It all seems so ridiculous because I do very much want to do the right thing for this Country and for my family – but I'm terrified sometimes of making a promise and then perhaps living to regret it.' (Bradford, 1997, p437) Nowhere in this lament was there any concern for the consequences for Diana.

While he was on a skiing holiday in the Swiss resort of Klosters, he telephoned Diana and told her there was something he wanted to ask her. He was making up his mind, he was ready to propose – in time for a summer wedding.

February

When he returned to Britain at the beginning of the month, he proposed and Diana said, 'Yes please.' He hadn't told her he loved her. 'There was never anything tactile about him. It was extraordinary, but I didn't have anything to go by because I'd never had a boyfriend. I'd always kept them away, thought they were all trouble,' she told Morton. 'I said: "I love you so much." He said: "Whatever that means." He said it then. So I thought that was great.' (1997, p34) So it was settled.

The *ingénue's* inexperience was the condition of his triumph: any woman who'd ever had a love affair would have known that this wasn't one. But even the reporters, whose preoccupation with Diana averted their gaze from the actual affair, hardly noticed. 'At the time it was remarkable how little courting was done,' noted Whitaker. 'Charles never went to her flat, to pick her up, he never sent chocolates or flowers. All the arrangements were made by his bodyguards or his valet.' If Charles had wanted to do things differently, now was the time.

Immediately Diana went to Australia to spend time with her mother and to think about the implications of the engagement. 'That was a complete disaster because I pined for him but he never rang me up. I thought that was very strange and whenever I rang him up he was out,' Diana told Morton. He did eventually respond to one of her messages. But she was by then blind, not available for re-thinking but only for reassurance. The unsettling evidence that this man didn't love this woman had already been revealed to Diana when she told him 'I love you so much' and he replied 'whatever that means'. He shared that thought with the world when the couple announced their engagement, after she returned from Australia, on 24 February 1981. Asked whether they were in love, she said, 'Yes, of course.' He said again, 'Whatever that means', and her face fell. So, the clues were there: something was wrong.

Courtship, like college, was a chance for Charles to enter his own life. The perception that he was a sensitive soul suffering from the *froideur* of his class and circumstances was only an excuse. The theory assumed that he *loved* this woman, that he wanted her. The appearance of a romance had been created by the royals, with their mania for control and secrecy, and by the tabloids, whose pursuit and eroticisation of Diana produced her iconic status as an object of desire. But the conduct of the courtship provided the clues to the masquerade: nothing was what it seemed. Everyone, including Charles himself, had agreed to the royal decree that the *Prince of Wales* needed a wife, a *Princess of Wales*.

Charles enlisted Diana to become a sexual soldier; having taken the Queen's shilling, she was to be drilled and disciplined in the service of her country. Her courtship had been a kind of conscription. Everyone in his circle knew it, they knew that this wasn't Operation Love, this was Operation Wife.

On Remand

When Diana arrived back from Australia, a member of Charles' staff delivered a bunch of flowers. There was no note. It came, she thought, from Charles' office, not from Charles. She packed her bags the night before the official announcement of her engagement to move to her new billet at Clarence House and then to Buckingham Palace, where she was to have a suite of rooms adjacent to the Prince's. She was escorted by an armed police bodyguard, Chief Inspector Paul Officer, who warned her, 'This is the last night of freedom ever in the rest of your life, so make the most of it.' (Morton, 1997, p118) It was as if she'd joined the Foreign Legion.

Once she was installed in palace property, she became palace property. No one welcomed the new recruit, except the servant who took her to her room, where she found a peremptory letter waiting on her bed inviting her to lunch. It had been written by Camilla Parker-Bowles before the official announcement. The lunch had one purpose. 'She said: "You are not going to hunt, are you?" I said: "On what?" She said: "Horse."' Diana was not going to hunt. That cleared the hunting community, which Camilla and Charles had reserved for their own rendezvous.

Once Diana arrived at Buckingham Palace, the Queen did little to make her prospective daughter-in-law feel at home. 'Diana, she quickly realised, was not her type of girl.' (Bradford, 1997, p349) The palace was full of 'dead

energy', a cold place. Diana began a kind of dying, she
became bulimic, and according to her friend Carolyn
Bartholomew, this was when 'the tears started'. (Morton,
1997, p119) Her belief was that the bulimia had been 'there
through her royal career, without a doubt'.

Diana's training began in earnest. The first lesson was to
be guided around the layout of the chintz barracks. Private
Diana learned about the seasons of the royal calendar, she
learned how to weigh her hems to defeat the wind on
walkabouts, and she learned what Charles didn't like. She
learned that nothing changed, 'the only thing the royal
family liked to change was their clothes'. (p120) But the no-
change clause was more than merely an effect of a cold and
conservative menage, it was a clear message: soldiers don't
confer with their sovereign. There was no *negotiation*.
Charles did not need to know what she liked, because
sovereigns are not obliged to negotiate with servants and
soldiers.

At the end of the first month of their official engagement, Charles was scheduled to visit Australia and New
Zealand for five weeks. It was unfortunate timing but it
provided a perfect photo opportunity: a parting. As his
VC10 glided away from its dock, Diana wept. Ahh, tears of
love, thought the watching world. But they were the tears
of a woman betrayed. She told Morton that a few hours
before Charles was due to leave, the pair were pottering in
his Buckingham Palace study. The telephone rang. It was
Camilla. Diana left him alone to say his farewells. She took
him to the airport, he kissed her before he climbed the
steps into the plane and as she watched him leave she wept
because her heart was broken. She went on weeping. 'I
couldn't believe how cold everyone was. I was told one
thing but another thing was going on. The lies and the
deceit.' She had challenged the Prince, who had barely been
able to reassure her.

A couple of weeks before the wedding, at the end of July,
she wandered into the office she shared with some of

Prince Charles' staff and noticed a parcel, asked what was
inside and proceeded to open it, despite the pall of panic in
the room. It contained the now notorious gold bracelet
with an enamel disc bearing the initials signifying Charles
and Camilla's secret intimacy, ordered by the Prince for
Camilla. Diana was devastated, 'Rage, rage, rage.' Charles
and Diana had a row. Again she was not reassured. (p38) On
the day before the wedding, Charles, in his incarnation as
the Prince of Wales, sent Diana a comforting card and a
signet ring engraved not with any *personal* insignia but
with his *princely* imprimatur of three feathers.

Bad Luck, Duch

The Prince began his wedding week by disappearing,
without his detective, to lunch with Camilla, bearing the
bracelet. Diana rushed upstairs to her sisters Jane and
Sarah, who were staying with her at Buckingham Palace to
prepare for the wedding day, and roared that she could not
possibly marry this man. Tough, they said, 'Bad luck Duch,
your face is on the tea-towels so you're too late.' (p124) She
was trapped. No one, least of all those closest to Diana,
could contemplate her withdrawal from the wedding of the
century. Thinking about the revelations in Andrew
Morton's book, my companion commented, 'They left her
in a cage, like a budgie. She had a mirror but she didn't have
a bell or even a mate.' She had to go through with it, even
if it killed her.

Eight hundred guests joined the royal family for a ball
that night. It did not go unnoticed that the prospective
groom danced only once with his future bride. His partner
that night – with their world watching – was Camilla.
'Diana was seen to be in tears. Charles danced all night
with Camilla.' (Bradford, 1997, p441) When Diana left to go
to Clarence House and to bed, alone, Prince Charles and
Camilla disappeared and spent the night together.

Dimbleby describes the Prince looking down on the Mall

the night before his wedding with one of his closest friends. He was 'not at all elated but aware that a momentous day was upon him, clear about his duty and filled with concern about his bride and the test she was about to face.' (1995, p348)

What does this mean? His behaviour at the ball had severely tested the young woman. Was it royal duty that preoccupied him? Or was he dumbfounded by Diana's discovery and her dissent?

His relationship with Camilla was not a phantom of her paranoia – it was well known. He had faced other women with the evidence of his prior passion for her. The scandalous stories about his behaviour in the week of his wedding have several sources, but the most important was his valet Stephen Barry. When caught up in conversations about the wedding week, the loyal servant would 'shake his head in disappointment. He told friends he could not believe Charles would take such a risk, carrying on with Camilla right up to the final moments of his bachelorhood.' He told James Whitaker, 'Sir had always been infatuated with Camilla since they first knew each other in the early 1970s. But when he took her to bed in the very week of his wedding it seemed incredible. Certainly, incredibly daring if not incredibly stupid.' Dimbleby scorns the story and insists that by the time it appeared in Whitaker's book, almost a decade had passed since the valet's death. So Barry 'was therefore never able to rebut the charge against either his employer or against his own integrity'. (Dimbleby, 1995, p348)

Crinoline Shroud

During the engagement Diana's body mutinied. She was throwing up. The day before the wedding she had dinner with her sister Jane. She threw up again. She didn't have a night out with her girls, her own community, the people she could cry with when his family got on her nerves. Instead of a night out getting drunk and having a last laugh, she was stuck at his place being sick.

On 29 July 1981 the deceitful and depressed engagement ended when this thin, wan, whiter-than-white woman walked down the aisle, propping up the aged patriarch who had got her into all of this. Neither her father nor her mother had taken care of her, enlightened her or warned her. They married her off to someone else's prince at St Paul's Cathedral before 2700 guests, watched worldwide by 750 million witnesses.

Her ivory silk wedding dress was a shroud. The dress was a crinoline, a symbol of sexuality and grandiosity; a meringue embroidered with pearls and sequins, its bodice frilled with lace and its sleeves ruffled. The 'something old' was lace that once belonged to Queen Mary; 'something borrowed' was a pair of earrings belonging to her mother; and 'something blue' was a bow, with a horseshoe, attached to the waist. The bridesmaids wore matching ivory dresses and the pageboys wore navy cadets' uniforms dating from 1863. That was the year when the last wedding took place of a Prince of Wales, when Alexandra of Denmark married the philandering Bertie.

Diana's body was displayed and desired by millions, the collective witnesses to her sexualisation – the world penetrated her with its gaze, and infused what it could not see with its own fantasies. And yet that dress didn't really fit properly, despite the efforts of the dressmaker. Diana's body was already shrinking, it was unloved. She knew that she was not the woman the Prince really wanted.

8. Virgin Queen

All that Diana was allowed to bring to the marriage was her body. She knew that her husband was a man with 'a past'. If he was not exactly candid about his history of pleasure, then she might at least have expected that the experience deficit might yield some reward for her – a man who could relax, reassure, forget his own needs and patiently pleasure her, in the sure knowledge that even if he was not completely pleasured there and then, he could be confident that he would be, in time. If a wife was to benefit from her husband's past then at least she could anticipate that his experience would service her great expectations.

There is no evidence, however, that the Prince was committed to *her* pleasure. He had adopted the great uncle's mantra: sow your wild oats and then settle for a woman who will know no better than you, who will, therefore, have no judgement about you. It was a mantra for mastery, a defence against *her* disappointment. By bowing to his family's commandment: thou shalt only

marry a virgin, he had also innured himself against a
knowing woman. A knowing woman would, of course,
have had a history. But the virgin is a woman without
history. In the Bible, according to Marina Warner's virtuoso
study of the virgin in Christian history, 'the amount of
historical detail about the virgin is negligible. Her birth,
her death, her appearance, her age, are never mentioned.'
(Warner, 1985, p14)

However libertine his *other* lovers had been was
irrelevant. He wasn't marrying a libertine. He was meeting
the royal family's pragmatic and political requirements.
But the royal project also plundered the religious cult in its
celebration of a virgin as the perfect woman. The royal
family, therefore, was not only gaining a daughter, but a
woman who embodied their concept of perfection. Yet in
the 'celebration of the perfect woman both humanity and
women are subtly denigrated'. (pxxi) The virgin is
developed in history 'to diminish not increase her likeness
to the female condition. Her freedom from sex, painful
delivery, age, death and all sin exalted her *ipso facto* above
ordinary women and showed them up as inferior.' (p135)
The virgin herself, even in her exalted state, was also
'subject and inferior to men, "thy desire shall be to thy
husband and he shall rule over thee". The cult of the virgin
therefore defines the masculinity for which it is a central
theme.' (pxxi)

The royal family, therefore, required their son to take a
wife whose identity was now and for ever to glow in his
grandeur. The women of his own generation had already
rejected this philosophy because they knew, as their
mothers and grandmothers had known, what it meant for
women: a poverty of pleasure.

The rush into thrill-seeking by Charles' generation had
not necessarily produced harmony or happiness, but it had
given women what they needed: experience and what went
with it, a critique of a disaster that Germaine Greer
prefers to designate the 'frightful British fuck'. Charles'

contemporaries were, like him, people with complex
sexual histories whose culture had produced a proliferation
of sexualities, a kind of sexual pluralism. They had put
sexuality, subjectivity, pleasure and personal power into
the language of politics; they had struggled to put 'the
luxury of candour' into the vernacular of personal and
public, political life. All of this Charles rejected, and thus
fortified himself and the class he represented against the
efforts of women to reform their relationships with men.

But Charles' endorsement – in practice – of the House of
Windsor's commandment also implicates him in a public
and political felony; it makes him the embodiment of a
millennial history of patriarchy, the institutionalisation of
sexual tyranny. Obviously, the patriarchal principle patrols
the bodies of young women, as a religious edict, among
many creeds in many countries. But in the West it is only
in the aristocratic milieux of the   royal family that
patriarchy is still the *law*; not merely the lore of sexual
syntax, but the law of the land. Parliament, the Church of
England and the House of Windsor require our queens and
the wives of our kings to live by this law. Charles decided
to live by this law at precisely the point when it was losing
its legitimacy, when his contemporaries were consigning it
to history. He could have chosen otherwise.

If virginity is taken as the specific sexual requirement of
patriarchal marriage, then the pool of virgin brides was
already drying up. British women of all creeds had
mutinied, *en masse*, against the prohibition of sex before
marriage. In 1994, the most comprehensive survey of
sexual behaviour ever carried out in Britain was published,
in which 18,000 interviews were solicited as a snapshot of
the entire population. Only 6 per cent of men and 15 per
cent of women were virgins when they married. But among
Charles' own age group virginal marriage had largely
disappeared. Among women marrying in Diana's category
– women between 16 and 25 years old – fewer than 1 per
cent had not been *penetrated*. This, of course, was the

prohibited sexual act to be perpetrated upon a royal bride only by the heir.

By the 1980s the sexual revolution had wrought a seismic shift, 'premarital sex was nearly universal'. This prompted the analysts of this study to conclude that virginity was so rare and irrelevant that 'there is little value in focusing on its prevalence in contemporary studies'. (Johnson *et al*, 1994, pp95–97)

Sexual Scandal

The sexual status of the royal bride might have remained an implicit clause in the royal contract, known and yet not known, had it not been for the royalists themselves who introduced its 'relevance'.

On 16 November the *Sunday Mirror* ran a front-page story alleging that Diana had joined Charles for a secret tryst on the royal train while it was stationed in a siding at Staverton in Wiltshire for the night. The story had come from a trusty, Jim Newman,who, as former policeman, had good police contacts. 'The idea of her spending a clandestine night with Charles, under the full scrutiny of SAS and police minders, seemed ludicrous,' commented Whitaker. Ludicrous because Diana's 'unquestionable virtue' was vital to her engagement to the heir.

The Queen's press secretary demanded a retraction. This was unprecedented. 'It was a very vigorous and definite denial,' recalled the feminist journalist Frankie Rickford, who was later to write about the row. But the *Sunday Mirror* editor Bob Edwards would not budge. He challenged the palace to send an official denial, and then he'd publish it, he said.

Meanwhile Whitaker went straight to Diana herself. She denied that she'd ever been near the train, backed up by her flatmates who confirmed that she had been at home having supper with them, nursing a hangover from the night before at Princess Margaret's party. He believed them:

'These were young, well-brought-up girls, who were not used to evasion.'

But the people involved in protecting the royal train were in no doubt: there was a blonde woman on the train with Charles 'and the telephone log', according to Whitaker, 'showed that a call had, a little earlier, been made to Bolehyde Manor.' Everyone resisted the conclusion that 'the woman that night – logged by the SAS soldiers on guard duty around the train – could be any other than Diana. But they were wrong. The woman on the royal train was Camilla Parker-Bowles.' (Whitaker, 1993, p11) Bob Edwards got corroboration many years later that there was a woman on the train – but that it was not Diana. A Christmas card from a former politician close to the court arrived at his home in 1986 and it said simply, 'It was Camilla.' Diana's denial was also confirmed years later by Prince Charles' valet, Stephen Barry. Before he died in 1984 he told James Whitaker that the woman was Camilla.

The royal family's response to the press reports about the blonde woman on the royal train were concerned only with Diana's reputation. The royal family, and particularly Charles, had created a crisis for Diana. Certainly, they respected her determination to refute the reports, but they did not take responsibility for enlightening her, telling her the truth, and thus giving her a choice: to be or not to be Charles' wife. Camilla Parker-Bowles, who had been a witness to Diana's selection, did not enlighten her either. Camilla's strategy placed her firmly on the side of her man, not his other woman. Sexual double standards were inscribed in her own family history. But it was Charles, above all, whose 'incredibly daring or incredibly stupid' tryst with another woman ignited an inflammatory sexual scandal.

Just at the very moment of royalist renewal, bestowed by Diana's impending betrothal, this scandal revealed the contradiction between the royals' dominance of public virtue – expressed in the demand that Diana be both unknowing and unknown – and the real behaviour of its own family members. Historically, this hypocrisy was nothing new. But by the late twentieth century, the discovery of Charles' affair with another woman was enough to bring crisis to the royal family. The scandal of the royal train drew attention to the woman who wasn't there – Diana.

What was at stake for Charles was the protection of his *secret* love affair with Camilla – an affair that was clearly not secret to his coterie. To sustain its secrecy he had to be silent about the identity of his visitor and yet strong in his denial that it was Diana. For if the heir was to have a virgin wife, then Diana's reputation had to be defended. Charles' prospects as a married, or indeed a marriageable, man were in jeopardy. What was at stake for Diana was her 'virtue'. Her 'virtue', however, mattered only to their majesties.

It was the crisis of the royal train that opened season on Diana – her reputation was not allowed to remain implicitly 'innocent'. Her virginity had now to become *public* knowledge if she was to have any chance of protecting the reputation that was *all* she had in her bargaining with the palace and the Prince. The focus on Diana also took the heat off Charles – Diana became a cover for Charles' relationship with Camilla. So Diana's body and its history became public property. By having Camilla on that train, the prince played fast and loose with property that didn't yet belong to him. He pulled people into a public debate that didn't belong to them either.

The Queen knew that the woman on the train was not Diana – her son had told her so. After the first outraged rush of correspondence with the *Sunday Mirror* editor Bob Edwards, the palace seemed to let sleeping secrets lie. A member of the public complained to the Press Council about the story but the palace had no interest in pursuing it.

Diana's mother, who was already a pessimistic observer,

felt provoked to write to *The Times* in December 1980 to
protest at the harassment of her daughter. Her brother,
Lord Fermoy, offered Whitaker a peroration about his
niece's virtue: 'Purity seems to be at a premium when it
comes to discussing a possible royal bride for Prince
Charles at the moment. And after one or two of his recent
girlfriends I am not surprised. To my knowledge Diana has
never been involved this way with anybody. This is good.'
Diana – unconsulted – was horrified. A motion signed by
60 MPs deploring the behaviour of the media prompted a
meeting between editors and the Press Council.

Don't Do It

Britain's feminist community, jaded by the eternal airing of
royal romances, was aghast at the atavistic presumption
that Diana's sexuality should fall under such scrutiny.
Frankie Rickford, a feminist journalist working for the
communist daily, the *Morning Star*, read the bizarre
pronouncements of Lord Fermoy with astonishment. The
paper was one of the few redoubts of Britain's rather
residual republicanism (together with the Labour MPs
Willie Hamilton and Tony Benn). But since the first
audacious flourishes of the women's liberation movement
at the beginning of the 1970s, the paper had also been a
focus for feminist activism. Frankie Rickford wrote a
protest piece in the paper, headlined 'DON'T DO IT LADY DI'.
This was the *only* national newspaper protest. The trail
was picked up by Mandy Merck, the feminist chief
subeditor at *Time Out*, the London listings magazine set up
in 1968. The magazine was a material monument to the
cultural revolution in the capital. It uniquely listed and
reviewed everything in the straight and alternative cultural
industries, from poetry to pop, and its news reporters were
famously put on trial for revealing the activities of the
secret services. Mandy Merck commissioned Frankie
Rickford to write for the magazine and *Spare Rib*, the

feminist monthly set up in 1970, took up the campaign and printed the 'Don't Do It Di' badges which were worn by thousands of women during the wedding year.

It was Diana herself who, in the very moment of her victimisation, discovered agency – she spoke up for herself. It was her first lesson in palace politics and she had to be her own advocate and the authority on her own life. Her honour remained 'intact' because *she* said she wasn't there. It did not matter that her life story placed her, like Charles, outside her own contemporaries. She brought to the scandal of the tryst on the train a refusal to be complicit in the conspiracy and by insisting on her virtue, by her repudiation of the rumour, she forced the palace to do something unprecedented: to respond. They should have known what was coming.

When James Whitaker wrote that the public wanted a virgin bride, he was wrong. The public long ago lost interest, it was only the royal family that had never renounced its requirement of the king's wife. But by focusing on Diana's sexual status, the incident ignited a slow-burning fuse. By bringing about the situation in which Diana could be the object of an inquisition, the Prince created the conditions in which royal sexuality became a matter for public interest.

Little Black Number

Diana's first official engagement was to be a turning point in the presentation of her sexuality. David and Elizabeth Emanuel, who had been commissioned to make Diana's wedding dress, also designed the evening gown in which she attended a charity gala for the Royal Opera House. She was photographed emerging from a car before entering the Goldsmiths' Hall, the cameras looking longingly at her strong swimmer's shoulders and royal bosom. This was the transitional moment of erotic excess.

According to the couturier Emanuel she had been discussing upcoming functions for which she needed to be dressed. She saw the gown in the showroom and 'she fell in love with it so we created one specially for her'. The dress was a black silk taffeta, a ballgown with a 'gravity defying decolletage'. Its composition was in the genre of the crinoline, with a full tulle petticoat and a boned bodice. The fashion history of the crinoline spoke for grandiosity, 'the woman is the property who displays property,' according to the fashion writer Brenda Polan, 'the clothing is a structure that the body inhabits, it is a huge, hierarchic presence'. Its meaning as a 'big frock' is that it eats space; it is only a frock for the rich, for femininity, as show, small lungs and statuesque inertia. (Evans and Thompson, 1989)

Britain's most radical fashion improviser, Vivienne Westwood, identified in the crinoline a riposte to twentieth-century functionalism and to hyper-feminine frilliness; and in its 'ponderous regality' she spotted an arch erotic aesthetic which she offered as 'a sort of vitality that has never been exploited'. She saw crinolines as 'very, very sexy, there never was a fashion *invented* that was more sexy, especially in the big Victorian form.' That's the imaginary space Diana walked into when she acquired that dress. She was still emerging from her Sloane Ranger cocoon, 'shy Di with a high neck and frills'.

But the dress was more than daring, it was dangerous. It declared the desirability of the woman it displayed. The dress did not deliver an ingénue to Charles, but it delivered the pleasure of beauty to Diana. When she saw herself she saw someone lovely. In that dress she could enjoy herself. If that were not risky enough in itself, the dress was also dangerous because it was demanding, it was an incitement, it said: Look at me, love me. Charles' response to the dress prefigured his response to her self. Charles said he didn't like the dress, but when he complained that 'black is for mourning', what on earth was he talking about? He couldn't reveal his real reasons. After all, he was a black and white man in a milieu which had reserved black as the defining colour of *classy* dress for men.

His complaint that day was not candid. That dress and Diana's pleasure in it were a challenge to her containment as an undesiring and undesired virgin. This ravishing gown suddenly announced Diana as a woman, as sexy, as a woman who deserved to be desired, whom anyone might desire. In his anger, was he confronted with his own struggle not to desire her, or the shame of arousal? His self-hatred, since he was not what he seemed? What did it do to his quest for mystery and mastery when the virginal cabbage-patch girl appeared before him wearing the outfit of a metropolitan diva, when the ingénue rather than the prince emerged as a majestic seducer? Did her meta-morphosis reveal that she was worth seeing? Since she was destined to be a subordinate prop, a woman to be seen with *him* and for him, her glamorous reinvention in a great frock unsettled the problem of power that circulated between both the the virgin and the prince and between the virgin and the public.

The irony at the crux of his crisis was palpable. Here was a regime that was quite incapable of improvising or revising tradition and propriety, a regime that 'changed nothing but its clothes', about to enjoy a remarkable renaissance through a woman who – in her iconic emptiness – simultaneously wore the mantle of virgin and vamp.

Instantly she became a sexual object *par excellence*, and since duped Diana had been merely an object, her notorious sexualisation that night announced a potent ambivalence that would haunt the rest of her days. The Diana dialectic had arrived: she was both empowered and endangered.

Virtual Virgin

Diana confirmed and simultaneously disturbed the template of virtue prescribed for her: she had kept herself 'tidy', she had denied herself experience, and so she was, in their eyes, unspoilt. But sexual virtue did not, for her, imply abject subordination; nor did it imply hiding her sexual potential. By appropriating the royal imperatives of public, if not private, virtue, and the royal family's commitment to display, she became a woman whose identity was available for multiple meanings: she existed to service their perpetuity, to be seen, to be displayed, but she was also available for reinvention and reinterpretation because her iconic identity as a virgin was simultaneously empty and eroticised. Instantly, ambivalence defined her appearance: she emerged as a 'virtuous' woman who *wanted* to be desired, and she was displayed as a woman who *was* indeed desired, if not by her man, then by her audience.

When Lady Diana Spencer became Charles' 'new girl', the tabloids reinvented her as jaunty 'Lady Di'. In September 1980 journalists tracked her down at the Pimlico kindergarten where she worked as a helper. She refused to give an interview but agreed to a photograph. 'She was posing in the garden with a child on each hip and the Nikons were rattling like machine guns when the sun suddenly came out from behind a cloud,' recalled the *Sun* photographer Arthur Edwards. 'In a trice her flimsy summer skirt became totally see-through.' It was pure fluke, 'none of the lads said anything, because the pictures were so great. They just kept blazing away while Diana patiently posed up.' (1993, p78)

The Dublin feminist academic, Ailbhe Smyth described Diana as the 'virgin of the century' and saw the picture the photographers produced, of Diana holding the two toddlers on her hip, as an ideal constellation of virginity. This was no old spinster, but an image of a virgin whose identity would soon metamorphose into motherhood, whose sexuality had been reserved for a man with whom she would have babies. Here was virtual womanhood, 'she had to be a bit of a baby herself'. She appeared as a woman with the touch, a woman who could touch babies, and in that kindergarten photograph she was portrayed already as a maternal virgin, a woman who could care. So, her virginity was not perceived as lack, but as a prized prelude to maternity.

Lord Snowdon's engagement photograph softly focused on an embracing couple, the woman (though taller than the man in life) nestling in the crook of her lover's shoulder. But the offical engagement picture restored the virginal allusion. Diana wore a frumpy lady's 'costume' bought, with her mother's help, from Harrods for the February engagement announcement. It was blue and white, the colour of heaven, the livery of virgins the world over. Here she had moved from her own terrain to the palace. Prince Charles stood behind her, holding her shoulders. He was not holding her so much as holding her in place. Once she was betrothed, her virginity, as a style, no longer mattered.

9. Food of Love

When Charles and Diana set off on their honeymoon, ghosts patrolled their already ruined partnership. They slept in rooms where they breathed the same air as *his* parents and *his* paramours, they even slept in the bed where his parents had slept in 1947. Everything about this honeymoon reprised the mania for repetition by which the Windsors codify continuity. Every place they visited positioned Diana in a Windsor ecology.

Instead of the blissful period of postnuptial intimacy a honeymoon couple might have expected, this was a pathological journey beginning at Broadlands, a significant historical dot on the royal landscape, and then on to the *Britannia* accompanied by 277 seafarers. Bizarrely their honeymoon located her in his – rather than *their* sexual history. Not only was Broadlands symbolically potent for the Windsors, it was also the space donated by the great-uncle for Charles' sexual initiations. *Britannia* too had hosted innumerable trysts, all testimony to the illicit intimacies sanctioned by royal patriarchy. Not that there was anything intimate about this voyage of discovery. 'A royal honeymoon could never have been entirely private,' notes Dimbleby, though couldn't it have been a little more private? Why would one of the most privileged men on the planet not arrange intimacy, if not intermittent privacy? Why couldn't he grasp that Diana's disappointment – represented as 'sudden shifts of mood' – was predictable rather than perplexing? Coming from the House of Windsor, the boundaries between intimacy and privacy, between public and private, bore no resemblance to the conventions of space and sexuality which were being negotiated in popular culture. And perhaps the last thing Charles wanted was privacy as a prelude to intimacy.

With brittle deception, the boundaries between old and new encounters were blurred and Diana's first sexual relationship with a man was entombed in the spaces that belonged to others.

This honeymoon was not what it seemed, it was not an old-fashioned, sentimental journey around the great moments in the history of a fond family, revelling in royalty's *transparent* traditions which, by being repeated were also being honoured. Repetition was, in fact, the royal way of disciplining this marriage as a pact with their own future – a future already defined by deceit about the most important thing in her life, *him*.

What did the Prince think *he* was doing? Was he giving his parents a marriage? Was his tour round the sexual traditions of the Windsors intended to reassure his parents that all was well, that he would do things their way?

Their palaces, their codes and ceremonies have to be seen as a 'space of enunciation', an environment in which *they* conduct the conversation; they decide who speaks and what is sayable, what is done and what is doable. To honeymoon in their way was, therefore, more cynical than it seemed – it wasn't just a gift to Charles' parents, it was an injunction to his new wife: that their life together was not negotiable; that it would not be *their* marriage, they

would not be making it up as they went along; that royal
routine would not risk disturbance by the honeymooners'
drama of self-discovery; that their life together would never
be *more* than, or different from, the life he was already
leading. The honeymoon made her sick.

The biographer Anthony Holden thought in the 1980s that
Charles hoped for a 'genuine love-match', he did not want
'like so many Princes of Wales before him, to watch a
marriage of convenience slide into one of arrangement'.
But this was already an arranged marriage – albeit one that
he himself had arranged. Holden came to think that the
arrangement appeared to the Prince as most inconvenient.
The distinction between this arranged marriage and other
openly arranged marriages was that Diana didn't know she
had been arranged. Deceit was what made the difference. It
was already, therefore, a marriage made in bad faith: she
wanted a companion, he wanted a marriage of convenience; she wanted babies, he wanted an heir; she
wanted some loving, he already had a lover; she wanted a
partnership, he wanted to be king.
    The Prince's friends were later to argue that the
difference in their ages and education left them with little
in common. But their honeymoon, like their courtship,
was conducted on his territory, in his family, a family from
which he was estranged and yet in which he was
enmeshed. Diana told Andrew Morton that she became
bulimic almost as soon as her relationship with Charles
began. (1997, p61) The body dominated her honeymoon
and she was sick several times a day. Her companion had
packed a clutch of books by his mentor Laurens van der
Post, in the hope that they would have improving
conversations at mealtimes, a pair of cufflinks given by his
paramour, and photographs of her which fell out of the
pages of his diary. He took to his bed for siestas, hoping for
a rest from it all. Diana playfully invited him to 'do his
duty' in the vain hope that he would make the earth move.

When they returned to Britain, they joined his family at Balmoral, where they stayed from August until October. Diana had become Her Royal Highness, and posed with her kilted husband by the River Dee. Married life was 'highly recommended' – she had to say that. Their long sojourn at Balmoral was, according to Jonathan Dimbleby, 'a blissful interlude, at his favourite home, complete with his books, his fishing rod, and his friends'. (1995, p355) But what about her friends? He couldn't stand them. And what about her books? He thought they were silly.

There is no evidence that anyone thought about who this stranger was, who she loved and liked, what she needed and what she wanted.

Fading Away

By October Diana was pregnant. Relief all round. But by then she was not only bulimic, she was feeling suicidal. When the couple holidayed with his family at Sandringham in the New Year, she seemed to have reached a point where she could no longer live in her own life. His family didn't know what to do with all this evidence of *feeling* and *frustration*. Had they ever seen tears before? She shouted her suicidal despair at her new husband and threatened to throw herself down the stairs. 'Charles said I was crying wolf and I said I felt so desperate, and I was crying my eyes out and he said: "I'm not going to listen. You're always doing this to me. I'm going riding now." So I threw myself down the stairs.' Her husband went out riding and his mother found her at the bottom of the stairs. The Queen was 'absolutely horrified, shaking – she was so frightened'. (Morton, 1997, p45)

The family's response to her distress was to erase the cause while seeking a solution in sedation. Doctors were called, pills were prescribed. Her gender, rather than his grandeur, was regarded as the genesis of their domestic crisis. She, not the prince, was the problem and she, therefore, had to be calmed and controlled.

The royal family's response to a bride who was not blooming but fading only dramatised Diana's body as a site of crisis. They only wanted her for her body anyway. And they only wanted her body for its reproductive faculty. But what was this young woman to feel about herself, about her body, when she knew that it wasn't the body he loved?

Charles created a hunger for nurture that he met with neglect; his indifference created a cycle of deprivation that demanded replenishment. Food for Diana, like everyone else on earth, is an elementary source of renewal, something life-sustaining. But the quest for gratification could also be the evidence of greed. Her husband's coldness could only induce a fear of her own feelings. Food became a metaphor for feelings and feelings, like food, were to be feared. Food became both friend and foe. Bulimia was Diana's survival strategy.

Historically, women's pain and anger, and their visible manifestations, have been pathologised as being a function of the female body. Women, supposedly at the mercy of their raging hormones, were labelled illogical, emotional, neurotic, temperamental, unclean. But when women have no sanctioned voice, or when that voice is not heard, anger and frustration have found an alternative avenue of expression.

Feminist theorists have made the connection between the mutiny of mind and body since the early 1970s. Susie Orbach, the pioneering psychotherapist who has popularised feminist insights into the crisis of the body, and the food it takes in and refuses, in her books *Fat Is a Feminist Issue* and *Hunger Strike*, describes a woman's food crisis as an expression of 'confusion about how much space she can take up in the world'. (1993, pxii) Women feel 'safer using their mouths to feed themselves than using them to talk and be assertive'. (1988, p68) The denial of food is driven by the need to control the body, 'which is, for her, a symbol of emotional needs. If she can get control over her body, then perhaps she can similarly control her emotional neediness. Submitting her body to rigorous discipline is part of her attempt to deny an emotional life.' If she experiences emotions as 'an attack on herself', then she may try to avoid being devoured by emotions by gaining control over her body and mind 'by creating an altogether new person out of herself. In other words she negates who she is – needy, hungry, angry, yearning.' In a context in which she feels assailed and powerless 'she gains strength from the knowledge that she can ignore her needs and appetites'.

The woman who suffers from bulimia, a form of compulsive eating and vomiting related to, but distinct from, anorexia, does not necessarily appear emaciated, and thus does not announce to the world that something is wrong with her life. The bulimic woman's survival mechanism is to gorge and at the same time she seems to have 'a way of seemingly not paying for what she sees as her greed'. But her success – an appearance that does not draw attention to her crisis – is precariously balanced. 'During the daytime fragments of emotional shrapnel pierce the bulimic woman's insides. She hurts but she has few resources for living with, or passing through her pain.' By night she binges, an 'intense experience. In it she may feel like a wild animal, foraging, searching, desperately looking for something to soothe and satisfy her. All the feelings that lay undigested by day, jump out at her as though the spring from Pandora's box has been released. But still the woman cannot embrace them or examine them.' (1993, pxiv) She goes towards food in an attempt to quell her feelings. But she finds little solace. She feels no better until she is full and then emptied. She needs to 'deny the need for soothing, to throw up and out of herself what she cannot digest. The process of not being able to keep what she wants inside her is reiterated.' The bulimia is an absorbing detour around the discovery of what is really troubling her. (1993, pxiv)

The response of a patriarchal society has been to take the

blame away from itself and lay it squarely on the woman and her physiology. This is the medicalisation of social conflict. Thus a woman who is depressed is represented as having a neurological chemical imbalance; a woman who self-harms has a personality disorder. This takes away the impetus for society to actually *do* something – instead of looking at the reasons behind behaviour, it is classed as a physical problem with physical (and pharmaceutical) solutions.

Susie Orbach notes that treatment models, from psychoanalysis to behaviour modification, share the assumption that the problem is the woman's wilful refusal to eat or digest her food. This so annoys practitioners and alarms family and friends 'that interventions focus almost entirely on attempting to make the woman give us the refusal'. Sometimes she is force-fed or subjected to reward-and-punishment regimes. But these approaches, based on forcing a woman to face her strategies, cannot reach her unconscious motivation 'except as further judgements' about behaviour that may not be so much a conscious act of will as an unconscious solution to problems that cannot be addressed in any other way. (1993, pxv) The feminist approach developed by Susie Orbach at The Women's Therapy Centre, which she co-founded, recognises that the woman's strategies represent a sense of accomplishment and pride. To attack her strategy would therefore merely attack her strength. 'Giving up a symptom and owning the power assigned to it means you are taking yourself seriously. Taking themselves seriously has been a risky business for women'. (1988, p83) The royal family only gave Diana their confusion and contempt. 'My husband made me feel so inadequate in every possible way that each time I came up for air he pushed me down again.' Even when she felt she was doing well, by eating, he'd say, 'Is that going to reappear again?' (Morton, 1997, p55)

How could she manifest her anger or her grief? If the discovery of her own disappointment could not be revealed, because it could not be tolerated, then it made sense to keep screaming and at the same time to starve, to stuff food into herself and to be sick. If food was a source of survival and at the same time a reproach, then eating and being sick was at least a way of manifesting and at the same time masking self-hatred, shame, relief, triumph and reward.

Blood Sacrifice

Later Diana cut herself, too. This was seen as attention-seeking, self-destructive and silly. Certainly, it was a shout from someone who did not feel attended to. Why wouldn't someone who sees this not want to wrap his arms around her and say, What's wrong, what can I do? Please don't hurt yourself because you are hurting the person I love.

What was happening inside her husband that made him so angry and able to turn away? He could have made a difference. He could have shared in her torment by validating her and taking responsibility for his part in her distress. He could have taken her side by being, at least, by her side. Instead he gave her blame. Her pain was an appeal and an accusation. By not taking responsibility for his action, he gave the responsibility back to Diana.

If you have been made to feel worthless, if you have come to hate yourself, then harming the body in which you live is an expression of that self-loathing. And if you are only allowed to shadow yourself, rather than *be* yourself, then the sight of your own blood may remind you that you do, after all, exist. It is also the evidence that you are living in a dangerous place. In her tapes for Andrew Morton's book, Diana reported throwing herself against a glass cabinet, cutting her wrists with a razor blade and scratching herself with a lemon knife. One night when she had tried to have a conversation with her husband, who didn't want to listen, she picked the penknife off his desk and slashed her chest and thighs. He didn't react.

He was later to represent his underreactions as the exhaustion of an exasperated man. During their Expo tour of Canada in 1986 she was holding very little food in her body and began to feel 'ghastly'. At one point 'I put my hand on my husband's shoulder and said: "Darling, I think I'm about to disappear," and slid down the side of him.' She had fainted and was carried off to another room by two royal aides. 'My husband told me off. He said I could have passed out quietly, somewhere else, behind a door.' (Morton, 1997, p55)

A soul that is being sacrificed by a power greater than itself is a soul in panic, caught in a frenzy of impossible options. It is neither life nor death, but a kind of living death. The restless refusal to lie down and die reaps no reward, only mutual reproach. Red blood spreading across skin materialises the drama of sacrifice, but it also has its own biochemical effects: cutting releases endogenous opioides, it induces insensibility and causes calm. Cutting is a strategy of self-harm that simultaneously soothes. Sacrificial survival is an existence that gains no reassurance or respect, there is no security or satisfaction. For the bulimic Diana, food, like feelings, had to be purged. If she was to be a good girl, then she had to renounce the possibility of gratification, she must not be greedy. And yet in the absence of love and satisfaction, what was she supposed to do? Leave him? Eat? Love him, bleed and make herself sick?

10. Sex

When the world watched Diana's wedding day, a galaxy of fantasies surrounded her sexuality. She had been preserved for procreation and now she was penetrated by a global gaze. She was penetrated, but was she pleasured?

By a self-denying ordinance she had been deprived of desire until her body was to be deployed in dynastic work. Her self-denial, her inexperience, was suddenly revealed as the necessary qualification: if she was to experience the mystical shudder, then she had to know nothing, she had to know no better. Just as the great-uncle had said it should be.

Suddenly she was sexualised, saturated in sexual light. Diana's sexuality was of course a fiction, incipient and imaginary, displayed in a spectacle from which her audience drew its own inferences and designed its own fantasies. That day Diana embodied the feminist problematic: her iconic sexualisation represented the defeat of women. Her marriage was being celebrated as the triumph of *modern* monarchy, and yet her transformation from 'virgin' to 'bride' announced that her value to the

royal family lay in the absence of experience and a history
of her own. Her value was defined only in reference to her
relationship to a man. And yet that day expressed the
heterosexual woman's eternal hope that it would be all
right on the night. Women that day and night will have
been wondering, despite their better judgement, did the
earth move? Women were fascinated by Diana as the
embodiment of an ideal and its impossibility. They went
on searching her face for evidence.

Diana was delivered to sexual disappointment at
precisely that point in our history when women, including
the women of her own generation, were exposing the
notion of the normal sexual act to the gimlet eye of their
own experience.

To make sense of Diana's story as a sexual tragedy we
need to remind ourselves that in contemporary Western
culture sexuality is represented as a force of nature. But
twentieth-century scholars in fields as disparate as science
and cultural studies now acknowledge that the body itself
has a history, the ways that the body has been lived in, used
and abused, treated and interpreted, have been the subject
of history. The body has been brought into being and
'incorporated into different rhythms of production and
consumption, pleasure and pain'. (Gallagher and Laqueur,
1987, p1)

Just as women's desire has been a shifting theme in
history, so has women's anatomy been subject to
representations and repressions, the meanings of which
reveal not so much an evolutionary struggle *for* knowledge
as a power struggle *over* knowledge, what can be known,
and who can know it. The female body gains and loses
faculties across this historical landscape. The clitoris, more
than any other organ, vaults in and out of the history of the
body and desire. In our own time it is feminism that has
disinterred this story of sexual anatomy as part of the larger
chronicle of control and containment. Women's bodies
have been interpreted and reinterpreted throughout 300

years of masculinised medicine. Until the eighteenth century women's bodies were interpreted merely as 'an inferior and inverted version of the male body'. But at least that fashioned a theory which gave the female orgasm its place, together with male orgasm, as an inflammatory event that *had* to be created if procreation was to follow.

The Enlightenment bequeathed to women a new story, one which 'ceased to regard the female orgasm as relevant to generation. Conception, it was held, could take place secretly, with no tell tale shivers or signs of arousal.' An idea which had prevailed for a thousand years was swept away in the quest for a new conception of human sexuality, predicated not on gender similarities but on gender difference. Orgasm 'moved to the periphery' of physiology. And so, something deeply embedded in the notions of how humans create life faded into a feeling, nice but not necessary. (p1) These hypotheses belonged not merely to biology but to the 'new claims and counter-claims regarding the public and private roles of women as distinguished from those of men'. A social struggle was, therefore, being expressed in biological debates.

Having confidently collapsed procreation and pleasure for men and yet erased that equation for women, patriarchal ideologies of sex were left with an enigma: how to explain an epidemic of sexual *dis*pleasure, and how to recruit women to active participation in heterosexuality in the face of a reticence which was deemed natural and yet demobilised feminine enthusiasm for the sexual act?

Sexologists throughout the twentieth century have been foraging among the detritus of women's disappointment to find the runes that might yield evidence to explain women's complaints, tears and estrangement. Indifferent to the autonomous site of pleasure in women's anatomy, men, from the man in the street to the masters of medical omnipotence, have been asking the same question as Freud; what do women want? The question responded to the phenomenon of frigidity which, until relatively recently, pathologised women's disappointment as if it were a disease. But sympathetic sexologists had also been suggesting throughout this century that far from being a feature of femininity, frigidity is not the absence of desire but rather the body's covert rebellion against 'wham, bang, thank you ma'am'. Frigidity came to be seen not as feminine failure but as feminine protest.

This intelligence later infused the ruminations of one of Britain's great polemicists for women's pleasure, Dr Helena Wright, an early advocate of fertility control as well as the pleasure principle. Her own work as a clinician providing contraception in one of Britain's first birth-control clinics prompted her to write a stirring attack on the ideology that produced the problem: the penetration principle, she argued, effaced the clitoris and amounted to a 'penis-vagina fixation'. Wright's work began in the waning days of early twentieth-century feminism, but she arrived at her critique of the fixation and its obliteration of orgasms for women in the 1940s, in the middle of the interregnum between the two great waves of Western feminism. Her conclusions were pilloried by 1930s sexual politics and left lying latent until women's liberation revived the great debate.

The great sex surveys of the late twentieth century were preoccupied by the same problem: how to explain the epidemic of ennui among women, and how to enlist women's enthusiasm for a sexual project that produced risk and unhappiness, babies but not orgasms.

The women's liberation movement brought feminist intelligence to feminine experience. In her mammoth survey of American women, Shere Hite echoed Helena Wright's earlier insight: we were asking the wrong question, she said. Instead of asking why women were frigid, we should be asking why anyone would think that the old fixation would make the earth move or the clitoris quiver. The Hite Report concluded that 'it is clear that intercourse by itself did not regularly lead to orgasm for most women. In fact, for over 70 per cent of women, intercourse – the penis thrusting in the vagina – did not regularly lead to orgasm. What we thought was an individual problem is neither unusual nor a problem. In other words, *not* to have orgasm from intercourse is the experience of the majority of women.' (Hite, 1977, p136)

The history of patriarchal heterosexuality is not just a history of triumphant conquest, but of failure, of restless effort expressed in encyclopedic texts, sex surveys and how-to-do-it manuals, in repression and resistance. Across the centuries, the history of the clitoris, that small but beautiful continent, is revealed as the crux of sexual crisis. Women were denied the knowledge of its amazing properties by 'phallic propaganda', a determination to either erase or infantilise it, or make it marginal to normal, heterosexual sex. The clitoris did not die, it slept, ached, laughed and threw arrows to the heart.

Experience Essential

Young women whose decade was shadowed by Diana's doomed marriage defined – more than Diana did – a process of permanent revolution in civil society, the informal social space in which we all live. But the map of their sexual safaris remained a generational secret. Young women leading open sexual lives at the end of the twentieth century organised their own access to sex, drugs and rock'n'roll, and their commitment to sexual pleasure was matched only by the hard work they invested in having it. 'My clitoris has cobwebs over it,' said one young woman who expected to educate her lovers because they never seemed to know where it was. These young women learned from their own experience – indeed *experience* is their essential qualifica-tion – and through it they thought they could improve their men, an optimism no one else seemed to share.

Lucky women made their own voyages of discovery and found the precious place themselves, and found lovers with whom its exquisite alchemy could be appreciated. Many or even most straight blokes missed the precious place, however, unless they allowed themselves to be enlightened by women's experience. Experience was, of course, what Diana denied herself in the line of destiny. Without experience a woman is left relying on good luck.

Within the patriarchal firmament there are, of course, men so mesmerised by women, so addicted to the scent of a woman, so rewarded by her whispers and roars, that they confidently give a woman what *she* wants, a lexicon of lovely lust learned from other women; thus his gift, and his power, is to share with her what she doesn't yet know about herself. This man is, of course, the gigolo. He doesn't do rape or pillage, and he doesn't do sex as a poke. He loves women. The gigolo and the patrician may be opposites sides of the same coin, but at least the gigolo knows how to give a gal a good time.

Diana's iconic sexuality – sleeping beauty awakened not by a fornicator but by a formal, fidgety but kindly prince – served a regressive fantasy, a fraud visited upon women for centuries by sexual ideologies that emptied them of their own desire, their own sexual anatomy and their own sexual fantasies, ideologies that left them in a contingent status, waiting for the royal wave of the willy. This traditional template enjoyed its day down the aisle at the very moment in history when it had been finally and fully exposed, by experience, as the scourge of women's sexuality.

The display of Diana as a sexual ingénue about to be initiated, awakened, by her prince, her deliverer, served a political project. It was not just bread and circuses, a diverting jamboree, that gave the wedding day its potency in the wan beginnings of the 1980s. The marriage suddenly and surprisingly was subliminally mobilised, at least in the royal imagination – who else cared? – to vindicate the ragged reputation of *procreative* sex as the only *pleasurable* sex.

On the eve of her marriage Diana discovered that Camilla was the love of Charles' life. Within a year of her marriage she was a mother. Her memory of her life between the birth of her first and second child became a blank. By the time her second child was born, she sensed that this marriage was over and within a couple of years it *was* all over bar the appearance. A silent, sulking holiday in Majorca in 1987 was followed by Charles' flight to his Balmoral bolthole, where he stayed for six weeks. She confronted him in a showdown with the question that revealed who had the power in this relationship to reassure or repudiate: 'Have you *ever* loved me?' (Dempster, *Daily Mail*, 5 June 1995). She already knew the answer, but the question was both an appeal and an accusation. He could have lied. But he is reported to have said no.

Diana's only experience of love, sex and passion had been with a man whose heart wasn't in it. Her personal history taught her not about love but about triangles in which she struggled for herself amidst dramas defined by other people's needs. Her childhood had been dominated by a man whose intermittent interest left her loitering for love in a schedule absorbed by another. Her marriage, likewise, promised a prince but gave her a reluctant romance and rudimentary courtship before settling down into an unsympathetic, uncomprehending impasse. Imprisoned in an inhospitable milieu, her body became the bearer of her crisis in which her distress surfaced not as a coherent story but as symptoms which accelerated dangerously when the reality of the marriage was unveiled.

Her husband also came to their marriage as a needy, uncertain victim, disempowered and yet entitled to personal dominion; brutalised as a schoolboy, schooled in the lore of sovereignty, a cult bequeathed to him, paradoxically, by a woman. How could such a boy be with a woman? Was he still seeking sovereignty? Or was he after the thrill of illicit impossibilities? The sexual tempers of both Diana and Charles were cruelly exposed in the publication of the transcripts of their taped telephone conversations with Camilla Parker-Bowles and James

Gilbey, both recorded in 1989. Charles' representation of himself as an unlovely Tampax doomed to swirl around the top of the toilet invited infinite interpretation. The grandeur of sovereignty was suddenly transformed by his identification with the visceral rubbish of womb-waste, a prince who saw himself as a soiled secret. Their long, late-night conversation, preoccupied by his problems, his arrangements, his sadness, his longing, was mediated by her lust, her attentive admiration, her administration of their shared secret life. Amidst his anxiety and self-absorption, her *raison d'etre* is revealed as *his* life.

'I'm so proud of you,' he tells her.

'Don't be silly, I've never achieved anything,' she replies.

'Your great achievement is to love me,' says Charles.

Diana's great tragedy, of course, was to love him – he was the love of her life. Her precarious, traumatised attachments as a child were repeated in this attachment to an adult who emotionally abandoned her as well, an attachment that she maintained for years, even at the expense of her own health and her own reality.

Illicit Intimacy

How could Diana gain either satisfaction from this unwanted attachment or safe, secure separation? Inadequate attachment skews the possibility of safety in separation. Diana's own experience, if it taught her anything, was that once aristocratic women were denied love or divorced, they risked losing everything: her own mother and stepmother both lost their children when they were divorced by their husbands.

Locked in a loveless place, judged and watched, where was she to find love? Flirtation could flourish among the men to whom she had access, old friends, married men whose sexual status did not, therefore, invite scrutiny, and staff. How could she avoid a pattern, described by Judith Lewis Herman, of 'intense, unstable relationships, repeatedly enacting dramas of rescue, injustice and betrayal?' (1992, p111) Unlike Charles, whose lovelife could be warehoused by a courtly class happy to provide the premises and the privacy, Diana was doomed to encounters in unprotected public places, the cloisters of the palace, or risky rendezvous in the real world.

Charles' relationship with Camilla Parker-Bowles and Dale Tryon – Kanga – enjoyed almost total immunity. The press peeped, but their rendezvous yielded little evidence of illicit intimacy. By contrast Diana's evenings out or country-house parties with friends like the banker Philip Dunne and Major David Waterhouse, who had been with Charles and Diana during their Klosters skiing holiday in 1987, were instantly snapped by the press. Her relationship with James Hewitt, a major in the Life Guards and her sons' riding instructor, was organised around the routines of riding lessons and ultimately exposed to the press, too, by his privileged girlfriend, who told their story to the News of the World, and by Hewitt himself, who cashed in on his connection by selling his own story, co-written with Anna Pasternak.

Her friendship with posh car salesman James Gilbey was spotted by photographers when they emerged from Diana's favoured London restaurant, San Lorenzo, whose proprietor, her friend Mara Berni, made her own flat available to Diana. (Whitaker, 1993, p52) Their relationship was also exposed when transcripts of taped telephone calls in 1989 were later published, revealing another romance riven by the frisson of risk and sexual panic. Whitaker reckoned that by the end of the decade she minimised her contact with other men; 'I do not know of another royal princess in the present House of Windsor who has exercised such exceptional self-restraint.'

In the 1990s, when Charles and Diana had already been living separate lives for several years, Diana began to break out of the supervised itinerary of everyday life – crucially, after withdrawing from public life at the end of 1993, she dispensed with royal police protection. At least now she could have a *private* life; at least she could sleep alone in her own apartment. Or she could choose to do otherwise.

Diana was at the centre of the closely watched collapse of the short-lived marriage of England's rugby captain Will Carling and his wife Julia in 1995. Carling had lightly referred in public to 'so-called trysts' and in September Julia announced the separation and said, 'It hurts me very much to face losing my husband in a manner which has become outside my control.'

In August 1994 the *News of the World* reported that Diana had haunted the home of a rich art dealer, Oliver Hoare, with anonymous telephone calls. Her friendly reporter on the *Daily Mail*, Richard Kay, published her denial, but the police records were unequivocal. A silent caller had been ringing the Hoare home. Diane Hoare was unnerved by the silent intrusions. When Hoare himself picked up the receiver it began to dawn that perhaps the caller just wanted to hear the sound of his voice. When the Hoares enlisted the help of the police the calls were traced to Kensington Palace. It was a devastating and damaging story. But at the time the press didn't ask itself what a woman who lived in a proverbial tower was to do. How was she to deal with her feelings and to escape a situation in which she had experienced disrespect? Having dispensed with the eternal eye of her palace guards she was still under scrutiny. And so in the middle of a romance how was she to 'have and to hold' a lover? She couldn't confront him, go hammering on his door, walk *out* or *in* on him, have a row, or a rendezvous.

Diana may have been repeating the traumatic patterns of her youth, patterns of attachment and abandonment, but she brought to them the one weapon she had previously been denied – experience. These men were not husbands or princes; they were lovers and with them Diana explored the landscape of her own sexuality. Having been dumped by her husband, she began to look for love. However, unlike other women, she was looking for love in an environment in which there was total denial and total surveillance. She may or may not have found love and she may or may not have been used, but by seeking love, sex and passion, she was at last doing what every other woman did.

11. Mothers and Fathers

The heir to the heir to the throne was born just after nine o'clock in the evening on 21 June 1982. He was a healthy baby boy, known as 'baby Wales' for a few days until his parents agreed that he would be named William Arthur Philip Louis.

The date for the induced birth had already been determined by Charles' diary; 'we had to find a date in the diary that suited him and his polo,' Diana told Andrew Morton. (1997, p46) She too wanted to get the pregnancy over with, because she was finding the pressure unbearable.

The baby arrived amidst great excitement. He was welcomed into the world by both his mother and father – Charles' presence at the birth was perceived publicly as a sign of his commitment and his modernity (uncontaminated by the private negotiations over his polo priorities). 'I am so thankful I was beside Diana's bedside the whole time,' Charles wrote to his godmother Patricia Brabourne, 'because by the end of the day I really felt as though I'd shared deeply in the process of birth and as a result was rewarded by seeing a small creature which belonged to *us* even though he seemed to belong to everyone else as well!' (Dimbleby, 1995, p368)

Diana, too, was pleased to have finally given birth. Her pregnancy had been an unhappy time, punctuated by bulimia, morning sickness and sadness. The beloved baby entered a palace peopled by adults deluded by grandeur and deprived of care. Sure, they were supremely serviced by their subordinates, but this was a community which did not bring to its children the labour of love and a culture of care.

Toffs, like many men, have not assimilated either the difficulty or the passion of parenting. But toffs, like many men, were participating – whether they liked it or not – in diverse debates about childhood and the politics of parenting, pioneered by the women's liberation movement, child-health and welfare professionals, and by Thatcherism. Thatcherism introduced a new political subject, the *parent*: children were represented as *virtual* humans whom parents were to patrol, train and police. By contrast the women's liberation movement and and welfare professionals encouraged adults to see children as a constituency deserving of resources and respect, entitled to expect companionship, rather than mere control, from adults.

Part of women's new expectations was that men should share the work of care. Modern feminism's critique of the polarisation between public and private spheres was also a critique of a sexualised landscape in which masculinity was deemed to belong to the public sphere and femininity to the private. Masculinity was, therefore, validated in a *separatist* sphere populated by other men – their work-mates and playmates – unencumbered by unruly and unpredictable women and children, who were to be safely sequestered in a secluded space: the home. The relationship that modern masculinity had constructed to children, based on absence and authority, was already losing its legitimacy when Charles became a father. But it was the women of his generation who propelled the new relationship.

Charles had no help from his own family. Even though they lived and worked at home, even though they enjoyed freedom of movement and – unlike most other parents – control over their own time, Charles' mother and father *both* visited upon their son the aura of absence and authority, expressed synergistically as sovereignty. What did a boy know about *how* to be a parent when he had a mother before whom adults bowed and a father to whom a sovereign deferred?

Although his class did not see itself, in its collective identity, as an indictment of poor parenthood, the prince was not without self-awareness. Both Prince Charles and Princess Diana knew, in some sense, that the parenting they had received was less than good enough.

The Prince was fortunate when he became a parent. His generation (if not his class) was changing the contract between children and adults, and he had married an enthusiastic woman who wanted nothing more than to be with him and have babies. And Diana had learned from the mistakes of her parents. She wanted to do things differently. But Charles wanted his children to be brought up by his own nanny. His cauterised imagination clung to the stalwart surrogate mothering he had relied on as a little boy and his script for his own child looked like a melancholy reprise of his own childhood, as if he could not conceive of himself as a confident carer. Still less could he acknowledge that if he and his wife could not be partners for one another, they could still be partners in parenthood. That might have salvaged something useful from their misconceived marriage.

Diana's memory of the years between the birth of William and her second son, Harry, is of 'total darkness. I can't remember much, I've blotted it out, it was such pain.' (Morton, 1997, p51) Her life was cloistered. Her baby arrived amidst riches, the best care money could buy. But the baby also exposed the everyday reality of her doomed marriage: deceit, disappointment and now depression.

Deprived and Depressed

Post-natal depression, it is well known, often visits women who have been inadequately nurtured in their own childhood, whose adult environment leaves their own mothering, though motivated and diligent, again unsupported. And yet depression, so common among mothers, as well as men and children, has routinely been met by a medical response in Britain that rarely addresses the existential and emotional. In a speech in 1982 Charles told the BMA's 'top men' that doctors should acknowledge that medicine is about more than bodies and biochemistry; illness is a 'disorder of the whole person' embracing mind, self-image, social environment and the cosmos; and the 'health of human beings is often determined by their behaviour, their food and the nature of their environment'.

Charles did not connect this critique with his own life. He mobilised his authority but not his personal experience of his wife's crisis to attack medical orthodoxy. He used his own power, rather than his wife's pain, to air an argument in the public realm. So it was in private.

This speech revealed a populist tendency in the Prince, an approach to politics that appeared to connect with popular consciousness but appealed to traditional authority rather than popular empowerment. Certainly, in his relationship to his wife and her lament about their life he was aloof and angry, reluctant to recognise that her anxiety had anything to do with him. In the search for a solution he looked neither to her nor to himself, but to the profession which he now assailed.

It was not as if alternative wisdoms were not available. Diana's distress echoed the experience of thousands of women who, since the 1960s, had been mobilising against the myopic medicalisation of their troubles. These survivor movements operated at the interface between women's pain and professional practice. They started with women telling their own stories and with professional women allowing their clinical environment to be transformed by these testimonies.

When Charles was calling in the psychiatrists to deal with his wife, The Women's Therapy Centre had already been functioning for five years. When it began in 1976 it was instantly inundated with queues of women. It was the clinicians' openness to women's experience, including their own, that produced a new discourse of women's body crisis, food and mental health which transcended the differences between women. In the 1980s this new archaeology of the mind accumulated more evidence of neglect, cruelty and abuse spanning women's life histories both as children and adults. These discoveries lent adult endorsement to a parallel process of revelation among children, whose long lament was also being heard afresh. A decade after The Women's Therapy Centre opened its doors, children's accusations, primarily against adults, found a new ear in Childline. Ten thousand calls are made every day to this listening line. When children's determination to tell their story gained access to adult allies and advocates, then the space from which they could speak, both to themselves and to the adult world, challenged what was known and what became knowable about childhood adversity. Indeed these survivor movements among women and children challenged everything.

It was not that The Women's Therapy Centre disowned the discipline of psychotherapy, but rather that it allowed the experience of women to interrogate it. The effect was to infuse the professions and popular culture with new ways of thinking about 'disturbance and distress'. The Women's Therapy Centre took risks, 'to be prepared to re-examine everything,' explained its clinical director Sally Berry. The confidence came from the women's movement, its culture of consciousness-raising and solidarity which revealed the extent to which women had, so to say, no ground to stand on. The centre wanted to 'create a sense of entitlement, so that women had space to examine their own issues in some safety, not being judged, defined, diagnosed, and to be confident about taking that space'. A new relationship between women as clients and women as clinicians yielded a confident challenge to a history of psychiatry which labelled women 'hysterical', 'greedy' and 'manipulative' – all terms that were deployed against Diana.

What the clients and clinicians discovered together was that women did not hurt themselves, starve, make themselves sick or cut themselves up 'unless they were in excruciating pain, suffering great anguish and loss, and under gigantic internal pressure'.

Jonathan Dimbleby's biography repeats the disrespectful response to Diana's difficulties that were used to discredit her. He minimises and, indeed, mischievously mis-represents Diana's self-harm: 'the cuts were always less serious than at first they appeared; they drew blood but a sticking plaster invariably sufficed to stop the bleeding.' (1995, p400) Neither the Prince nor his biographer, it seems, bothered to find out what the professional community and a massive constituency of women already knew about self-harm.

The biographer reports what the psychiatrist was told when he was commissioned, an account that came from the Prince, presumably. It points to a predictable culprit: there was a woman to blame! The psychiatrist was told that Diana's mother 'left her husband to marry another man'; Diana's grandmother cautioned the court to 'give custody to her son-in-law rather than her own daughter'; Diana's father was 'doting but disconsolate' and these traumas 'blighted her entire upbringing'. (pp400–401) Presumably the psychiatrist was not told, because Dimbleby doesn't tell us, that Diana had a 'doting but disconsolate' mother and a father whose violence made her mother leave. Nor is he told that Diana was deceived by a husband who was never able to love her. The biographer, of course, does not believe that Diana was deceived. These omissions are an index of strategic storytelling, mobilising Diana's pain to redeem the reputation of a self-pitying prince.

The biographer, like Charles and his family, blames Diana for the failure of a marriage that, he concedes, was always flaky: 'she was able to escape only intermittently from a pattern of behaviour that steadily wore away the insubstantial foundations on which their marriage had been constructed.' (p401) Dimbleby describes her as displaying 'erratic and arbitrary behaviour' and 'waywardness' during her post-natal depression.

It is notable that those who backed Charles' view of the marriage were mostly men. When the male prerogative is threatened, when women's claims endanger the status quo, men, unsurprisingly, close ranks to protect their own interests. Many of Charles' friends who support his view of Diana would have been well aware of his relationship with Camilla, but chose not to allow this to impinge on their interpretation of Diana's distress.

Adopting his subject's protestations of innocence, Dimbleby does acknowledge that in this relationship that 'lacked intimacy and mutual understanding' the Prince 'was not always solicitous. Burdened by the workload of his own official life, lacking the emotional support at home to which, in his romantic fashion, he had for so long aspired, and drained by the persistence of his wife's reproaches, he did sometimes rebuff her.' (p399)

Diana was living in the classic conditions that create post-natal depression. It is a common condition affecting about 10 per cent of women. 'It is often minimised by medical doctors as *just* post-natal depression,' says Professor Lynne Murray, 'but it is just as severe as depression.'

Professor Murray's research on depressed mothers and their children shows that the women rendered most vulnerable are those who did not have experience of being taken care of in their own childhood, 'because they haven't built the same robust self-esteem you get when you have someone on your side'. The impact of this history is particularly poignant when a woman becomes a mother herself. Her vulnerability to depression is increased if she lacks support from her partner and other confiding relationships. These elements can be disastrous for a young mother if her world has been emptied of affirmation and yet she has a needy baby. Professor Murray points out that the absence of a *supportive* partner is the one consistent variable in all the research on post-natal depression. 'Every single study that looked at the quality of a woman's relationships found an association between the woman being depressed and difficulties in her relationship.'

All these conditions prevailed in Diana's life, marooned as she was in the palace with the Prince's family, the Prince's friends, the Prince's priorities and the Prince's pleasures.

It is not uncommon for women, like Diana, to resist medication during their depression. Professor Murray suggests that this is often because these mothers are well-motivated women who want to be attentive to their babies. They don't want to be drugged up. They want to wake when their child wakes in the night, they want to be in their child's life. And 'they probably sense that the cause is not physical'.

This is confirmed by the speed with which post-natal depression lifts if a woman has access to *any* support. 'There is really good evidence that these depressive disorders can lift very quickly if emotional support is put in place.' It would have taken very little for Diana to get better. Indeed it was as soon as she began to feel *heard* and *understood*, rather than 'judged, defined and diagnosed', that she did begin to get better.

Bliss Goes Bang

Diana dispensed with the psychiatrist briefed by the royal family. Prince Charles and his family continued to blame

Diana's distress for destroying their marriage. He was never able to bring to his wife's depression the qualities he had demanded of the BMA's good doctors.

The couple's second baby was born in September 1984. 'Harry appeared by a miracle,' she said later, but then 'it just went bang, our marriage.' That year Charles, under pressure from Diana, agreed to spend more time with his children. According to James Whitaker, 'Prince Charles started to take more and more time off his official duties – ostensibly to be with his children. With his public engagements cut to virtually zero, the prince suddenly underwent a barrage of criticism from the press and Parliament.' Kensington Palace explained that the Prince was not shirking, he was 'taking a breather to be with the boys'. But Whitaker, who believed that the Prince had already decided to resume his relationship with Camilla a couple of years earlier, reckoned the Prince had another reason: 'he was hunting regularly, and not just foxes.' (1993, p137)

Charles used his children as an alibi in the face of public criticism. While Diana was probably the first royal mother whose relationship to her children resembled the norm among British parents, Charles' performance as a father continued to match that of a class eternally estranged from the world of childhood. As a *father* Charles could have rescued something from his wretched family life. And as a father he could have matched his dramatic polemics about doctors, architects, planners and teachers with a robust intervention in the great debate about fatherhood. He didn't.

In 1991 the differences between Diana and Charles were ruinously revealed. Prince William was rushed from Ludgrove School to hospital after being hit on the head with a golf club by a fellow pupil, leaving an indentation in his skull. He was moved from Berkshire to Great Ormond Street Hospital for Sick Children in London, where consultants decided to operate. His parents, both of whom had rushed to the the child's bedside, were reassured that he would recover. His mother stayed with him through the night. His father went to the opera with European environment commissioners and the following day to Yorkshire for an official visit. Charles explained, in his own defence, that the doctors had reassured both parents that the boy was not in danger. But the response of these parents touched something bigger than themselves.

For decades child care professionals had been campaigning to change the militaristic routines of hospitals which had left children enduring minor operations, typified by the routine removal of tonsils, in a kind of solitary confinement. A legacy of loss and sadness was lodged in the collective memory of childhood. In 1971, the British psychoanalyst John Bowlby identified the crisis for children caused by forced separation from their parents. His insight was confirmed by research into the impact upon children of hospitalisation conducted in the 1950s. (John Bowlby, 1971, p14) Working with this data, hospital social workers launched the National Association for the Welfare of Children in Hospital to campaign for more supportive environments for parents and their children. This campaign successfully created the conditions for parents to remain with their children in hospital. Love, rather than life itself, was at stake. Parents reacted to the Prince's brittle self-defence with bewilderment. Why wouldn't he want to stay with his son after an accident, whether or not his life was at risk? 'What kind of dad are you?' asked the *Sun*.

Although William seemed to have adopted the over-conscientious care that children of depressed mothers often exhibit, Diana appeared to be a normal mother, and for this her commitment to her children came to be sanctified. It was only in the context of her class, who routinely got rid of their children, that she seemed so special. Charles clearly loved his children, but could not or would not use his position, his power and privilege, to extend his time with them.

It was the couple's relationship to their children that finally exploded their marriage. Half-term holidays change the populations of Britain's buses and trains, museums, swimming baths and theme parks. Public transport and public places, usually packed with adults, teem with children, hand in hand with diligent and delighted grandparents and fathers who have taken the day off work. Charles decided that the children's holiday from boarding school in November 1992 should be spent at Sandringham, where he had organised a shooting party for friends. Diana told him that she wanted to take the children to Windsor for a weekend with their grandmother, the Queen. Charles enlisted the Queen's support to make Diana deliver herself and the children to Sandringham. The Queen agreed. Diana did not. If it wasn't Windsor, she said, it would have to be Highgrove.

'It does seem odd that he should think such a weekend a good plan,' commented Sarah Bradford. 'He snapped,' wrote Dimbleby. He refused to cancel his shooting party and when his wife refused to give in, he refused to go on with his marriage.

After his separation from their mother, Charles spent around 30 days a year with his sons. Equivalent to a holiday.

12. Warfare

After the wedding of the century, the couple made their triumphant tour of Wales in the royal train. Although bulimic and suffering from morning sickness, Diana showed 'a deft touch with the crowds'. (Dimbleby, 1995, p356) The royal family received their first lesson in the new order: the crowd was less interested in the sovereign than someone else, not one of *them*, but his shadow. It was the crowd who discovered that the shadow was actually a sphinx.

They pressed against the barricades for a glimpse of her, holding out their hands and calling her name 'as if for a blessing. She stooped to talk gently with children, touched the blind, and embraced the elderly.' (p356) But this representation of Diana as a saint misinterprets the crowd's connection to Diana as a celebrity. She behaved as if she was royal and yet one of the crowd.

For the first time, an ingénue gave to the monarchy what it could not give to its subjects. It had taken a non-royal to embody that elusive equation proposed by Lord Altrincham, 'being at once ordinary and extraordinary'.

The lesson was that an outsider, a 'commoner', gave the royal family the allure it could not give itself. For this she was never forgiven. The royal family's reaction to her investment in the family firm – her self – was salutary. They were jealous, they were affronted by the ingénue's assault on their *supremacy*. Ultimately they went to war, mobilising a mighty propaganda campaign to promote their prince while sabotaging her efforts to emerge from the ruins of her marriage as a useful ambassador and advocate for the troubled and dispossessed.

The royal family treated Diana as someone they didn't think was worth teaching, nor – as she struggled to find her own form in royal encounters with the public – emulating. They didn't countenance the possibility that the ingénue had anything to teach them. As Dimbleby recognised, she, literally, had the 'touch'. Whitaker believed that 'jealousy has a large part to play in this story. Both Prince Charles and the Queen were jealous of Diana's instant acclaim, trained as they both were for sovereignty.'

The royal family could have mobilised her as a partisan for a modernised monarchy; it could have enlisted her feminine aura for a newly fashioned royal project, patriarchal and yet populist. There had been plenty of precedents for Diana's potential as a first lady, a star whose light might shine upon an unpretty prince.

The Other Churchill

A hundred years earlier Jennie Churchill offered a prototype of the aristocratic pin-up, who discovered her agency as a public figure in the service of her husband's political career. Randolph Churchill was a promising mover and shaker in upper-class politics. Jennie Churchill's reputation as an exciting and magnetic mobiliser for her husband's cause was acclaimed for helping to keep the Tories in power for 20 years at a critical moment in the modernisation of British politics.

Like Jennie Churchill, Diana seemed set to keep the royal family popular for the rest of its lifetime. Like Jennie, Diana loved her public performances because they took her into the 'realm of the unexpected, of association with people of all classes and kinds, of commitment to a cause'. (Campbell, 1987, p11) And like Diana, Jennie Churchill rode into the public domain on behalf of her husband – in her case as a stunning surrogate candidate in Randolph Churchill's election campaigns in the 1880s.

Randolph Churchill had been a founding member of the Primrose League, a coterie of aristocratic men interested in the reinvigoration of Tory politics on the eve of a democratic era that threatened the party with political meltdown. Although her husband barely bothered to campaign, Jennie enthusiastically entered the lists on his behalf and recruited the resources of aristocratic women for the creation of a new social base for the Tories. 'There was no escaping us,' said Jennie. (p11) The Primrose League had seemed set to become just another club of Tory gents. But once the men admitted their wives, the women transformed a clique into a mass movement: they created the scientific electoral machine which became the Tories' secret weapon amidst a volatile electorate, and they created a social space in which women could connect with a political party. The league became an indispensable auxiliary to the Tory machine.

In less than a decade the women attracted 1 million members to the Primrose League. According to the political historian Ostrogorski, they formed 'a formidable Tory militia', which surpassed the Tory party's regular army of members, both in numbers and political élan. (Cornwallis West, 1908, p98) This auxiliary to the party was the first mass movement of women attached to a political party in mainland Britain. It utilised these titled women's tradition of good works and philanthropic visiting to lock the Primrose League into the social life of communities throughout the countryside and the cities. The league became a scandalous success. It was accused of overreaching itself, of transgressing propriety by campaigning in public and politicising the elite's historic power in community life. It infused politics with pleasure – regularly organising fêtes at the 'big houses' and putting on performances of singers, jugglers and conjurors together with waxworks and 'oriental illusions'. It was the Primrose League that created Tory culture as cross-class sociability and as a space in which women and men could mingle – unlike the embryonic Labour movement, which, despite its rhetoric of equality, institutionalised the separation of the sexes and the polarisation between public and private, paid and unpaid work.

Of course the Dames of the Primrose League were accused of vulgarity. 'Vulgar, of course it's vulgar,' Jennie proclaimed. She was more than ready not only to appear at the league's great public presentations but to perform – she played the piano at one Hackney celebration. While Randolph Churchill faded from the political firmament, Jennie became a star. The league even distributed cheap pin-up pictures of their heroine for the members.

Driven to Extremity

This historical parallel is suggestive. Randolph paled by comparison with his glorious wife, but because she claimed her place in the public arena, the Primrose League, as a political project, was transformed. Jennie and the aristocratic sisterhood secured the Tories' transition into a modern mass party. These women, whose only power lay in their proximity to power, became indispensable to the men: they engineered the Tory triumph at the very moment when the party faced electoral extinction. It was only their desperation and their fury, commented Ostrogorski, that led 'men to this extremity'. (Cornwallis West, 1908, p98)

The history of the royal family and its faithful political following among the Tories has depended on its embrace of femininity. Charles, living in another era of profound

political contestation, could not sustain even the
appearance of an alliance with women and children.

His muffled misogyny responded to Diana's celebrity not
with gratitude but with envy, and then rage. Reporters
were among the first to notice his splenetic reaction to his
wife as an object of public interest. A journalist who
covered a royal visit to Germany, Brenda Polan, saw them
at a fashion gala where the Prince looked rather archaic,
wearing patent-leather pumps, and the Princess looked

> stunning, very glamorous. They were surrounded by a
> crowd and as they were ushered away he wanted her to
> get into a lift with him, but she was still surrounded and
> said 'I'll go down the stairs darling.' He went purple and
> shrieked 'No! Come here this minute.' She didn't know
> her place, two paces behind him. He was out of control,
> intimate and inappropriate.

Royal tours provided the perfect occasion for the display
of a modernised monarchy. The royals didn't have to
believe it, all they had to do was pretend – a faculty for
which their class was already famous. Instead Charles'
royal tours in the mid-1980s revealed royal jealousy. In
Australia in 1985 the couple were showered with attention. The Australians adored Diana. 'So infatuated was the
throng at every walkabout, that as they got out of the car
to "work", an involuntary moan of disappointment would
rise from the crowd which turned out to be nearest to the
prince and furthest from the princess.' (Dimbleby, 1995,
p463) Instead of prompting a new way of 'working' the
crowd, with the Prince acknowledging and basking in the
adulation, he recoiled, depressed and greedy. It was the
same everywhere they went.

Patrician Politics

Charles bitterly resented the response to his attempts
throughout the 1980s to present himself as a 'rational man'

in contrast to his 'emotional' and 'erratic' wife.

He began his career as a controversialist soon after he became a husband and father. However, neither his wife nor his child seemed to inform the priorities of his new political career, which began to appear more like flight and fury than the wisdom of a holistic man.

He made his first dramatic attack on the medical profession a few month after the birth of his son William, when his wife was sequestered in the palace suffering from post-natal depression, bulimia and the agonising fear that her marriage was a fraud. In the autumn of 1982 he had arranged for Diana to consult a psychiatrist. Psychiatry was one of the more closed and conservative disciplines within medicine, in which distressed women were seen, but not heard, by men who contemplated the physiology of dysfunction, passed judgement and pushed pills. Psychiatry, like much of the medical establishment, was already forced to defend its own impenetrable hierarchy and restrictive practices from critics seeking to integrate the social and the physical conditions that produce illness and recovery.

But it was not his personal experience of a woman's pain that prompted Charles to take on the medical establishment. It was the mystical ideology of natural balance and harmony picked up from his friendship with the patriarchal Laurens van der Post which guided his missiles against the British Medical Association. As the BMA's president, he marked its 150th anniversary with a speech advocating intuition and intimacy with 'nature'. Doctors were to understand their patients and enter 'sympathetic communication with the patient's spirits'. The triumphant edifice of medicine, 'for all its breathtaking successes, is like the celebrated Tower of Pisa, slightly off balance'. With the wisdom of what would, by the end of the century, be regarded as common sense, and touching the chord of alternative approaches flourishing across the West, he argued that health was often determined by behaviour, food and the environment. These were not thoughts that enlightened him about the pain and agony in his marriage. It was as if domestic fury found another direction, targeting the purported inhumanity of public professions. Thus the Prince presented himself as a 'prince with a conscience', not a closed, confused, angry, frightened and sometimes fleeing father.

It was a poignant speech, remarkably allusive and yet evasive, so suggestive of sympathy, 'feel' and 'touch' and yet so aggressive in its attack on a public profession in the name of a humane science of health and healing. This exegesis was regarded as exemplary of the Prince's approach to politics – intuitive, holistic and catholic. It was also emblematic of something more sinister; a young father's evasion and externalisation of difficulty and distress that was dominating his own domestic domain and defeating the mother of his baby.

Indeed this public presentation implied that the Prince himself was intuitive, holistic and sympathetic at a time when he was aloof and alienated.

Her Majesty's Opposition

Charles' first strong challenge to Thatcherism was provoked by the riots against racist policing in British cities at the beginning of the 1980s. Prince Charles hosted a weekend encounter between 60 British business leaders and the same number of bright young black people. 'Chastened white businessmen – bankers, for instance, unused to being laughed at when they protested that they did not discriminate in their employment policies – listened intently,' wrote Holden, while young black people told them how life was really lived. (1988, p185) That Windsor conference was a watershed for its participants.

By the middle of the decade Charles threw himself into Business in the Community, an organisation set up after the riots to sponsor small black businesses. 'It was to be the making of him,' wrote Holden, because by then his own economic initiatives appeared, like his marriage, to be going nowhere. He appeared to speak for dispossessed black communities, and he appeared to be doing something useful. In 1986, described by Holden as 'a crucial year of transition', his Prince's Trust, which had flickered for a decade, took off with a summer concert at Wembley Arena, supported by a great galaxy of pop performers including Tina Turner, Mick Jagger, David Bowie, Paul McCartney and Elton John. The concert raised more than £1 million.

His connection, through charity, to the dispossessed in the inner cities led Charles to an alliance with architects who were working with the mutinous tenants' movements in local-authority housing. His endorsement undoubtedly encouraged the expansion of a more democratic engagement between planners, providers and tenants, exemplified by John Thomson's refurbishment of the Lea View estate in Hackney. His sponsorship of 'community architecture' fuelled the increase in public angst about the state of the cities, speculative tower blocks, the architectural establishment and craven or corrupt local government. The movement seemed to speak for what was already a mass mutiny. But it was a hybrid coalition harbouring democratic design alongside a populist assault on modernism in the name of traditionalism.

In 1984 Charles had been invited to address the Royal Institute of British Architects and made a speech which revealed the contradictory feelings nestling in his approach: he affirmed the housing co-operative movement in Liverpool which challenged the Fordist standardisation and authoritarianism associated with public housing. But in the 'most outspoken moment of his public life so far', he assailed the proposed extension to the National Gallery in Trafalgar Square: 'What is proposed is a monstrous carbuncle on the face of a much-loved friend.' At the same time a consortium headed by Peter Palumbo was pitching for permission for a site at Mansion House in the City of

London to build Britain's first Mies van der Rohe building. This 'glass stump' would be better in Chicago than London, Charles told the RIBA. Charles' speech was not an innocent intervention – he lent his specific support to his friend in the community-architecture movement, Rod Hackney, who stood, successfully, for election as the RIBA's president. The speech gave new meaning to the treasured words 'By appointment to ... '

Several years later Charles returned to his lament about London and protested that developers had done to the capital what the Luftwaffe had failed to do: the city's skyline had been wrecked, the great dome of St Paul's had been lost in a 'jostling scrum of office buildings'.

Power Without Responsibility

Without doubt Charles was identifying himself with challenges not only to the architectural establishment, but also to professional cartels in other fields, including medicine and education. In that sense he was engaging with great debates of the time. But his critics were alarmed that his critique was essentially conservative, populist and an abuse of his royal prerogative. The Prince was more than a commentator, he became a participant in planning controversies with an expectation that the protagonists would take heed. His Mansion House speech had been preceded by an invitation from the developer Stuart Lipton, who was proud of the artistry that adorned his major projects, to look over the plans submitted for his Paternoster scheme. The Prince hated the seven schemes that had been submitted, and said so. After the competition produced a winner, it was announced that his views would be taken into account. (Dimbleby, 1995, p541) But what qualified him, any more than any other interested citizen, to have a say?

He had acquired power, without responsibility. A sentimental view of Charles' interventions, that he was voicing our collective common sense, is challenged by Anthony

Holden's rigorous record of Charles' impact not only on the reputation, but also the livelihood, of planners and architects. They were professionals working for a living. He was a prince. 'At a time when Britain could boast three of the world's greatest living architects – Richard Rogers, Norman Foster and James Stirling – the prince's bad-mouthing was forcing them to do their best work abroad, while cowering British planning authorities kowtowed to their future king by sanctioning a 'toytown' suburban landscape full of hypermarkets and superstores artificially clad in lurid brick and embellished with cutesy bell towers, Corinthian columns and dormer windows,' wrote Anthony Holden. (1994, p240)

Richard Rogers threw down the gauntlet to the Prince when he noted that the royal family, despite their enormous personal wealth, had 'a poor record as patrons of the arts and sciences'. Jonathan Dimbleby, revealing where his own sympathies lay, commented that Rogers' 'silky venom' extended to the Prince personally when Rogers complained that Charles was no exception to a royal family with no reputation for great works on their own properties; 'He has an extraordinary opportunity to commission buildings for his large estates. But he has yet to produce a noteworthy construction.'

Charles did, however, commission Leon Krier to be his master planner for a development at Poundbury, edging on Dorchester, in the Prince's Duchy of Cornwall. He hoped that community consultation would inform the develop-ment, which would in any case be subject to the usual planning requirements. But Krier's grandiosity matched that of the Prince – he didn't want mortals mucking up the master plan. Ultimately the Prince offended the master, too: Krier's neoclassical monument was not only financially reckless, it did not fit in with the Dorset vernacular. (Dimbleby, 1995, p565) Another struggle between Prince and master planner modified the design. Ultimately, Poundbury emerged as less than a grand plan, more of a housing estate like any other.

Charles also lent his royal weight and resources to a new architectural journal, *Perspectives*, designed to give ideological space to the critics of the architectural establishment. But by 1997 the journal was in trouble and in 1998 it folded.

Ultimately Charles was faced with the contradiction at the crux of his position: he was personally powerful and yet politically weak. His personal volleys were not meted out with professional knowledge or institutional backing. Beyond his personal domain, he lacked the means to translate critique into construction, to convert petulance into positive change. His strength was also his weakness – he was not a professional, he was only a prince.

Disarray and Disorder

Charles had become an eloquent protagonist, but appeared to sustain only intermittent presence in his great crusades. His officials complained that it was hard to hold his concentration, that he was flaky.

Dimbleby is candid about the chaos in Charles' private office. The Prince's enthusiasms and vaunted intuition 'too often bore the imprint of the last conversation he had held or the latest article to have caught his eye'. The public saw order and precision 'conveyed by the prince's entourage' but this 'concealed a disarray in his private office that he found hard to comprehend and impossible to rectify'. He had four officials, a dozen secretaries and typists, and yet 'disorder was rife'. Foreign Office classified documents would often lie around the office for days, unread. Charles' private secretary Edward Adeane 'liked the efficiency with which the Princess dealt with her paperwork (which he contrasted favourably with the Prince's more spasmodic approach)'. And Adeane did not approve of the *personal* services his colleague Michael Colborne rendered for the Prince, 'Colborne was the provider of secret cufflinks and flowers for ladies.' (Bradford, 1997, p457)

Despite Adeane's efforts to create order and routine, the Prince's office remained a mess. According to a palace aide, 'Adeane tried to get the Prince to work and stick to his plans but it was like nailing jellies to the wall to get him to stick to a programme, and a lot of deceit used to go on to make out he was doing a lot of work when he wasn't – he was off playing polo or something.' (p457)

The Great and the Good

Despite Charles' disrespect, Diana, through her traditional work as a lady of leisure visiting the sick and the disadvantaged, began to connect with a new, radical culture in the voluntary sector. Where his interventions tended to be ambitious, aggressive and ultimately traditional, hers were modest, empathetic and finally radical. Voluntary organisations and charities mushroomed in Britain during the 1970s and '80s and, though scarcely articulated in political discourse, expressed a vigorous civil society. This became the space in which Diana began to transform the idiom of aristocratic philanthropy and patronage, and developed a *humanitarian*, rather than *patrician*, orientation with which the public completely identified.

One of Diana's first and most memorable gestures as the new face of the great and the good was in April 1987 when she opened the first dedicated AIDS ward in Britain, the Broderip Ward at Middlesex Hospital, with Professor Michael Adler. She was visiting the Middlesex as a friend of the National AIDS Trust, an organisation campaigning to raise awareness about AIDS which uniquely enjoyed government support.

Diana did something unprecedented: Her Highness shook the hand of a man suffering from HIV. Flesh touched flesh. No gloves. The impact was instantaneous in breaching the touch taboo that then prevailed in Britain, cordoning sufferers off from the rest of their community.

Within London Lighthouse and the National AIDS Trust itself, campaigners like Adler and the director Margaret Jay discovered that Diana was not the dunce that her royal critics claimed. Margaret Jay often repeated her experience of this woman as uneducated but quick, curious, competent and dedicated to being well briefed. She hosted their Concerts of Hope in 1993 and 1994 and, apart from visiting AIDS organisations around the country, adopted a confidently ambassadorial role as an advocate for sufferers. The trust became one of the half-dozen voluntary organisations with which Diana maintained her public profile after 1996 when she downscaled her public duties.

She began her association with the Royal Marsden Hospital in 1982, and also kept the connection after 1996. When she had discussed with her son William what to do with her wardrobe – which had, predictably, been the object of both celebration and criticism – he suggested an auction, which would raise money for the cancer hospital. The Royal Marsden, in its tribute to Diana, praised her enduring links with people suffering from cancer, HIV and AIDS, and leprosy. She had helped to remove the stigma, taboo, and fear associated with these diseases.

Centrepoint, a service for young homeless people, was launched from a crypt in Soho, in the shadow of the towering Centrepoint block squatting on an island at the junction of Tottenham Road and Oxford Street. The block had been an emblem of London's housing crisis and the speculative building boom, because it remained empty for many years, free of tax liabilities, while homeless people sheltered in the doorways and alleys below.

Since half of Centrepoint's clients were between 16 and 17 years old, they had no entitlement to state benefit and thus were living without any income whatsoever. Half of the young people staying at Centrepoint shelters were young women, and half of these women were on the street, having left their parents' homes – nearly 80 per cent had been forced to leave.

Centrepoint was among the new voluntary organisations which not only provided services for the disempowered, but also sought to empower them. It belonged to the radical culture of new charitable movements that acted as advocates, including Childline, the helpline for abused, neglected and bullied children, and Refuge, the Chiswick sanctuary for women battered by their men. Many of Diana's meetings with Refuge were private and personal. There, too, she was known for wanting to know, the Refuge director Sandra Horley recalled that Diana would scan the bookshelves and borrow academic texts about the impact of domestic violence on women and children. The books were always returned, read, it seemed, from cover to cover.

Damage Limitation

After Charles and Diana's separation at the end of 1992, in the wake of the publication of Andrew Morton's book, she enjoyed massive support from the public, and private hostility from the royal family. Her work for charities and the dispossessed had begun to establish her in the public eye as an independent woman. She wasn't going quietly, despite evidence that Buckingham Palace was undermining her work while Prince Charles was employing *nine* public-relations officers to hoist his ratings. There was a war going on behind the scenes, and the effectiveness of using the media as a weapon was not lost on anyone.

A new woman began to emerge in 1993. She was still hunted by the paparazzi and her increasingly confident commitments to her hundred charities were, if anything, making her more interesting. In April she made a speech which was described in the media as a 'spellbinder'. It was about bulimia, at the International Eating Disorders 93 Conference in London. Although careful not to cast her comments in the first person, she said wryly that she had it 'on very good authority' that the 'quest for perfection our society demands can leave the individual gasping for breath'. She spoke memorably about the crisis of self-respect that could lead to eating disorders: 'From early childhood, many have felt they were expected to be perfect but did not feel they had the right to express their true feelings to those around them – feelings of guilt, of self-revulsion and low personal esteem, creating in them a compulsion to *dissolve* like a *Disprin* and disappear.' Aristocrats never talked like this.

The keynote speaker at the conference was Susie Orbach. For years Diana had heard her name as a leader in the field. For years clinicians had treated Diana either by dispensing pills for depression or by making her eat to treat her eating disorder. Now she encountered a democratic exposition of the relation between clinician and client. The patient, said Orbach, had created 'a new persona, an admirable person, a need-free person, subject to no one's control'. But 'by seeking treatment she fears she must submit and surrender. She wants someone who will understand her. But she is scared of being patronised, of having control wrested away from her, of being invaded and made to comply with a treatment that compromises everything that she understands as central to her.' Although she might be desperate to give up her 'lonely struggle', she might also feel she must conceal it from the clinician. 'She doesn't know how to feel ambivalence, let alone express it. She doesn't know how to stand up for herself.'

Addressing the clinicians' dilemmas, Orbach explained, 'We are frightened when we have to confront such extraordinary self-denial ... we find ourselves in wonderment. How does someone survive so long on so little?' Why, amidst plenty, should some women starve themselves? she asked. 'Why and how have young girls and women come to feel so bad about themselves? Why have they understood at their place depends on diminishing themselves, on depriving themselves, on starving? For we would do well to recall that she does indeed feel hungry. She registers it and she then vanquishes it.' The woman has understood that 'while food is love when she gives it to others, it is dangerous when she eats. She has understood that while processing or soothing the emotional lives of others is valued, her own needs are taboo.' Her bargain, her protest and defiance, 'this surrender and complicity are finally too much to bear and her body and her psyche collapse under the pressure of trying to solve the dilemmas of giving without being allowed to receive inside herself and through transformations of the self and the body ... She says with her body what daren't be heard and daren't be said in the wider body politic.' It is the task of clinicians 'to give her that body back as a place to live in and from ... and to reflect on the psychically internalised dimensions that make eating problems the quintessential protest and accommodation of women and girls to their place in Western society'.

Diana, the emblem of 'what daren't be heard and daren't be said', had already begun to take control over her own life, by telling her story. She was fighting back. She met Orbach at this conference and then began to work with her therapeutically. This began a new phase in her quest for a different future – although by 1995 her visits to the clinician's north London practice were haunted by photographers who set up on the street outside, and by helicopters which hovered above whenever there was a purported IRA alert. It was as if the world would never leave her alone or let her keep her secrets.

In June 1993 Diana made another speech which affirmed that women were the care providers who were themselves deprived of care, the carers whose unpaid work was estimated to save the country £24 billion annually in wages. 'Women in our society are seen as the carers, the ones who can cope. Whatever life throws at them – they will always cope,' she told a mental-health conference.

Women might be 'suffering themselves from post-natal depression, violence in the home or struggling in a daze of exhaustion and stress to make ends meet,' said Diana, 'but they will cope.'

'The suffering behind their anxious eyes so often goes unseen.' Millions of women had been 'locked into a terrible torment', dependent on tranquillisers, tending to 'make a woman more passive "to help her conform to the norm". But whose norm is it?' she asked. If women were continually disabled by the belief that they should exist only for the benefit of others, 'they will live only in the shadow of others'. This speech prompted suggestions in the press that Diana had 'finally signed up with the feminist cause'.

That month Diana was not to be seen at royal rituals. In July, however, she went on a tour of Zimbabwe. This was due to be followed by another African tour, but the second tour mysteriously never materialised. A projected Red Cross trip to Bangladesh was also inexplicably cancelled. 'Someone, somewhere was determined that the Princess of Wales would no longer outshine the rest of the royals,' commented the *Sun* photographer Arthur Edwards. (1993, p324) While the royal family's most charismatic ambassador was being edged out and her reputation soiled, Charles' role as a roving envoy for Britain around the world was assiduously promoted. While his companion Camilla Parker-Bowles was making appearances at aristocratic events, Charles' prospects as a divorced monarch were duly debated in the media. Diana was still being hunted by the paparazzi at the same time as she was being disparaged as an unstable wreck. By the end of the year she was reaching the conclusion that she should withdraw from public life, but early in November she challenged the disparagers at a fund-raising event for Birthright, a health organisation that sponsored research into, among other things, post-natal depression. Birthright was relaunching itself as Wellbeing. She contacted the

organisers early in the morning and warned them that there
was something she would like to say. They had not expected
her to make a speech but were happy to provide a platform;
'the prevailing opinion at the time was that she was a
cracked vessel and she wanted to put the record straight,'
recalled the Wellbeing director Vivienne Parry.

'Ladies and gentlemen,' Diana told her audience, 'you are
lucky to have your patron here today. I was supposed to have
my head down the loo for most of the day. I'm supposed to
be dragged off in a minute by men in white coats. If it's all
right with you I thought I might postpone my nervous
breakdown.' Many of her audience were moved, but the
speech confirmed her critics' conviction that the vessel was
indeed cracked. 'You can hear the shrill pulse of a rising
hysteria,' commented the *Guardian*.

In December Diana decided to announce that she was
withdrawing from public life. She informed the Queen and
sent her the draft of her proposed speech. She was going,
but she wasn't going quietly. She insisted that the public
had the right to be told. The Windsors were worried, and
urged her not to go public, yet they welcomed her exit.

On 2 December Diana appeared at a Red Cross fund-
raiser. It was the day before she planned to make her
announcement. The director Mike Whitlam, a man with a
long association with voluntary organisations working
with children throughout the world, and with penal
reformers and offenders, encouraged her to think again and
proposed a fresh approach to her work for the Red Cross.
He suggested that she might like to go on a management
training course which could open the door to a different
and practical profile within the organisation. She didn't
have to be just a pretty face.

The next day she arrived at the Hilton Hotel for a charity
lunch, where she announced that she would be reducing
her public engagements and concentrating on a small range
of activities, 'seeking a more suitable way of combining a
meaningful public role with, hopefully, a more private life'.

Her audience gave her a standing ovation. But Charles' supporters were outraged by her public assertion of autonomy.

If 1992 was the Queen's *annus horribilis*, then 1993 was Diana's nemesis: her reputation was being savaged. She had tried to bear witness to her struggle to survive the House of Windsor but still stories surfaced which presented her as a self-absorbed and superstitious woman who seemed to spend as much money on astrologers and psychics, as ordinary mortals might actually earn.

By the end of 1993 and early 1994, however, she was becoming a more strategic survivor. Despite her 'much-mocked patronage of psychotherapists, psychics, alternative therapies and new Age hygeines,' argued the feminist scholar Elaine Showalter, she came to live not as a 'querulous, self-protective neurotic, but a courageous activist'. Indeed 'she was one of the great success stories of contemporary psychotherapy. She had achieved independence against enormous odds.' (*Guardian*, 6 September 1997)

Landmines – Fighters That Never Miss

Diana's transition from a traditional, though warm, patron to a more confidently political position as an advocate, matured in the year before her death. It was her endorsement of the worldwide campaign against landmines that confirmed her as an enemy of the Establishment.

The Red Cross remained one of the half-dozen charities to which she continued to lend a public profile. It was part of a coalition of charities, voluntary organisations and campaigns against the arms trade. Its critique of anti-personnel mines was unequivocal: 'Mines may be described as fighters that never miss, strike blindly, do not carry weapons openly and go on killing after hostilities are ended. In short, mines are the greatest violators of international humanitarian law. They are the most ruthless of terrorists.' Since World War II landmines have

killed more people than poisonous gases or nuclear
weapons and they have left a deadly trail across the
landscape of some of the poorest, most ravaged countries in
the world. In 1995 the International Red Cross launched a
global campaign, together with about 80 other organisations, against landmines and enlisted Diana to visit Bosnia
and Angola.

After Angola's liberation from Portuguese dictatorship in
1974, the potentially rich landscape had been saturated
with landmines laid by Unita, a movement backed by the
USA and by South Africa during the apartheid regime. In the
decade after independence it was estimated that destruction
amounting to $10 billion had devastated the country.
Despite the formidable combined might of South Africa,
Henry Kissinger and Unita, the government of Angola
survived raids, mines, British and American mercenaries,
and terror tactics directed at the civilian population.
Limbless peasants bore evidence of the country's suffering.
'It added up to a catastrophe, but a catastrophe out of sight,'
wrote Victoria Brittain, the *Guardian*'s deputy foreign
editor and one of the few international experts on post-
colonial attrition in Africa, sponsored by the West. (1998,
pviii) Angola was broken by Unita, which, without enjoying
a mandate from the majority of the people, managed to sap
the will to live. Red Cross clinics and sanctuaries were
among the targets exploded by the movement.

The profile of this campaign against landmines was
internationalised when Diana visited Angola with the Red
Cross in 1997. Her visit outraged the British Conservative
government. She had breached the propriety of her position,
complained former foreign secretary Lord Howe. *The Times*
columnist Richard Deedes parried that Howe's point
bizarrely 'boiled down to the fact that the Princess was
highlighting the scandalous loss of life, limbs and land.'
(*The Times*, 26 June 1997) Labour MP Ann Clwyd responded
to the Tory attack by tabling a motion signed by seventy-
three Labour, Liberal Democrat and Plaid Cymru MPs.

Diana later invited Clwyd to Kensington Palace to discuss the issue. According to the MP, when she told Diana that Foreign Office briefings about Cambodia had been inaccurate – the government has since revealed that it had been involved in training the deadly Khmer Rouge – Diana 'jumped up out of her chair: "The briefing I got on Angola was useless."' Under pressure Diana had felt compelled to withdraw from a House of Commons meeting on landmines. The campaign itself was a mark of her own transition from a celebrity to a humanitarian.

At the beginning of September campaigners organised a picket by hundreds of supporters at the Farnborough airfield to halt Britain's biggest annual arms fair, the Royal Navy and British Army Equipment Exhibition. The fair opened the day after Diana's death. The new Labour defence secretary George Robertson called off his visit to Farnborough to open the exhibition because of Diana's death. He did not, however, criticise the international trade in landmines. The government's support for the exhibition – despite foreign secretary Robin Cook's inauguration of a new 'ethical' era in Britain's international relations – was not lost on many mourners. The Campaign Against the Arms Trade was caught by surprise when many people called its London office making the contradictory connection between Diana's campaign, Tony Blair's tribute to the 'people's princess', official foreign policy, and the government's endorsement of the arms trade.

The international community finally banned landmines – Britain's international development secretary Clare Short signed the Ottawa Treaty in December 1997, although, like most of the rest of the world, Britain did not actually follow up with ratification – and the Nobel Peace Prize was awarded to the American campaigner Jody Williams, co-ordinator of the international campaign. The ban was acknowledged as the world's tribute to Diana. Her robust identification with the worldwide campaign against landmines had attracted the Establishment's ire and politicians' protests. She had gone too far. Landmines, like bulimia and suicidal lack of self-esteem, were too challenging. She could no longer be construed as an empty icon, flooded with our fantasies; Princess Diana was political.

Part III
Seen and Heard

13. Silent Shots

Diana became the most seen woman in the world. Her body was subjected to unprecedented scrutiny – never in the history of the world had a young woman been so publicly sexualised. Even before her body belonged to herself it was delivered to a man who seems not to have been sure whether he wanted it, and to a world that welcomed her into its own fantasies.

The romance with Diana broke the ceremonial shroud which hitherto protected the royal body: it was like a corpse, or a saint, a body somewhere between heaven and earth, a body to be seen but scarcely touched, addressed only with awe, grace or grief – but not with desire. Diana's body dramatised the tension between seeing and not seeing that lay at the heart of the royal project's success and its decline. Royalty acquired the status of stardom when she entered the royal enclosure. The pursuit by the press exposed the distinction between royalty and stardom: ceremony covered the body, celebrity exposed it.

Historically the royal body's potency lay in symbolism

rather than sexuality, a body invested with divine and
dynastic mystique, a body treated as if it were a treasure. It
was a fetish, viewed by its spectators with a kind of
suspended disbelief, within a culture that disavowed what
it *knew* in order to sustain a *faith* in monarchy. Their
bodies were, after all, the same as ours. They sweated or
ached in the same way. The royal body connoted
sovereignty that could never, finally, transcend its own
mortality; in real life the rituals of royalty held it in a
revered domain, seen but sheltered from view, touched, but
only lightly.

The politics of seeing, and being seen, are about power as
well as pleasure, voyeurism and exhibitionism, censorship
and surveillance, knowledge and ignorance, celebrity and
harassment, espionage and jealousy. The politics of seeing
the royal family were played out in the decline of deference
and the royal family's own response to the dawn of
democracy with a feast of ceremony: their duty to be seen,
and our duty to watch.

What was enacted in the twentieth century was a
historic struggle over seeing and knowing. The technology
of mass spectatorship expanded the audience. But in the
late twentieth century the tabloids – unlike television and
the broadsheet press – exposed the tension between
coverage as reverence and as reportage. Robust reporting by
the tabloids, unconstrained by the decorum of deference by
which the respectable media continued to co-operate with
the royal family, inaugurated a historic battle over rights
which were not reciprocal. What the tabloids implicitly
asserted was the people's right not only to watch but to
know, to know everything. The tabloid agenda tested the
boundary between public and private which had, in any
case, been breached by the royal family in their celebration
of Diana's virginity.

That ethereal frontier is where the monarchy lived for
almost two centuries. Deference and the monarchy's power
to police that frontier had secured its extraordinary control

over its audience, over when and how the royal family were to be viewed. The love affair between Edward VIII and Wallis Simpson exemplified the craven self-censorship of the British press, compared with the scabrous splendour of the press during George IV's inquisition of Caroline. But by the 1960s deference was dying: the royal family were becoming fair game for a new generation of satirists, from *Private Eye* to Steve Bell, *Spitting Image* to Sue Townsend. And the most intrusive demand for patriotic deference in everyday life – the national anthem played in the nation's cinemas – faded when the audience simply skedaddled at the end of the film.

The Diana era accelerated the death of deference and created a new tension between censorship and curiosity. That tension was sprung to its limits by the Windsors' determination to display the Princess of Wales to royal effect, and by the tabloids' competitive quest to maximise their control over what could be observed – a quest that was simultaneously sexist and democratic. Their own desire to see Diana became the instrument of a democratic imperative to seize control from the palace. Surveillance of the royal daughters-in-law became the tabloids' secret weapon.

Magic and Majesty

For two hundred years the royal family has been recuperating its peculiar rites of privacy, expressed in Walter Bagehot's celebrated caution: Do not let too much daylight in on the magic. It has invented its own rites of spectacular seeing, choreographed in the ceremonial *mise en scènes* which frame what can and cannot be seen. The equation between magic and majesty lifted the monarchy beyond the material reality of the body: the condition of its symbolic existence was its opaque, not-like-us otherness that could only be sustained, of course, at a distance and through the decorum of subservience. What was to be watched was not just pageantry, but the 'Holy Family'. The domestication of the monarchy functioned to humanise it, and the register of its humanity was its appearance as a family, but not as an ordinary family. 'They represent us by sheer *analogy*, an *iconic* sign,' argues the cultural theorist Judith Williamson, and the representation of this parallel family, like us but not us, 'is the heart of its representative function'. (1986, p76) The royal family was therefore attempting to couple irreconcilable objectives: domestication and deification.

It was not technology that created the tension that became a tragedy, it was the royal family's own addiction to both sovereignty and spectacle. The monarchy in Britain eschewed the modesty of European representations of royalty – famously Holland's bicycling royal family – and opted instead for the spectacular display of its dynasty as the strategy by which it could transcend the problem of its limited powers. Being seen became the Windsors' *raison d'être*. The triumph of this strategy was the renaissance of spectacular ceremony in the twentieth century, and the consummate episodes: the coronation of Elizabeth in 1953, which (albeit reluctantly) secured saturation visibility while preserving the deification of the dynasty, and later the wedding of Charles and Diana in 1981 which trumped the tabloids' coverage by allowing live global coverage of an 'intimate' family event.

The coronation was an emblematic moment in the history of seeing. The Coronation Commission, headed by Prince Philip and the Earl Marshal of England, the Duke of Norfolk, who 'viewed human beings with little unnecessary respect', (Bradford, 1997, p181) was preoccupied by two problems – the date and the audience. The date had to be squeezed into a convenient slot in the horse-racing calendar to satisfy upper-class racing fanatics; and the organisers had to decide whether or not to maximise the world audience by televising the event.

At first the commission agreed to satisfy the racing

community but not the global audience. The date was to be 2 June, the day before the Derby. The audience was to be satisfied with a delayed 'cinematographic film'. According to Sarah Bradford, in this, 'the first pitched battle of her reign between the traditionalists, those who wanted to preserve the "mystique" and magic of royalty, and the modernisers, who wanted to let light in on the magic, Elizabeth sided with the traditionalists'. She said no to television. 'She may have felt that certain moments of the ceremony were so sacred that they should be private.' (p182)

But the media mutinied, in the confidence that the people, the national audience, would want to see the ceremony live now that they had access to the technology that could bring the coronation service into every street. The people triumphed and the palace compromised. The public would be allowed to see the crowning of the Queen live, but the 'sacred' parts of the ceremony were to remain 'private'. 'For the first time the public had insisted on its right to seats at the royal spectacle.' (p183) But the Queen had triumphed, too, in her demand that the 'sacred' episode remain secret.

It took more than a decade for royal domesticity to be televised. In the aftermath of the Suez crisis of 1956 and an unprecedented (in the twentieth century at least) controversy about the snobbery, seclusion and philistinism of the Queen, she reluctantly agreed to televise her Christmas Day broadcast. The controversy had been ignited in 1957 by Lord Altrincham, who penned a populist critique of the royal family at a point when upper-class condescension was aired only in private, and republican objections were confined to Irish Republicans and British communists. (Pimlott, 1997, p276) Altrincham's critique of royal stuffiness, priggery and indolence, and imperial insouciance concluded with a call to the monarchy to modernise itself with the 'seemingly impossible task of being at once ordinary and extraordinary' (p278) as if that

elusive distinction – the marque of most of the rest of
humanity, as it happened – was all that remained of the
ideal of monarchy.

In the late 1960s Elizabeth was persuaded to allow the BBC
to spend a year trailing the royal family at home and on tour.
This created an illusion of intimacy and, most importantly,
appeared to convey the royals as human. The massive
audience watched, not out of deference, nor necessarily
royalism, but out of curiosity. A fascination with the
ordinary, with whatever it was about them that resembled
us, and whatever it was that made them not like us.

The coverage of Charles and Diana's wedding at St Paul's
in 1981 provided a perfect opportunity to reprise television
coverage as propaganda, as reverence rather than reportage.
The royal family already knew from the tabloids that
Diana was the object of obsessive attention. It could have
staunched the obsession by insisting upon a private
wedding. This would only have resumed the eighteenth-
and nineteenth-century tendency of the wealthy, analysed
by John Gillis in his history of British marriages, to
withdraw from the elaborate public performance of
betrothal and marriage. This derived from the desire to
escape rowdy congregations and crowds. 'Having defined
marriage as an essentially private legal act, the upper
classes were determined to eliminate those elements of the
big wedding that symbolized the collective interest in
nuptiality.' (1985, p142) But by the twentieth century
marriages were part of the material of royal propaganda.
Certainly, Charles' wedding was, like his investiture, most
important as a royal rite that *needed* an audience.

We now know that there were two dimensions to that day
– a ceremony and a crisis. The crisis was impeccably
censored for more than a decade. Later, the paradox of ten
years of voracious viewing became evident: what *was* seen
revealed as much about what could *not* be seen and what
could *not* be known. We, the audience, did not see what

Diana was desperate *not* to see: close to the end of her walk down the 625-foot aisle, holding on to – and holding up – her ailing father, she looked across him to her left and saw the lady in the grey pillbox hat whose relationship with her fiancé was driving her crazy. We didn't know that her wedding week was dominated by treachery, discovery and confession. We didn't know that her great day had been ruined.

14. Tabloid Democracy

By their own account, tabloid journalists repudiated the rules by which royal reporting had functioned as a symbiotic relationship between the monarchy and media. Represented as intruders by both the royal family and their defenders in the deferential media, they confounded conventions of good taste but, more importantly they breached the garrisons which policed public knowledge of royal life.

The first photographer to trespass across royal control was Ray Bellisario, who identified a new market for his pictures of the Queen and the other young royal women in the late 1950s and early '60s, when the technology of colour photography made it difficult to catch people in motion. He improvised his own lighting techniques which dramatically maximised the light, enabling him to photograph the royals out and about, arriving and leaving their destinations. His pictures appeared in women's magazines and he became a successful and ingenious member of the pack. But royal coverage was still being

managed by Commander Richard Colville, who served
Buckingham Palace from 1947 until 1968. The dyspeptic
commander guarded his employers fiercely and press
enquiries were 'met at best with guarded courtesy,
sometimes with impatient disdain, never with good
humour'. (Bradford, 1997, p246)

In 1961 the Queen undertook an important tour to
India. Bellisario hoped to cover the tour and got his
accreditation from the Indian High Commission. Colville
arbitrarily refused to include Bellisario in the press team,
refused to negotiate and refused to budge. Bellisario recalls
that Colville told him, 'I will see to it that you will never
get another photograph of the royal family and you will
never get a press pass.' Bellisario didn't go to India. He
continued to turn up for the royal routine at home, but
then found his access to the royals' appearances being
blocked. 'Colville was keeping his word and I was
beginning to have a hard time.'

Royal influence worked through their Establishment
links with the press to close down Bellisario's contacts. So
he tried another strategy: long lenses and informal
contacts with people working for the royal family. He took
pictures of the royals out riding or shopping and began
writing stories about the life and times of palace life
which painted a less than flattering picture of their
behaviour, particularly towards their staff. His work had
an enthusiastic market in the European press, but he was
effectively boycotted by the British media – except by the
Daily Worker, the communist daily, which regularly used
his photographs. His abiding ambition had been to work as
a photographer in the Third World, but by the late 1960s
the mild-mannered but irrepressible Bellisario – a socialist
whose people were Italian immigrants – had become
notorious as 'the peeping Tom the royals dread'. Although
he had improvised audacious techniques as a news
photographer, his livelihood became increasingly
precarious. The royals did more than dread him, they

destroyed his career. However, there were others to take
up where he had left off.

The new genre of royal coverage was created when Diana
arrived in the world of the Windsors. The rat pack was
initially a small posse of photographers and journalists
which expanded and which enjoyed spectacular investment by the tabloids. The pattern was established by James
Whitaker and Harry Arnold, and photographers Arthur
Edwards and Kenny Lennox, together with freelancers Tim
Graham, Anwar Hussein, and the only woman photographer in the rat pack, Jayne Fincher. They spotted Diana
at Balmoral and Sandringham in 1980. In November Jayne
Fincher noticed Diana's red Metro at Sandringham and told
her colleagues who filed their stories about the new girl in
Charles' life: 'I was only in my twenties, they didn't regard
me as significant, but I told them I'd seen her. They filed
the story and then the police said "she's not here" so they
rang their editors and had to pull the story. I got blamed.'
But then Whitaker and Edwards saw the Metro leaving the
Sandringham estate, escorted by the police. According to
Arthur Edwards, 'James, who was at the wheel of his red
Cortina, drove alongside Lady Diana while I hung out of
the back window with my camera.' Once she was out of
royal territory, 'the police car abandoned her, and we had
her all to ourselves. At speeds touching 80 miles an hour on
the single lane road, I snapped away as we tore along side
by side. Until she spotted us, Diana was under the
impression she had got clean away. And I beautifully
captured her shocked expression when we roared up beside
her.' As Edwards admitted, 'press harassment of the
Princess-to-be had begun'. (Edwards, 1993, p82)
    Tim Chapman, Arthur Edwards and Harry Arnold
chartered a jet to follow the couple during their honeymoon. 'It was the most cushy way to go hunting the royals
we had ever experienced,' recalled Edwards. They raced
from Sardinia to Sicily, Rome, Athens, Crete and Egypt

before finding 'our quarry' and their 'arch-rivals' Whitaker and Lennox. (p103)

A secret holiday in the Bahamas, before the birth of the Waleses' first baby, was targeted by the rat pack. Lennox, of the *Daily Star*, and Edwards, of the *Sun*, found treasure a quarter of a mile away on the beach: the pregnant princess in a bikini. When Edwards arrived back at the *Sun* offices in central London, a staff driver shouted that he was ashamed to be working for the same organisation, but his boss, Kelvin MacKenzie, swept him off his feet and said, 'You come back to this office a fucking hero.' The *Sun* declined to attend an unprecedented meeting called by the Queen to persuade the press to call off the rat pack.

Her appeal was in vain. By the middle of the decade the rat pack had established itself as an intrepid institution in tabloid journalism, supplemented by freelance photographers who were guaranteed a regular income from royal tours and syndication rights to snaps stolen from 'private' episodes. The royal rat pack, though disparaged, could be placed alongside industrial and political correspondents as chroniclers of national institutions. They monitored royal seasons and routines, and read the clues pointing to the collapse of the Prince of Wales' marriage.

James Whitaker began writing about the wan, wasting Princess as early as 1982 and when he speculated that she might be suffering from an eating disorder, he caused an outcry among respectable journalists and outright denial by the palace. Whatever the evidence, the rat pack were not put off by the bullying of the palace and its spokespersons, particularly Vic Chapman, who roared at the rat pack's intrusive insights.

It didn't matter that at that time Whitaker had the evidence of his own eyes and corroboration from a member of Diana's family. Nor did it seem to matter that the palace was prepared to lie, point-blank. The fact was, however, that the tabloids had tapped into the material evidence of emotional oppression that neither they nor the indifferent broadsheet press knew how to interpret as a problem of politics and power. They simply classified it as tabloid trivia and soap opera.

But now public as well as 'private' occasions began to provide the press with the runes in which to read the evidence of a marriage in big trouble. These were supplemented by the stories they heard from staff who were close to the couple. In 1986, when Charles and Diana's marriage was effectively over, they took a holiday with King Juan Carlos near Majorca. Whitaker followed the King's £3 million yacht, the *Fortuna*, and watched, 'completely mesmerised', through his binoculars for five hours. 'Everything I believed was happening in the marriage of the Prince and Princess of Wales was demonstrably true. Not once during this lengthy period did Charles or Diana sit anywhere near one another, let alone speak.' He felt vindicated, the five-year-old marriage 'was dead'. Although his story was headlined 'ARE THEY STILL IN TUNE?' and although he felt that the evidence was unequivocal 'it was inconceivable that that marriage could go wrong. On all levels on these stories there was caution. Because the chance of it ending in separation were *infinitesimal*. It was impossible, unthinkable.'

Andrew Morton was one of the journalists who followed the royal tour of Portugal in 1987 and, after checking the accommodation arrangements, realised that the couple were sleeping in separate quarters.

Making Up a Story

The rat pack not only recorded situations, they constructed them. In these coercive improvisations the press created a parallel narrative, a fictionalised inventory, which confounded notions of fact and fantasy by telling some kind of truth.

The official tour of India at the beginning of 1992 provided two photo opportunities which were manufactured by the press people themselves. By then the couple were staying in separate palaces, and 'we were thinking "shit!" But even then separation was 'unthinkable, it didn't even enter my mind,' said Whitaker.

Charles spurned the opportunity to visit the Taj Mahal, built in the seventeenth century by the Mogul Shah Jehan as a monument to his wife. Years before Charles had vowed to take his own wife to the temple of love. But not now. He went instead to address a meeting of industrialists. Diana was taken to the Taj Mahal but did not want to be photographed in her iconic isolation, and so kept her Indian hosts with her while they were photographed. 'I swear to you that's true,' insisted Whitaker, who was there with the rat pack. 'She insisted that the Indian officials be in the picture.' But the photographers harassed her and howled, 'Get those cunts away, get the wankers out.' In the face of this brutal behaviour, her Indian host suggested a solution: perhaps she might sit on the very bench where Her Majesty the Queen had posed many years earlier, and quietly contemplate the beauty before her. The journalist Judy Wade asked her, 'What comment have you got?', Diana replied, 'It's a very healing experience.' When asked what she meant, she said, 'You'll have to work it out for yourself.'

The photographers got their picture, but its history as an event was erased. It was precisely because the evidence of alienation between the couple was so compelling that the rat pack pressurised the royal press representatives for a picture of the royal couple kissing. 'The palace line was: this is shit, ridiculous, you've got it wrong. There was a huge battle between what our own eyes were telling us and the palace,' said Whitaker. Eventually the palace bowed to the 'give us a kiss' lobby. 'The palace knew that if they didn't do something about it then the hounds of hell would have said "Diana refuses to kiss the Prince." So the palace had the problem of saying to the Prince of Wales: "Sir – a kiss!" Charles agreed to kiss his wife and take the hounds of hell away.

This brief encounter took place a couple of days after the

Taj Mahal visit at a polo match in Jaipur in front of a crowd of 3000 officers of the 61st Cavalry, dressed, the Prince recalled, in blue blazers and Hermès cravats, and regimental grooms looking 'like a Raffles painting', as if 'time had somehow stood still'. The Prince played with the winning team and went up to the Princess for his trophy.

Apparently Diana had reluctantly agreed to kiss her husband in front of the crowd and the cameras. According to Dimbleby, Charles 'evidently had little idea what was at stake'. (p591) But everyone else knew what was at stake. As he leaned towards Diana to kiss her cheek and as the photographers pressed their shutters, she moved her head away, so slowly that his face followed hers in an effort that seemed eternal. The crowd caught his humiliation.

The India tour consolidated the rat pack's authorship of the royal story: they created the pictures, in particular the Taj Mahal picture, which was then read as an image of sadness and solitude; they were also the agents of Charles' humiliation by coercing him to make the unwanted kiss gesture. But by creating these fictions they were also making visible what they could already see with their own eyes.

From the beginning it was the tabloid economics of competition that drove the pursuit of the royal daughters-in-law. Although the rat pack created narratives, such as the Taj Mahal and Jaipur débâcles, they also worked with the material yielded by other interests. The tabloids did not create the taped telephone conversations between Charles, Diana and their lovers, they merely exploited other agencies' surveillance in what, by the 1990s, had become games of double and treble jeopardy involving the secret services.

But the tabloids' claim that they were only serving the public interest with material that they insisted was newsworthy, also shielded their own desire: by seeing Diana, they were able to have her, capture her, control her. Thus these men were able to exercise their sexual fantasies about a future queen. 'Most of them were in love with her,' said Jayne Fincher. The very process of sexualisation, which masqueraded as reportage, had a privileged audience – the photographers themselves. Throughout their history in the construction of her as a celebrity, their own desire was rendered invisible. They were always *behind* the camera. They loved looking at her, they loved chasing her, frightening her and, simply, staring at her. Their work also revealed a determination to dominate her, by never taking no for an answer. In the 1990s the tabloid troops retreated and relied on paratroop photographers – the paparazzi – who worked in teams to track down and trail Diana 24 hours a day.

One of the News International media empire's contributions to British culture was to pioneer a news aesthetic which, through the medium of the 'family newspaper', domesticated their own fetishistic iconography of femininity borrowed from a closeted genre of soft pornography in which the photographers' desire saturates the pictures at the same time as their desire as men is rendered invisible. The male photographers were always behind the camera while the women were on display. This relationship has been critical to the construction of masculinity in relation to femininity – men see, women are seen. Their desire was camouflaged by the press claim that the women set themselves up to to be seen. At a stroke the photographers were relieved of their responsibility for revealing their own relationship, both as newspapermen and as men, towards the daughters-in-law, as women. The tabloids found an unlikely ally in their monarchist critic Max Hastings, a friend of Charles and editor of the *Daily Telegraph*. When he later repeated their excuse commenting on Diana's decision in 1993 to retire from public life, he said that she would have been 'unhappy if she'd been left alone'. This was only another version of 'she asked for it!'

The aggression of the paparazzi, the mercenaries in the war over the royal women, was ultimately discredited after their deadly pursuit of Diana and Dodi Fayed through the streets of Paris on 31 August 1997. 'Men killed her,' said Andrew Morton after Diana's death, 'it was the male ego that killed her.' Jayne Fincher had by then pulled out: 'From 1994 it was just hopeless. She was hassled every day, it was awful, terrible, some behaved like animals, pushing, shoving, swearing. It was like being with a pack of football hooligans. It ruined our profession.' She said that, together with Diana, she had tried – in vain – to take action against the paparazzi, 'but you can't tackle it on your own and Buckingham Palace didn't challenge it. They could have kept tabs on the official photographers, but they just accredited everybody!' Her withdrawal was a 'hard commercial decision,' and the decision not to photograph Diana in Bosnia and Angola was tough, 'but once Diana had moved out of the official circle there was no protection. It would just be pandemonium.'

By then the rat pack's pleasure in the chase, the adventure, the lavish scale of the royal tours, their rivalry, all served to enhance their reputation as the masculine seers, the 'hounds from hell' whose audacity merely augmented their authority.

His Royal Hulk

If the tabloids conquered the royal daughters-in-law, they showed surprising deference towards the body of the heir. The press bowed before Establishment pressure to protect the unpretty Prince Charles' body from our sight. Although samizdat copies of fuzzy photographs of His Royal Hulk at play circulated on the continent, they were censored in Britain – because his body was too important to be seen.

The press which had been so keen to expose the bodies of the unruly daughters-in-law recoiled from showing us the future king in the raw. This uncharacteristic modesty revealed the degrees to which the media dissembled and became disoriented when it came to the opportunity to strip the royal family of its final fig leaf, the body of a man.

Clothes draw our attention to the power of men who would be kings. To strip him, to do the full Monty, would direct us to his sexuality. Millions of people would have been allowed to contemplate his precious bits and his pectorals, taking ownership of him in our fantasies, comparing him with the Chippendales, with ourselves and our lovers. This could not be borne because men have so long protected themselves from sexual scrutiny while maximising their own right to subject women's bodies to their gaze. Richard Dyer's study of representation of white masculinity in the context of Christianity and colonialism shows that although 'the white man has been the centre of attention for many centuries', there has always been a problem about the display of his body which reveals the paradox of whiteness and visibility. 'A naked body is a vulnerable body', a body unprotected against the elements and stripped of the accoutrements of social rank. 'Clothes are the bearers of prestige, notably of wealth, status and class: to be without them is to lose prestige. To expose the white male body is to problematise the legitimacy of white men's supremacy.' (1997, p146)

The prospect of pictures of the Prince in the altogether would have drawn attention to the sovereign as a man like other white men, it would have drawn attention to the unlikely prospect of the unpretty Prince as stud. His nakedness would have emphasised the ancient destiny he shared with his wife: he could be dull or deceitful, but his body remained his prize possession as a producer of heirs.

Just as Charles' masculinity had to be veiled from view, his relationships with his confidantes were also protected, in stark contrast to the tabloids' pursuit of the royal daughters-in-law. His relationships had been *known* during his marriage, but rarely *seen*, or rather, rarely seen by the world beyond the royal perimeter. Charles' time with Camilla and Kanga was secure in the 'safe houses' of their friends, or in royal kraals at Balmoral and Sandringham.

Horrible!

The Queen declared 1992 her *annus horribilis*: in March the press leaked the decision by Sarah Ferguson and Andrew to separate. In April Mark Philips and Anne decided to divorce. And in June Andrew Morton's book telling Diana's story was published and serialised in the *Sunday Times*. Unlike the two earlier separation stories, Morton's book revealed the duplicity at the centre of Charles' marriage and represented a searing critique of the Windsors' manners. That month the Queen confidently gave a public seal to her son's liaison with Camilla Parker-Bowles when she invited her to join the royal family at a polo lunch. In August the *Daily Mirror* published pictures which compromised Sarah Ferguson and scapegoated her as a 'scandal' who was ruining the reputation of the royal family. At a stroke the reputation of the Windsors themselves was redeemed while attention was redirected towards the daughters-in-law.

It did not matter that Sarah and Andrew had managed to negotiate a new life and a commitment to co-operation in the care of their children. Nor did it matter that their relationship had been rocked by the behaviour of the royal family. Fergie still loved her husband and they had been discussing a separation 'not because we'd stopped caring for one another but because I had reached the end of my royal rope'. In the six years of her marriage she had been hunted, like Diana, by the press, and, equally importantly, 'I'd endured the barely veiled hostility of the royal household, the courtiers who run the show. Gradually, relentlessly, they'd beaten me down. They were killing me by inches: it was time to save my life.' (Duchess of York, 1996, p4)

During the summer Sarah holidayed near St Tropez with John Bryan, 'an American who started out as my financial adviser, then became something more'. She acknowledged later that the trip was 'a stupidity' – rotten timing for

Andrew, 'a man I still loved'. When she returned to London, Bryan warned her that the *Daily Mirror* had the photographs and although he promised to get an injunction to prevent publication, she went, as usual, to join the royal family at Balmoral, where she told Andrew the bad news. Unlike Charles, her relationships were fair game: the pictures of Fergie on holiday with John Bryan were published in August. The result was her effective expulsion from the family. When the pictures appeared in the *Daily Mirror*, the paper also editorialised that Sarah had made the royal family a laughing stock, Andrew had been humiliated and Sarah should be sent packing. There could be no more scandals, the paper pronounced, 'if the royal family is to survive beyond the queen's reign'. Sarah went to see Elizabeth to apologise. The sovereign was furious. 'I curtseyed my retreat, then I went and found the one woman who understood what it meant to marry into the royal family' – Diana. Three days later Sarah was due to leave Balmoral with her daughters. That very day the tabloids were full of the Squidgy tape. 'I went into Diana's room and thanked her for taking me off the front page; it was our private, rueful joke.' (p14)

The monarchy's morals were screened from our sight while only the daughters-in-law were unprotected from prying eyes. Indeed the responsibility for the royals' reputation was, once again, dependent on the discipline and sexual subservience of women. Since appearances were all, the tabloids broke the code by which the royal regime of appearances was maintained. In the 1980s and 1990s the tabloids began to take control. They, like the royal family itself, put pressure on the shocked, superstitious daughters-in-law struggling for their own survival, and ultimately ruined the reputations of these women who were already, by any measure, free to enter into other relationships.

But this drama of royal sexual politics and scrutiny was bigger than a contest between the tabloids and the monarchy. Diana's history as a sexual object exemplified the tension between the authors, the photographers, and the audience, their readers, who brought their own ambivalent interest to their spectatorship. The readers, whether appalled or attentive, were drawn by a desire to see what could be seen, while some were shocked by the sexist use of women as the wedge that opened the door to a secret life; the public had its own legitimate preoccupations as it brought itself into the circuit of surveillance. Public fascination with Diana, almost instant, searched for evidence of the success of triumphant heterosexuality, and when the evidence evaporated, searched instead for the evidence of failure.

The tabloids used their own sleuthing skills to decipher the clues to the disintegrating marriage. The fictions by which the family firm controlled women, the set-up family holidays and compulsory royal tours, were now challenged on two flanks: by the women themselves, and by the tabloids scavenging around their lives and liaisons. The royal mania to master what could be seen, and therefore known, produced an open season.

Pandora's Box

'A secret thing may be hidden away, in a concealed place, but a secret meaning must be transformed into a code. One can be simply discovered by the eye, the other has to be deciphered.' (Mulvey, 1996, p53)

While the box might be prised open, allowing its secrets to be seen, the meaning of those secrets, in terms of feminine dilemmas and survival strategies, had yet to be deciphered. The questions unasked and unanswered (until Andrew Morton's book) were: Are these women mad or merely bad? Are the daughters-in-law just daft or dangerous? What are they dealing with, and what can they do with their distress and their dissent? The distressed daughters-in-law confronted their society with a historic difficulty: how to understand the pain and protest of women who had been rendered powerless.

The revelations seemed to destroy the two women, and yet, what was being unmasked by Morton was also revelatory of royal marriage and manners. Without the work of the tabloids we would not have been allowed to know what was going on behind the appearances choreographed by the royal image-makers. The royal Establishment, however, deflected blame back upon the tabloids and the public. The readers were accused, by the protectors of royal privacy, of reducing royal life to soap opera, of inciting the tabloids' penetration of royal sexuality, of opening Pandora's box and emancipating evil. The public's insatiable curiosity was maligned as idle voyeurism and as transgressive trespass across forbidden territory. But it represented something much deeper: both a desire to see and also the thrill of deciphering the enigma of femininity. What the readers' critics in the straight press and in parliamentary circles repudiated was the salience of sexual politics. And what these critics could not interpret was what the mass audience brought to this process of revelation: its own experience, its own attitudes and ambivalences, the pleasures of seeing, the satisfaction of seeing a royal mess, the recognition that royal family life was not immune from strife and struggle. The public was not merely prurient, it was interested. It was entitled to be fascinated by a symbolic family around which a structure of sovereignty and subordination had been earnestly renewed throughout the twentieth century, and which was abjectly protected by a system of secrecy to which Parliament itself bowed.

Perhaps the readers could recognise the perils, the secrets, the megalomania and sexism at stake in sexual politics – this being a realm in which we are all experts and explorers. Through the medium of the tabloids we, the public, were not only acting out 'a transgressive desire' to see ourselves in them, and to see them through the prism of our own experience; it was also looking at a larger landscape, 'the

erotic economy of patriarchy'. (Mulvey, 1996, p62) That was
what made the tabloids' rivalry, the readers' curiosity and
the royals' participation in the process of revelation such a
devastatingly dangerous liaison.

It did not matter that not everyone shared the same
interpretations or investments; what the tabloids
unthinkingly did was bring together sexual and political
transgression to open up private palace life to public
attention. But there was something else going on. Their
desire for this woman animated another desire: to defeat
the royal family's injunctions, their privileged privacy and
personal immunity.

For ten years the tabloids knew that the romance of the
century was a lie. They could hardly believe it, but they also
knew what they saw with their own eyes: seeing was
believing. But seeing the story was only a subsidiary effect of
watching the women. Their smugger broadsheet brethren
protested that the royals had a right to privacy, but that
masked the royals' right to preserve their ancient sexist rites
from public interrogation. Both the tabloids and the
broadsheets shared a sexist discourse, of course, but the
tabloids' sexism perversely pioneered revelations that harassed the daughters-in-law while simultaneously detonating
the patriarchal sexual politics of the royal family.

Their pursuit of the daughters-in-law, whose distress and
disaffection was indeed a story, also masked their own
desire as men. The heroic quest for their quarry – not on
official parade but at play – connects virtuoso hack
photography with art photography when it glimpses its
subjects when they're not looking and catches life *au
naturel*. That, too, excites our curiosity – our search for
what might be normal in their weird lives. Our pleasure in
the act of looking is freighted with ambivalence: we saw
Diana through their lens, our curiosity was, therefore,
mediated by their perspective. At the same time Diana was
a woman the public enjoyed watching. People wanted to

know what was happening to her. In all this the women were 'silenced as subjects', unable to speak or to control when and in what conditions they might be seen.

Diana, finally, took control by insisting that she not only be seen, but heard.

15. Testimony

For the first time this century a woman called a future king to account for his behaviour as a man. It was Diana herself who came to see that survival depended on telling her story.

The revelations which have fissured the reputation of the royal family and created the conditions for republican feeling in Britain have all involved acts of deception. The conspiracies enabled and empowered a victimised woman to bear witness. The story of these stories also reveals the difficulty of testimony. Andrew Morton's book *Diana – Her True Story* is one of the most important pieces of social history in 1990s Britain. It was created in conditions of secrecy and entered the world as an audacious affront to royal control of our collective conversation.

Martin Bashir's *Panorama* television interview with Diana is, likewise, one of the most important social documents of its time. Unlike Andrew Morton, who has revealed the difficulties of telling the story, protecting both the text and its subject, *Panorama* has been rather silent. It has refused to answer the vexing questions which haunt one of the television *coups* of the century: How did it pull it off?, how did it triumph over other, apparently more commodious, contenders?; why did Bashir commission fake bank statements purporting to show that the Murdoch media were on to the Spencer family, bank statements that were never, and could never have been broadcast?; why did the plan for a programme about her *work* never materialise?; why did Bashir, the young journalist who instantly became a star in the television firmament, fade into BBC obscurity and why was he significantly unseen in the mass media in the aftermath of Diana's death?

Diana gave testimony because she sensed that she was at risk from her enemies in the Establishment, and because by speaking out she could secure her own safety. Her spectacular subordination – muted only by her refusal to utter the word *obey* in her marriage vow – had been witnessed by millions in the summer of 1981. Now, to the chagrin of the Establishment, the recovery of her self-respect was to be witnessed by millions, too. By telling her story Diana joined the 'constituency of the rejected' – the survivors of harm and horror, from the Holocaust, from world wars and pogroms, from Vietnam and the civil wars of South America and South Africa, from torture and child abuse – who have transformed the work of storytelling in our century.

Before Morton's book and *Panorama*, there were tabloid reporters and photographers who also bore witness, but who harassed Diana. Even as they accumulated an archive of royal cruelty and complicity, they tormented her because they desired her and sought dominion over her. The political paradox is that they used her in a quasi-democratic quest to breach the royals' control over what she, and we, could say and know. Both the Morton and Bashir narratives liberated a secret history. Paradoxically, Bashir, who was sponsored by the bastion of British broadcasting and its flagship current affairs programme,

Panorama, has been trailed by suspicion, while Morton, the man whose biography empowered Diana and left the monarchy exposed and accused, came from the vulgar tabloid tradition.

Another chronicler, Anthony Holden, started from a different position: his role as unofficial biographer to Charles took him to a critique of Charles' self-pity, his flaws as a father and his negative use of his power to assail professionals – architects, teachers and doctors – who did not have the same power to defend themselves.

All of these men risked their own integrity as professional listeners. Their integrity as men risked being contaminated and compromised by their commitment to a woman's narrative; their status as observers risked the same stigma that attached to the wounded woman herself; the stories they told were in danger of repudiation by the royals and a complacent coalition that embraced Diana's enemies in the Establishment and indifferent agnostics in all political tendencies, who regarded Diana as preposterous, a ridiculous or irrelevant 'rich bitch'.

These men became the couriers of a dangerous story where sexual politics met royal and republican politics. It found no articulation in parliamentary political discourse and yet it animated this society's conversation with itself and prefigured the amazing heterogeneity of Diana's mourners – women and men, gay and straight, black and white, Muslims and Christians, royalists and republicans.

But for a decade these chroniclers had also been bearing false witness: much of what they knew could not be processed, it wasn't thinkable or printable. That meant that they were bystanders watching a crash, making a living from the mess: did they bear responsibility not only for not recording the crash but also for not trying to stop it?

Andrew Morton had been writing material at the end of the 1980s and early '90s that was alerting readers to Charles' habits as a husband and father. He was well informed, had good contacts, and he was careful. He'd been trailing the royal family for years but always safeguarded his contacts in the royal household – and he had become confidently critical of the chauvinism and political unaccountability of the monarchy. As a member of the rat pack he had, like Diana, been close enough to become a critic. Her choice of Morton as collaborator put her in safe hands.

He began his career as a royal reporter on the tabloids with reluctance: 'It was like being in the Army and being asked to volunteer. I knew nothing about them and wasn't interested in them. I wanted to be a political reporter.' He worked with the rat pack, mostly monarchists, following the same people, chasing the same stories, fiercely fighting for the front page, driven by the contradictory ethic of competition and co-operation that defines journalistic communities. He wrote books on Prince Andrew, Sarah Ferguson, the royal yacht, royal finances (pointing out that the royal family had never enjoyed so many privileges with so few legal and fiscal responsibilities) and of course Charles and Diana.

His first clues came from the *News of the World* reporter with whom he worked, Fiona Macdonald Hull, who noted that all was not well at the palace and who was the first to suggest that Diana was desperate. She was

> ridiculed by the palace and her rivals, because the image was so much at variance with what she was saying. Being the *News of the World* people didn't believe it. Her stories never had great facts – there weren't a lot in the '80s – but she was insightful and had a sense of the unhappiness in the marriage that was disguised by the royal system. I met some of her contacts and realised she was right. She is the unsung heroine of this scenario.

As a jobbing reporter Morton covered the usual tours, broadcasts, marriages, and as he became familiar with the royals he recognised their landscape as unpleasant,

> hierarchical, deferential and male dominated. It was transparent that they were male dominated because of

the way they behaved and the response of the media:
royal men were judged by what they said, women by
what they wore. There were no Jews and black people, no
ethnic minorities of any kind, so we were seeing a world
that didn't reflect the make-up of modern Britain. The
queen has never walked down the street on her own.
She'd have tremors if she was set down alone in Oxford
Street and told to find her way home.

The rat pack noticed in 1986 that Charles spent much of
his time away from his wife and children and by 1987 they
were confident that there was trouble at Kensington
Palace. Reports appeared in the tabloids registering the
amount of time Charles didn't spend with Diana and his
sons, preferring the company of his old comforters and
confidantes, Camilla Parker-Bowles and Dale Tryon. At the
end of the summer Charles holed up in Balmoral for a
serious sulk – he didn't see his wife and children in London
for more than a month. 'It was the morality of the rutting
stag. If the royal family were on a sink estate you'd be
talking about the "underclass",' said Morton. There was no
equivalent in the broadsheet press or the BBC to the rat
pack and thus no debate in the 'serious media' about the
royal family. In 1990 Morton wrote 'Diana's Diary', a
portrait of everyday life among the Waleses'. I wasn't
negative about the marriage, that would have been
unthinkable.' He also wrote a story in the *Sun* that Camilla
Parker-Bowles had secretly gone to Italy, where Charles
was on holiday. 'Nonsense,' she told the press. In 1991 he
revealed that Charles had sacked his private secretary, Sir
Christopher Airey, appointed only a year earlier as 'a safe
pair of hands' to manage the chaos in Charles' office at St
James's Palace. Charles himself shrank from telling the
man, who was taken aside by one of his Business in the
Community colleagues and told it was time to resign.
(Dimbleby, 1995, p602)
There was an investigation into who might be Morton's

source. This was training for the *True Story*. 'I knew it would happen.' He also knew that to protect Diana's 'deniability', her chronicle had to be confirmed by others and he would have to lay false trails and false clues. 'You've got to know the enemy, so the question you ask yourself about every sentence is: is this going to compromise Diana?'

Morton began writing a biography of Diana expecting it to be dominated by three themes: a girl growing up knowing her parents had wanted a boy, becoming a 'high-school drop-out' and then the most famous woman in the world. Diana knew he was doing the book. Feeling 'trapped by her image, by an unbending royal system and an unravelling marriage', and spiced perhaps by a Spencer recklessness, she was eager to collaborate. 'She was dead keen for the book to come out. The enthusiasm took me aback,' said Morton. Although she was paralysed by palace constraints, which made her feel like a 'butterfly stuck on a pin', and by the paparazzi, he also had a sense that 'she could be empowered' by telling her own story. Undoubtedly she was working hard to recover her self-respect, and Sarah Ferguson's critique of the royal cult was already leading her out of the family. 'So the whole thing was very unstable.'

Morton's interviews with Diana were conducted through a go-between, their mutual friend James Colthurst. Among other places they met in an inelegant café in Ruislip where they agreed on the conditions: the book had to appear as if she had no involvement. To ensure Diana's 'deniability' Morton would talk to her friends so that her version of events could be corroborated – without anyone necessarily knowing of her involvement. 'For the first time she could tell her story to the world. Otherwise, why would she have done it?'

Her friends had seen her become 'sad, desperate, sorrowful, at the end of her tether, treated as a second class citizen'. They knew that she had difficulties, suffered from low self-esteem, they knew about her bulimia, her self-harm, they

knew that Charles was only an intermittent father, and that
he was involved with Camilla. No one knew the whole story
but everyone knew fragments, 'it was looking at a glade
through the trees'.

Much of this was new knowledge for the reporter,
however. This story had never been told before. He
revealed that Diana had been delivered to the palace before
the wedding where, instead of being welcomed, she felt
abandoned; that she had evidence of the enduring
relationship with Camilla, the cufflinks, the photographs,
the phone calls; that Charles was enmeshed with his
relatives; that they kept his secrets; that they responded to
her survival struggle and her self-harm as if they'd never
seen tears before. It was a terrible tale.

Bugs and Denials

Morton had to protect not only his sources but himself
during 1991. The palace had become paranoid about leaks,
which were, in any case, difficult to control in a world no
longer ordered by deference.

After his stories on Camilla and Airey he was alerted by
members of the rat pack warning him that the Royal
Protection Squad was under orders to uncover Morton's
mole. In May 1991 – when he began working on the *True
Story* – his office was broken into, a camera stolen and
someone rifled through his filing cabinets. He had his
office in Drummond Street swept for bugs, and made
sensitive calls from an outside telephone. Upstairs on the
first floor, with blinds at the windows and an intrusive air-
conditioning system, he felt safer from burglars and
bugging devices. 'It's like being a spy. You have to know
your opponents – my opponents are in the palace.'

The deniability strategy worked. Diana could, in all
honesty, say that she had never met Mr Morton. Still, the
palace wanted to know who was talking. But what the
royals did not seem to register was that the world around

them had changed, 'women have changed, that's the point,' said Morton. 'Neither Fergie nor Diana were prepared to sacrifice their one chance of happiness and end up like Queen Alexandra: accepting Edward VII's infidelities and getting on with her sewing.'

What Diana had to say about her own experience, so easily consigned to secrecy, stunned Morton: 'It was like someone in the Middle Ages discovering for the first time that the world was round.'

Morton's book was serialised in the *Sunday Times* in June 1992, after the paper rigorously checked his sources and came to the conclusion that Diana had sanctioned its publication. On 8 July the Press Complaints Commission bowed to a tide of pressure and denounced this 'odious exhibition of journalists dabbling their fingers in the stuff of other people's souls in a manner which adds nothing to legitimate public interest in the situation of the heir to the throne'. When the PCC chair Lord McGregor telephoned Sir Robert Fellowes to read him this statement, he explained that editors were complaining that far from the press dabbling, the source was Diana herself. He wanted an assurance from the palace that this was not true. Fellowes gave him the assurance. The PCC statement was published, but provoked the *Sunday Times* to contact the PCC and explain why they were so confident. Charles' side of the story also appeared in the press. Fellowes had been wrong, and was forced to apologise. The PCC, a limp quango, judged complaints from ordinary citizens by standards rather less stringent than print and broadcasting ethics. The PCC received 2712 complaints in 1997, but upheld only 34. Wronged or misrepresented citizens – unless rich enough to bring legal actions against the media – are thus largely unprotected. But here was the PCC being pro-active in the protection of citizens against media harassment. In the name of privacy, however, it was protecting private power and in the name of ethics, it was defending the Establishment.

After Diana's death Morton's book was reissued with transcripts of the taped interviews. Morton was accused of cashing in on the tragedy, but his reply was that since there was now no need to defend deniability, something else had become more important: the tenor of the revisionist historians, he argued, was that the book was an aberration, a regrettable act by a desperate (and deranged) woman, rather than 'an integral part of her life'. After her death her story was already being buffeted by the campaign to discredit her. It became important to challenge this emerging orthodoxy. 'The argument from my publisher, Michael O'Mara, and myself was: are we going to let their distortions run?' Diana's own words, which prefaced the new edition, offered a clipped, unadorned tone to her testimony. 'Those words now stand as a boulder that any Establishment historian has to get around,' Morton explained.

A year after Morton's book first appeared, his fellow rat-packers James Whitaker, Arthur Edwards and Judy Wade published their inventories of years of royal-watching for the tabloids, Edwards revelling in rat-pack chases and Whitaker making sense of what he'd seen over a decade that wasn't sayable.

Whitaker, a monarchist, came to believe that Diana was used in a cynical exercise in social engineering; that Charles 'has been an adulterer throughout his marriage'; and that the royals did not apply themselves to an amicable settlement after their separation. 'Diana is regarded as the enemy,' he wrote in 1993. He was convinced that Diana's movements were closely monitored. This was confirmed by the secret recordings of both Charles' and Diana's private conversations in the 1980s and '90s.

The 'Squidgygate' tape was published in the *Sun* in August 1992, Whitaker believed, as a riposte to the *Mirror*'s Fergie photo spread. But it did much to discredit Diana after the impact of the Morton book. Whitaker regarded the release of the bugged conversations as battles in a 'vicious war' between the royal family and Diana, which extended to putting anything into the public domain that could 'diminish her'.

There were rival forces not only in Fleet Street but also within the secret services, including those who believed they were doing the royal family a favour by doing in Diana. 'Camillagate' and 'Squidgygate' appeared in very different conditions. The Squidgy conversation took place on New Year's Eve 1989, and was recorded that night by a radio ham, Jane Norgrove. A retired bank manager living in Abingdon, Berkshire, Cyril Reenan, heard the conversation on his £900 scanner four days later. He thought he was listening to it live, and sent his tape to a national newspaper. Other copies turned up at the *Sun* and the *Daily Mail*. The *Mail*'s royal correspondent Richard Kay received his copy in a brown envelope which had not come from Reenan. Furthermore, Reenan's tape was analysed by a specialist hired by the *Daily Mirror* who concluded that it had been taken from a wire-tap and processed to mislead the listener by sounding as if it had been taken from a mobile phone. In fact it had been recorded from Diana's home line. The disguise merely hid from the public and, presumably, the royals, the fact that the royals were being bugged. 'There is no question that it was transmitted three or four times,' added Whitaker.

The Camillagate tape was recorded by another amateur, a Merseyside man who used to record telephone conversations picked up by a scanner and roof aerial trawling the frequencies used by mobile phones. He played the tape to friends before taking it to the press. According to Steve White, a journalist in the *Daily Mirror*'s Manchester office, this man had identified Prince Charles' voice but did not recognise the woman. 'I knew immediately who she was when he played it,' recalled White. The *Daily Mirror* checked and double-checked the authenticity of the tape. The man's story checked out and the paper ran the story in

December 1992. The government in March 1993 denied
that the secret services were spying on the royals.

Thinking the Unthinkable

Whitaker reckoned that the war with Diana started 'from
the word go. She didn't fit in, she wasn't an easily manipu-
lated person. She proved that very fast.' She'd proved it by
refusing to have Charles' confidantes Kanga and Camilla at
her wedding breakfast, 'Charles must have been absolutely
gobsmacked that this 19-year-old innocent said "piss off, I
don't want these women there".' She had already shown
that she could put up a fight during the royal train
controversy. That episode revealed the difficulty of
deciphering what was going on. 'Diana might have had her
suspicions, but it never entered any of our minds. If
someone had got on that train it must have been Diana.' He
knew that Diana found it unbearable to think that Charles
may never have loved her – at least loved her as she'd
hoped – but he suspected that the Charles–Camilla
relationship had resumed swiftly.

The royal train story, and the suspicions that Charles and
Camilla were always an 'item' rumbled around Fleet Street
for years. Indeed Whitaker remembered discussing it with
his editor, but neither of them knew what to do with it
because 'it didn't seem credible'. Despite what they were
seeing, the reporters recoiled from the obvious
conclusions: 'it was impossible, unthinkable'. So, contrary
to myth, the tabloids held back.

Diana's decision to tell her story through Andrew Morton
suddenly made sense of long-held suspicions. The tabloids
were vindicated. A year later Jonathan Dimbleby's biography
of the Prince, researched by Clare Hargreaves, and his
television interview, represented Charles' counter-attack.

After the tabloid tradition was shown to have successfully stormed royal defences, *Panorama*, the BBC's flagship
current-affairs slot, began prospecting for its own royal gold.

Diana was known to be interested in doing a television interview, but she had been blocked by her office at the palace. The *Panorama* team approached Andrew Morton a couple of times. 'They think they're the pantheon,' said Morton, 'they were arrogant and supercilious, they'd say "we're thinking of doing a programme on Diana" and I'd say "I'm thinking I'm not interested in helping you."'

The pantheon had sneered at a decade of royal reporting in the tabloids only to find that the 'scum' had been right all along. In 1995 cameras were hidden in hold-alls and smuggled into Kensington Palace, where Diana was interviewed secretly by the BBC.

Britain stayed at home on Monday evening, 20 November 1995, when the BBC screened Diana being interviewed by Martin Bashir. The palace and the public were astonished. Although the interview tracks the terrain in the Morton book, the spectacle of Diana *speaking* her own story was arresting. But more than that, with this freedom of speech, she explained self-harm as a strategy for survival in a menacing milieu in which the Establishment treated her as an enemy. By bearing witness Diana revealed that she had once been in danger, and now she was dangerous. This is what she said:

- Her husband responded to her huge popularity like a man, 'a proud man' who minded, who felt low, 'instead of feeling happy and sharing it'.
- It was good fortune that she gave birth to boys, 'it would have been a little tricky if it had been two girls'.
- She had never been depressed before, but she had been slain by post-natal depression. 'I received a great deal of treatment but I knew that actually what I needed was space and time.'
- 'Maybe I was the first person ever to be in this family who'd ever had depression or was ever openly tearful.'
- Bulimia 'is like having a pair of arms around you, but it's temporary. Then you're disgusted at the bloated-

ness of your stomach, and then you bring it all up again.' It was 'a regular pattern to jump into the fridge'. Bulimia was an 'escape mechanism, and it worked for me at that time'. The illness was 'a symptom of what was going on in my marriage. I was crying out for help but giving the wrong signals'.

- Asked what the Prince of Wales, portrayed in Jonathan Dimbleby's biography as 'a great thinker' thought of her interests, she replied, 'I don't think I was allowed to have any.' No one praised any of her achievements.

- When she discovered Charles' love affair with Camilla, she was devastated. It provoked 'rampant bulimia'. There had been 'three of us in this marriage, so it was a bit crowded'.

- 'Friends, on my husband's side, were indicating that I was again unstable, sick, and should be put in a home of some sort.'

- 'I was so fed up of being seen as someone who was a basket case, because I'm a very strong person and I know that causes complications in the system I live in.'

- After the separation was announced in 1993, 'I was a problem, I was a liability', and the palace was pre-occupied by '"how are we going to deal with her?" This hasn't happened before.' People in the royal household perceived her as the problem. This became palpable when she discovered that 'visits abroad were being blocked, by things that had come naturally my way being stopped ... my husband's side were very busy stopping me.'

- The Squidgy tape was published 'to harm me in a serious manner' and make 'the public change their attitude towards me'.

- Because she would not 'go quietly' she fell under intense media harassment and in 1993 decided to take a temporary break from public life. 'The campaign at that point was being successful, but it did surprise the people who were causing the grief – it did surprise them when I took myself out of the game. They hadn't expected that. And I'm a great believer that you should always confuse the enemy.'

- Who were the enemy? 'My husband's department.'

- Jealousy produced a strategy to undermine her. 'I think it was out of fear, here was a strong woman doing her bit, and where was she getting her strength from to continue.'

- Her relationship with James Hewitt went beyond friendship; 'I adored him. Yes, I was in love with him, but I was very let down.'

- As a 'free spirit' she hoped to become an ambassador. 'I'm not a political animal' but she had acquired great experience; she didn't expect to become queen, but aspired to be the Queen of Hearts.

- The monarchy needed to change its relationship to the public, 'they could walk hand in hand, as opposed to being so distant.' She hoped that her sons would appreciate people's emotions, insecurities and distress.

- She had doubts about whether Charles would want to be king because he himself had conflicts. 'My wish is that my husband finds peace of mind.'

Diana's description of bulimia was revelatory. Women across Britain watched, amazed.

If anyone had been in any doubt about the fury of the palace towards truculent women, Diana revealed that old royal habits die hard: an institution that had put women in the Tower or under the axe was still working on the assumption that an unwanted princess could simply be put away. In comments that connected her with contemporary feminism, she counted herself among the 'strong women'. What did that mean? It faced the Establishment with an alarming, unnerving prospect – she had a social base beyond their comprehension and outside their control.

16. Frighteners

How did *Panorama* get this scoop? On 7 April 1996, a few months after the programme was screened, *Mail on Sunday* reporters published a remarkable story: Martin Bashir *had* produced fake documents as part of the planning for his Diana programme. 'Was he hoping to convince Earl Spencer he was the right person to interview his sister?' the paper asked. A year later the press was still worrying and wondering. 'As both Diana and Spencer believed that they were being spied on, possibly by MI5,' wrote the *Sunday Times* on 7 May 1997, 'they might have been receptive to "evidence" that confirmed their suspicions.'

Bashir had several meetings with Earl Spencer in the weeks before the interview was secretly filmed on 5 November 1995. The BBC denies that their conversations alluded to 'evidence' that GCHQ had been bugging Diana and that Ruport Murdoch's News International were on to the family and paying former staff to sell their story.

A month before Bashir filmed the interview he asked a designer, Martin Wiessler, to do a quick job for him.

Wiessler often did graphics for *Panorama*. Bashir told him he would be arriving with the material that night and needed the job done by the morning. The task was to create two bank statements which were to look like photocopies of genuine statements, dated March and June 1994, in the name of two men who ran a security firm. One of them was Alan James Waller. Waller had been Earl Spencer's security chief, but Spencer had obtained a High Court injunction against him in March 1994 to prevent him revealing anything about the Spencer family. This injunction followed a story in *Today* based on a leaked letter from Spencer to his sister Diana in December 1993 – when she was under intense media pressure. The letter suggested that she was being damaged by her public appearances.

Wiessler was asked to design into the bank statements credits purporting to be from News International. The graphics were to be dispatched for collection by Bashir at Heathrow Airport the following morning.

Since Diana had already been the victim of dirty tricks and the press had published leaks of bugged telephone conversations, it would be credible that News International had approached employees of the Spencer household. However, these payments had never been made to the Waller account. This did not come to light until colleagues of Bashir were puzzled by another alleged payment to the Waller account that Wiessler had been asked to include in the mock-ups. This payment purported to come from a company called Penfold Consultancy. Penfold was a company Bashir and his colleagues at *Panorama* had encountered in their investigation into the financial activities of Terry Venables and Tottenham Hotspurs football club. This payment was totally inexplicable as it was supposedly made three months after the real account had been closed. Colleagues 'remembered the Penfold's connection in the Venables programme and asked how it could have turned up in the Waller bank statements,' reported the *Mail on Sunday*.

Soon after the Diana interview was broadcast, the designer Wiessler got worried, too. He had trusted *Panorama*'s credentials and 'had no reason to doubt that the information provided by Bashir was genuine'. (*Mail on Sunday*, 7 April 1996) He now took his worries about the ethics of the scoop to *Panorama*'s editor Steve Hewlett, and was later told that the matter 'had been settled'. Early in December 1995 Wiessler tried to find his original graphics, stored on a computer disk. They were gone. This time he approached the head of weekly programmes at the BBC, Tim Gardam, and was told that everything had been sorted out. But what exactly was being sorted out? Why had the fakes been commissioned? Why hadn't they been screened? And since they could never have been broadcast – because they were fictions – what on earth were they for?

The BBC's explanation is disingenuous. Asked to confirm that the documents were created as part of the Diana project the BBC has admitted that 'they were set up for graphics purposes in the early part of the investigation' but that there was 'never any intention for the documents to be published' and they were 'discarded when some of the information could not be substantiated' – hardly surprising since the information could *never* have been substantiated. Waller told the press that the payments had never been made. Asked to explain the production and purpose of the graphics, the BBC is silent. And why did the BBC not disclose that there were two internal inquiries into Bashir's activities? (*Sunday Times*, 7 May 1997) Colleagues continued to worry that the documents had been produced to procure the story. The question persists. But the corporation has refused to give an answer. 'That question is never answered and never will be,' said a spokesperson for the BBC.

The BBC hierarchy's response to the media interest was: there's no story. After the *Mail on Sunday* report, the editors of BBC's radio current affairs programmes found this e-mail on their screens: 'If anyone asks about Bashir, the official line is: "It's not interesting."' (*Sunday Times*, 28 April, 1996)

Morton made a fortune. Bashir became a hero. But not for long, it seems. His star seemed to fade in the television firmament in the wake of these questions and he was significantly unseen on our screens during the saturation coverage of her death and her funeral.

Froideur

While the tabloids were squaring up to the separate bedrooms, separate holidays and separate lives of the Waleses, Charles unofficial biographer, Anthony Holden was the first writer to offer a critique of the very things that had made Charles a compelling figure: his politics and his wife. Holden had already written a biography of the young prince and published his second to mark Charles' fortieth birthday in 1988. Holden worked for the *Sunday Times* during the great days when it was edited by Harold Evans. Usually the Court Circular would be binned, but Holden was becoming a serious 'celebrity' journalist who followed the great and the good and recorded their twitches and bald patches. After a couple of years working in Washington for the *Observer* he returned to the *Sunday Times* – but walked out in 1982 in protest against editorial interference by the proprietor, Rupert Murdoch.

Holden was around the same age as the Prince and read Charles' life through the filter of his own experience as a well-educated middle-class professional. 'I started envying him and finished it thinking it was boring and lonely, eating dinners on a tray watching television.'

He covered Charles' tour of South America and acquired a reputation as a man Charles was close to. Not true. Holden was never his friend. But it was a useful starting point for his second biography. The 1980s Charles was a married man, a father, and a prince finding his place in politics. It was these changes that Holden subjected to searching analysis: he mobilised a scholarly critique of Charles' emotional attack on architecture, and he dared to suggest that his marriage was in trouble. When the book was serialised in the *Sunday Times*, coinciding with Holden's television programme about the Prince, Charles denounced it in the *Observer* as 'fiction', full of recycled lies and barely based on any conversations with those close to him, an attack that was supported by Charles' representative on the Prince's Trust, Tom Shebbeare.

The problem was that the rat pack always had to rely on their reading of royal body language, and 'the staff were all primed to lie. The royals have all sorts of ways of shutting people up.' Holden was pilloried. He was outraged and consulted the prestigious libel lawyer Carter Ruck, who acknowledged that he had a case but wouldn't win. 'From then dates the *froideur*,' said Holden. (Almost ten years later Shebbeare apologised for 1988.)

Charles' trip to South Africa in 1997 gave the palace an opportunity for revenge: Holden was refused accreditation for the royal party. These royal tours were critical events for royal correspondents, in the absence of the briefing or lobby structure that institutionalised the circulation of information. Through accreditation, the royals controlled access to the itinerary and to accommodation. Tours are the way royals do what they do: be seen. To be denied access was to be denied the right to work. Holden went anyway.

Holden had watched Charles and Diana's behaviour during the Australian tour in 1987, its bi-centenary year. When Diana moved towards a piano, at precisely the point when Charles was about to play his cello, and astonished the audience with some Rachmaninov, Holden thought to himself, 'Blimey, these two are in trouble.' He met her occasionally and found her bright, intelligent, witty and knowledgeable about classical music, despite her reputation as a disco kid. 'No wonder she polaxed them,' said Holden, 'she was a regular human.' Later he felt he initially misinterpreted their relationship. Charles, after all, appeared to be a serious person. Diana didn't. But Holden came to think Charles 'never even gave it a chance, and never intended to'. When he first knew the Prince 'he was full of potential to make the royal family a decent institution, and change his children's nappies, but I was wrong. I became more angry about that than anything.'

Sexism and Sovereignty

Holden was not only relying on body language, he was seeing the royals through the filter of his own experience as a father who was dealing with a divorce, a new relationship and the care of their children. Charles' behaviour when William was injured by the golf club appalled him. 'If one of my children had a crisis, that would be my priority,' he said. 'That's why I got so pissed off with Charles – because of the way he treated his wife and children.'

How Charles treated his wife and children had a lot to do with the reason for Diana's collaboration with Andrew Morton, and later with *Panorama*. It had everything to do with her hazardous confrontation with the palace. She had entered this family without being enlightened. When she discovered that she wasn't wanted, she was offered no choice but to fade away and suffer in silence. She obliged.

She may have screamed in sorrow, made herself sick in the privacy of her palace, but she still put on a good show. When she was required on parade, she put on a frock and did what she was supposed to do: show off. The palace, in pique, wanted more, they wanted a show trial: she must go out there and testify in public that she was really only her husband's shadow. (Holden, 1988, p258) Her silence was supposed to remind her public and the men from the media, who would rather look at her than listen to her husband, that she was only his shadow. Her job, she said, was 'to support my husband'. She explained later, in her

Panorama interview, that her husband did the speaking while she shook hands.

Thus was the language of sexual subordination mobilised against her by the palace. It almost destroyed her. Royal manners had certainly done in all the 'commoners' who married into the House of Windsor after World War II: Lord Snowdon, Mark Philips, Sarah Ferguson and, of course, Diana Spencer. The royals retreated into their laager and blamed the commoners for failing to cope. Diana was the first one to protest in public. Her decision to tell her story to Andrew Morton was her protest against royal sexism and its cult of sovereignty. It was also a protest against a regime that made her mad.

The *Sun* photographer Ken Lennox, who had followed Diana from the beginning, said, 'The courtiers were saying she was a mad woman, they were putting out stories at dinner parties that she was a mad woman.' That's why she decided to speak out.

According to Judith Lewis Herman, whose distinguished book *Trauma and Recovery* discusses the impact of traumatic events on the survivors of war, disaster and abuse, recovery depends on safety, space for remembrance and mourning, and testimony: the survivor piecing together her own story, her own version of events. This is particularly problematic for women since it requires them to repudiate the social demand for submission. And it is tough for survivors of family tumult because they are under orders to maintain the family rule of silence. By 'preserving the family secret they carry a weight that doesn't belong to them'. But by confronting the family, the survivors 'renounce shame and responsibility and put the burden where it belongs'. (Herman, 1992, p200)

History, like families, has depended on its victims to be the 'bearers of the silence' argue the historians of the Holocaust Dori Laub and Shoshona Felman, and through their silence the secrets of contemporary society are kept through 'denial, reticence or canonisation'. (pxix) The 'task of 'testimony', therefore, cannot escape the history of the tormented body and thus the act of bearing witness faces the listener with the intimate 'carnal knowledge of victimisation'. (p111)

To confront the royal family by telling her story, Diana made a conscious choice to speak of the suffering of her body and soul. Her 'task of testimony' was to face danger. The *Panorama* programme intimated that she was in danger. Her survival depended upon calling attention to her pain and to the perpetrators. Some viewers saw it as soap. Some saw it as a woman scorned. Many feminists saw it as the extreme difficulty of voicing dissent in her environment. Modern movements of survivors, from Siberia to Sloane Square, have redeemed pain from the psychiatric wards via the fridge and the phone, the samizdat and the secret services, to redefine it as public, political discourse. Diana positioned herself not as a victim but as a survivor, among a constituency of women, ill-treated and ill, whose unruly rebellions have, until now, brought them not care but contempt.

She was believed because what she revealed was how they had made her mad, and how they represented her mutiny as madness. The Tory minister Nicholas Soames, an old friend of Prince Charles, announced on television after the *Panorama* programme that Diana was clearly 'in the advanced stages of paranoia'. He was only saying what had already been said at those aristocratic dinner parties. She was accused of malice and madness only by people who could not extend empathy – her enemies in the Establishment.

When her disappointment about something so simple as lack of love demanded sympathy, she was rewarded with 'treatment'. If not the Tower then the pharmacy. No aristocratic woman had been so eloquent about pain as protest, about bulimia as accusation and explanation, as survival and self-destruction. The drama of self-destruction unmasked the impossibility of protest. The reason she was

believed was that behind her were the ghosts of thousands
of women sent to the attic, to solitary confinement. The
Establishment has been locking up women for centuries.
The confidence that they'll go quietly is confirmed by the
bumbling megalomania of Charles' marriage. He thought
he could get away with it. He thought he should, or could,
love another while scouring the shires of England for a
sweet and suitable girl who would give him sons and
secure his mission to be king.

I watched the *Panorama* programme with a group of
women friends. Everyone was astonished – we all knew
women who were in pain but had never heard an
aristocratic woman address them as if she were one of
them. That night my companion was seized by a suspicion.
'She's in danger!' she said. I had to send her for the
Southern Comfort. But of course, we said to ourselves, the
Establishment had already tried character assassination.
Why wouldn't someone want to 'take her out'? A car crash?
A rogue fantasy-fixated assassin? It had happened to
presidents, why not to a princess?

Falling in Love Again

After her divorce from Charles, Diana was stripped of her
title Her Royal Highness, and she was no longer monitored
by the detectives who shadow the royals at all times. In
1997 she whirled into a ravishing romance with Dodi Fayed,
a film producer who had been born in Alexandria, educated
in Switzerland, trained at Sandhurst, lunched at Harry's Bar
and the Ivy, and of course in LA and everywhere else, and
had produced six films, including the emblematically
English hit *Chariots of Fire*. His father gave him his stake –
Mohamed al-Fayed owned London's Harrods and the Paris
Ritz. He gave Dodi the money to bankroll David Puttnam's
film and its success earned Dodi $7 million.

This new romance opened season on Diana once more.
Diana's choice of lover increased her potential threat to

the Establishment. The English rose had fallen in love with the scion of the Fayed family, whose quixotic place in British politics had exposed the English Establishment's frosty feelings towards a rich Muslim who wanted to be one of their number. Worse, the Anglophile had created the 'payment for parliamentary questions' crisis which wrecked the reputation of the Tory government. Although Diana was by now a 'free' woman, she was still tailed by the paparazzi and her relationship had been snapped, despite the Fayed family's hot security, by an Italian photographer during the summer. The paparazzi never gave up.

'It's a hunt,' she told her good friend Rosa Monckton when they holidayed together and were trailed by the paparazzi (shortly before Diana's last fatal visit to Dodi). She had often told Monckton about having to 'fight for every second of privacy' but until then, Monckton had not experienced this herself and 'I was horrified.' (*Sunday Telegraph*, 7 September 1997).

But Diana was enjoying her love affair and happy to be with a man who also seemed to love the loving – though, according to Monckton, his predilection for giving expensive presents irritated her.

Dodi was different; he wasn't a soldier or salesman or Sloane Ranger, he was a rich *lover*. He had acquired a reputation as a dilettante movie-maker who loved being on the set, as if he were more than his money, and as a sweet playboy who was loved by women because he loved women. But it was prejudice that gave the relationship its frisson in Britain. The man was a Muslim!

Living dangerously

Diana and Dodi moved in worlds that were obsessed by security but weren't safe. Diana had been trailed everywhere by detectives during her life with the royals. Her private life was now private – except in public spaces.

She still wasn't safe. Dodi loved fast cars but didn't feel safe
in them; he loved having security men stationed upstairs
and downstairs; indeed he lived *in* a security system. But
on a summer's night in Paris the organisation couldn't keep
calm or safe.

Afer dining at the Ritz the couple were surrounded by
the paparazzi when they tried to leave for Dodi's
apartment. An alternative driver was enlisted to help them
escape by the back. The photographers were taunted and
Dodi and Diana in the back of their car, the driver Henri
Paul and the security man Trevor Rees Jones, sped off into
the Paris subways. 'She asked the driver repeatedly to slow
down,' but 'Dodi appeared to be enjoying the situation.'
(*Observer*, 7 September 1997) Chased by paparazzi roaring
behind them on motorbikes, their car going at 100 mph
crashed into a concrete pillar under the Pont d'Alma. Dodi
and the driver were killed immediately. Some of the
hysterical paparazzi crawled over the wreckage and kept
shooting; (*Observer*, 7 September 1997) the ambulance
workers scrambled for space and had to wait until Diana
was cut loose from the back of the car before they could try
to save her life in the ambulance.

17. Queen Caroline – Making a Cause

When the Prince of Wales purged Caroline from the court in 1814, she wandered, with intrepid curiosity, around the courts of Europe and the monuments of Africa. In exile she was emancipated from her husband's bilious harassment. But when George became king he could not contemplate the prospect of her return and his coronation with this woman by his side. He had grabbed her property and her jewels; he never informed her when their daughter Charlotte married and later died. Now he resolved to rid himself of this troublesome wife once and for all. To divorce her he had to discredit her, so he forced a House of Lords inquiry into her alleged and treasonable adultery. Although the King's ministers were desperate to avoid a divorce, the House of Lords dutifully ruminated upon the evidence against her in a high-treason case put by the Attorney General in the summer of 1820. Although the case secured a narrow majority in the Lords, it was clear that it would not be confirmed by the oppositional Commons.

Caroline had been encouraged by Radical politicians to return to London at the end of the hearings, and so she was spared the deliciously dirty stories that were rehearsed in the Lords and recycled in a voracious popular media, the equivalent of today's tabloids, satires and soaps. Although there were remarkable and rowdy demonstrations of support for the wronged queen, she was, nonethless, banned from attending the coronation in 1821. Undeterred, she rode to the ceremony only to find every door barred by prize fighters. She left, humiliated, apparently abandoned by the great movements of 1820.

The King may have felt he was finally rid of her when she died only three weeks later. But her indefatigable spirit revitalised the mood of 1820. The King ordered that she should not be buried at Windsor with her daughter – Caroline had anticipated this and had already indicated that she wished her body to be returned to Brunswick. Only a week after her death, the King ordered that the body be dispatched immediately across the Channel, 'scarcely decent in those leisurely days'. (Brand, 1986, p133) Nevertheless London donned black and gave public expression to a great grief. From Hammersmith the cortege, by now a mile long, moved through pouring rain to Kensington, where it was to turn north and east to avoid the City and the queenite crowd. But the crowd commandeered carriages and cobblestones to block the route and throughout the day, despite being attacked by troops, chaperoned the cortege towards the east end of the capital, sheltered by 'a vast crowd of umbrellas'. The people along the way seemed to have anticipated the procession and mobilised every cart and wagon to make up a dense escort for the dead queen. The Lord Mayor, hastily summoned from Guildhall, led the procession through the City. Deputations of men – merchants, cobblers, coopers and carpenters – fell in beside the cortege; bands played amidst the crowd; women were staunch and sad; and entrepreneurs hawked pincushions sporting the Queen's head.

The 'ramshackle cavalcade' rumbled through Essex on its way to Harwich. There the sun shone, the sea was calm and 'the piers were crowded, the harbour choked with boats of every size (Fraser, 1997, p465) The coffin was tipped over the jetty on to the deck of the frigate which took Caroline's body out to the open sea.

A crush of mourners met the cortege when it reached Brunswick for the consignment of her body to the cathedral vault and 'a hundred maidens holding flowers and tapers lined the aisles'. (Fraser, 1997, p466)

New politics

Despite her unforgiving exile, Caroline, an enthusiastic and entertaining spirit, had found her voice, which engaged a vast community of friends and a coalition represented by *The Times*, the Whigs, and the Radicals. The vitality of plebeian popular culture which sponsored this movement created 'a new political language that could speak both of high royal politics and of family crises in the same breath'. Even the apolitical or the illiterate could not avoid the Carolinite ballads sung on the streets and the caricatures in print-shop windows. It is claimed that two million copies of Caroline's *Answer to the King* were published. (Laqueur, 1982, p429) Anna Clark argues that Caroline functioned as a complex symbol that 'allowed her radical supporters to project on to her a variety of moral interpretations in disparate genres of popular literature, from libertine satire to moralistic melodrama'. (1995, p165) Challenging the frequent dismissal of this movement, Clark argues that 'instead of trivialising radical politics the transformation of popular literature into overt political language made mass mobilisation possible'.

The King's inquisition had inserted sexual politics into

the parliamentary domain and public debate. Caroline's reputation as a sexual innocent did not emerge intact, but 'did the British public care for that?' wondered the historian Elie Halevy. Apparently not. They cared much more about the King's unpardonable treatment of a woman. His inspection of her behaviour brought his own predilection for philandering with married women into public discourse. 'She forced issues of sexuality and gender into politics.' (Clark, 1995, p165)

Caroline herself addressed public meetings of supporters 'identifying with her as a mirror of both their woes and their virtues'. Georgian censorship was 'helpless against so massive a mobilisation.' (Laqueur, 1982, p421) The Caroline movement created a great debate about a moral manhood, which became a model not only for the middle class but for plebeians too. The tumult settled into a polarisation between respectable masculinity and domesticated femininity that defined the chauvinism of later proletarian politics. But what the movement around Caroline had revealed was the *potential* of sexual politics and a multiplicity of gender roles.

There has been much debate among historians about the Carolinian movement, so audacious and yet so brief. The eminent historian of the aristocracy, David Cannadine, has resisted the parallels between Diana and Caroline and has repudiated the suggestion that these women were 'one of us'. Although Diana did seem to be 'an authentically anti-establishment figure', he argues, both Caroline and Diana were daughters of the aristocracy, Diana married the son of 'one of the wealthiest women of the world, and her divorce settlement was reckoned in millions of pounds. (*Guardian*, 6 September 1997). But Cannadine does not excavate the dangerous popular resonance of the *sexual* politics which transcended class and political alignment and, albeit briefly, animated a mass movement that endangered the Establishment.

Then, as now, the limitations of progressive sexual politics – as politics – were that its language did not translate into parliamentary discourse. Its roots were, and are, in civil society, in women's 'woes and virtues'. Since it proposes the reform of masculinity, it is not surprising that it was not championed in parliamentary or party politics.

Elie Halevy has argued that the 'noisy farce of 1820 masked the failure of political agitation'. (1961, p105) But for the feminist historian Anna Clark, the Carolinian movement 'expanded the possibilities for women's political participation' and, far from merely defending 'traditional communal morality', created an inchoate search for 'a revision of traditional values'. It also transformed a 'public' that was masculine into a 'people' comprising both women and men. (Clark, 1995, p174)

The place of the Carolinians in British history and the debates about those inflammatory events reveals the resistance of 'official history' to the importance of sexual politics – Caroline's life and death has scarcely been encouraged to resonate across two centuries. But Thomas Laqueur argues that the Carolinian Cause was 'popular as no previous popular movement had been.' (1982) After the withdrawal of the Whigs' support in 1821 the movement lost its most powerful champions in the Commons. Then, as now, the sexual politics invigorating civil society depended – in vain – on champions in Parliament.

18. Dead

In the early hours of Sunday 31 August 1997, the news crossed the Channel that Diana had been injured in a car crash in Paris. The royal family were telephoned at their Balmoral retreat. Charles didn't tell his sons until they awoke in the morning. Prime Minister Tony Blair was telephoned in his Sedgfield constituency. Late-night viewers and listeners heard the news through the night and called their own loved ones. We all remember where we were and how we knew.

The news was dominated by the cause of the crash and the response to it: How and why did Diana die? How were the posse of paparazzi to be apprehended? Were the paparazzi to blame? As the scene was pieced together, it emerged that Henri Paul was not only drunk, he had been taking pills. It was inconceivable that an organisation with a mania for security should be sloppy enough to have a drunk driver on its staff. The Fayeds denied it, but forensic tests were unequivocal – the man had been drinking. So, was Henri Paul to blame? But his boss and a British security man were also in the car. Didn't they stop him or ask him to slow down? Don't chauffeurs do what their bosses tell them to do? Whatever caused the final collision between the car and the concrete pillar, there was no doubt that the paparazzi were in pursuit and their chase ended in the crash.

The determination to have this woman exposed, endlessly seen and subjected to surveillance, destroyed her. But her death cannot be debated as if it were simply a disastrous dilemma of privacy and the public interest. She died because a posse of men would not take no for an answer. When a woman says no she means no. This is a mantra of the modern woman. It is very simple and yet so subtle, one of the emblematic phrases of our era, one that expresses women's great efforts to take possession of their own bodies; a struggle to save their own skins.

Diana's fate exposed women's precarious possession of themselves as a matter of life and death.

Nothing it seemed, was more important than the paparazzi's right to look. Photographers resisted the demand to curtail press freedom by representing Diana as a capricious gal who caused confusion among the lads because sometimes she'd have tantrums when she didn't want to be photographed, and yet on other occasions she'd invite the press along. That Diana sometimes said yes seemed to drive them to distraction.

Her polite injunctions during private holidays with her children came to be represented not as authoritative and assertive but as aggressive. Clearly, her choice was experienced as an unacceptable challenge. In a sense they were right. She had challenged them to have a democratic, negotiated relationship. There had often been a sneering, leering contempt in the media for Diana, as if the media were affronted by the sheer nerve of a woman who should have remained a pretty face, an everlastingly exposed body. To banish the private from public articulation was never

her project. But that also never meant that she was not
entitled to have her privacy protected. She was no longer a
member of the royal family; she simply wanted the right to
choose when and where to be seen. After all, she was not
Neil Hamilton or Jonathan Aitken. The press, rightly and
bravely, pursued these men's corruptions and crimes. They
weren't interested in the men's bodies. Privacy laws would
have been no protection for Diana because they would not
have dealt with the deadly disrespect in which she, like
millions of other women, are held.

Conspiracies

In the aftermath of Diana's death, conversations were
dominated by the culpability of the paparazzi and
speculations on conspiracy. The evidence, or lack of it, was
irrelevant: what mattered was that the unthinkable was
already being thought. From taxi drivers to hairdressers,
television reporters and teachers, talk turned to the
possibility that *they* killed her, and if it wasn't Diana they
were after, it was Dodi. After all, the Fayeds had helped
bring down one government, so they could bring down
another. *And* they were Muslims. Either way, the royal
family had been relieved of a dangerous ex-daughter-in-law.

The Channel 4 News anchorman John Snow was woken at
1.20 a.m. while he was away in the country and was told
that Diana had been seriously injured and Dodi was dead.
By 3.30 he learned that she was dead. By six o'clock he got
in to ITN's glass-fronted building in Gray's Inn Road and
stayed close to the story for the rest of the week. Like many
others in the capital, he went to Kensington Palace with
his partner and their children. When the week of mourning
and the funeral were finally over, Snow was to broadcast
the rumours about royal dissent as *news*, not fantasy.

On the morning of Sunday 31 August people turned on
their televisions and left them on. The first live coverage

that morning was of the sepulchral saloons swinging out of Balmoral on their way to church. Royal ritual prevailed despite the fact that the family had lost a former wife, a daughter-in-law and a mother. There was one conversation that morning, *everywhere* but in that church. Diana had already been purged from the litany when she lost her status as a 'Highness'. Balmoral, like the Star Chamber or the Kremlin, could still render a protagonist an unperson, a 'disappeared one'.

A kind of monarchical madness prevailed. The royal rows began immediately. Something was more important than Diana's death and that was royal routine. Or rather it was the Queen's routine: Mrs Majesty prevailed and did not allow the ordinary respects to our dead to pass her lips.

When Diana's sons awoke to hear the worst disaster that can befall a child, they were conscripted for the standard church service at Crathie. Charles was unsure but Mrs Majesty overruled him. A middle-aged man was not allowed to make decisions about his own children – it was as if these children didn't belong to him. Something was more important than the feelings of Diana's sons – and they were, above all, *her* sons. Something was more important than Charles sorting out his shame and redemption, and that was the Queen. This was not the first test of her humanity during her long life, but it was the clearest – and she failed.

The very occasion for which the royal family's dysfunctional, dissociated state, their manners and their protocol prepared them now left them reeling. The monarchy was unmasked: the royals weren't well-mannered they were rude and rough; they weren't just cold and conservative, they were crass, full of fury, envy and spite. They weren't well prepared, they were just programmed.

Why hadn't it occurred to them that Diana's death was, if not *inevitable*, then predictable? How were Diana's children to feel about the rows roaring around the castle between their father and his family? How were they to feel about a grandmother who didn't think she should be taking care of their father? He was, at last, standing up to his mother. He was trying to be humane, or at least honourable, but when he flew off to collect the body from France, the boys were left with people who had ousted their mother. It was not until later in the week that any of these people were seen touching each other, when Charles was seen in public, for the first time, holding the hand of one of his sons.

Charles arrived back at Northolt with Diana's sisters, Jane and Sarah, who were blank-faced with shock. They and the coffin, covered in the royal standard, were greeted by a line of dignitaries. Men shook hands. Among these men the sisters seemed like strangers. The one man who didn't love her was bringing her back home. It was, as the writer Elaine Showalter noticed at the time, an 'indeligible image of patriarchy.' (*Guardian*, 6 September 1997)

The Great British Crowd

In the real world outside the Balmoral bunker, people were worrying for the safety and sanity of Diana's children, unsettled by a sense that they were already 'like the Princes in the Tower'. It was the public who transformed the landscape around the royal gulags. The people reinvented the concept of the crowd. Of course they were practised in the art of congregation: we are good in queues, marketplaces, school corridors, at football matches and raves. We know how to do crowds. But *this* was something that had faded and had become unfamiliar, like gas masks, public meetings, pinnies and bellbottoms: this was a *political* crowd. The people made for the palaces. In paying respects they were also making a protest against royal disrespect.

Diana's death was *the* conversation. The mysteries of the Pont d'Alma and the role of the paparazzi subsided as the media became mesmerised by an even greater mystery – the people. For days the media reported a national 'outpouring of grief', critics and cynics complained that the people were being whipped into a state of hysteria by the tabloids. But this was projection and a poverty of expression. Perhaps it was embarrassment. The crowd took the commentators by surprise because it was calm and contemplative. The tragedy invoked the crowd's own griefs, people recalled the deaths of *their* mothers.

'My mother died when I was 15 and me and my brother never spoke about it.'

'It started to well up that I wanted to be here,' said the 29-year-old singer Emma Rolph who camped at Westminster Abbey. 'Everyone here is surprised by their own unfolding feelings. She was privileged ... but she chose to spend time with people suppurating with sores on their bodies. She made it dignified to have bulimia. And self-harming is an issue in every women's prison. She stood up, the future queen, and said: "I have felt that bad about myself that I wanted to disappear."'

'It's like a peaceful revolution, like the Berlin Wall coming down,' said one mourner. A middle-aged man joined the crowd because he wanted to be 'part of it, we're not just spectators. We were just subjects to stand by. People feel we should be citizens not subjects.' The crowd recognised that this woman had not merely sympathised with sufferers, she named herself as one of them.

A homeless woman who was a familiar figure begging – politely – around King's Cross railway station appeared on television as an adviser to travellers visiting the capital to pay their tribute to Diana: she explained what they'd need for sleeping under the stars, how to keep warm, where to get a wash. A pauper belonging to the community of the dispossessed much maligned by Home Secretary Jack Straw, when he attacked beggars and 'squeegee merchants' became an expert, not an exile. Her survival skills, shared with the respectable, settled and housed, transcended the brittle nuances of class which have infused British political culture. During that week 'travellers' comprised the homeless, eco-gypsies and workers from Arbroath to Plymouth. They were part of the same community: street sleepers and suburbanites were all on the move and they all had something to say to each other. Gay people touched by the way that Diana touched AIDS sufferers, women whose bodies were in crisis, toffs who thought that Charles was a cad, all mingled with Afro-Caribbeans and Muslims mourning their own Diana and Dodi, with more generosity than the British, who grieved for Diana but didn't know how to think about Dodi. They, at least, could imagine sexual desire and intermarriage producing 'a new generation of racially indeterminate Britons.' (Grace, 1997, p5)

Republicans who had been arrested by her critique of royal cruelty took flowers to the palaces and placed them alongside flowers laid by monarchists who were mourning the woman who had been 'the best of the lot of them', the 'flower in the royal forest'. 'Every flower outside Buckingham Palace is a vote against the desert within,' wrote Elaine Showalter.

There had never been in this country such a blithely complicated or cosmopolitan crowd. This was Britain. People appropriated public spaces, invented vigils and memorials. 'Their success in forcing real, measurable change by popular collective action is unlikely to be lost on a people which has lost so much conventional political space,' wrote David Edgar (*Guardian*, 10 September 1997). It was not so long ago, and yet it seemed – and was – another era, when the location of Cruise missiles at Greenham Common harvested a mass movement that feminised a military arena, by planting photographs, Baby-grows, toys and the memorabilia of loved ones upon the perimeter fence.

The Salvation Army organised free teas for the people queueing for eight to ten hours, sometimes overnight, to sign the condolence books – there were never enough

condolence books – and the St John's Ambulance distributed foil covers for the overnighters. The people in the
palaces left the charities to take care of the people.

By Wednesday the crowd's feeling was interpreted by the
media as a set of demands: Raise the flag half-mast at
Buckingham Palace! Join us! Show some feeling! Pay
respect in death to the woman you disrespected in life! The
tabloids that had subjected the royal family to such
tasteless scrutiny gave their front pages to the rustle of
republicanism, or rather a neo-republican feeling, and
reinterpreted it. The people didn't *need* the royal family at
all. 'It's too late now,' muttered people in the crowds,
'they'll never get it right.'

The royals had to bow to their subjects. The palace
protested that the royal family had been 'hurt' by their
subjects' suggestion that 'they are indifferent to the
country's sorrow'. But the people didn't care about their
hurt pride. Downing Street's appeal that week that the
royal family be left in peaceful privacy missed the point.
People didn't believe that they *were* grieving, people
suspected that they were hiding in their bastille at
Balmoral.

New Labour, who had briefly seemed to exemplify
national feeling in the wake of their marvellous election
victory on 1 May, were in fact working with the royal
family to restore its ruined reputation. 'Blair is not a
republican democrat and saw the attacks on monarchical
hauteur as unfair,' noted the *Observer* on 7 September.
Every day that week a committee comprising representatives from Downing Street, the palace and Westminster
Abbey met to plan the funeral. The Queen's representatives insisted on the presence of Alistair Campbell, the
Prime Minister's bruising spokesperson. On Wednesday
Downing Street fielded Campbell to criticise the media 'for
seeming to think the royal family were extras in a media
show'. But the *Observer* noted that for all their

determination to impose order, the government 'also had
to bow to popular pressure, and frankly told Charles that
the queen had to give a broadcast and the royal family must
meet the crowds'.

This was an intimation of the new map of Britain – the
people who formed the culture of civil society were having
one kind of conversation, and presenting to the
Establishment a 'frightening mixture of sentimentality,
grief and rebelliousness' (*Observer*, 7 September 1997)
Frightening? Far from expressing mass hysteria, the crowds
were calm, they didn't rage, they simply 'demanded that
space be made for them'. Commentators interpreted the
crowds' commitment to their feelings as a loss of control;
an engulfing, feminine rush of sentiment. The crowds
mystified the media. However, Diana's death and the
crowds' response to it made 'deep narrative sense' to the
public themselves, who seemed to understand that her
grim death was somehow inevitable; 'there was, simply,
nowhere else for a woman "on the edge" to go.' (Barcan,
1997, p41)

Among the mourners was an elderly woman who
explained, 'I came to say sorry.' For what? a reporter asked
her. 'For wanting photographs of her. For wanting to know
what she was doing ... I bought all the papers and
magazines. She just never had a moment to herself. I just
didn't think. Now it's too late.' Ruth Barcan, a gender-
studies lecturer in western Australia, reckoned that 'in this
late-industrial, post-Thatcherite, highly urbanised country,
people were weeping for *everything*'. (Barcan, 1997, p42)

The crowd in history has been routinely represented as
'an unpredictable and malevolent force' but this was a
benign, quiet, still crowd that made itself immovable. It
did, however, command a response.

The royal family, in desperate retreat behind their
fortifications at Balmoral, were forced to come out: they
agreed to let the flag fly at half mast at Buckingham Palace
at the end of the week. 'In eastern Europe they burnt holes

in flags, in Britain they politely insisted that they be flown,' wrote David Edgar. (*Guardian*, 10 September 1997) The royal family agreed to surface sooner than Saturday – the day of the funeral – by returning to London. The original route for the funeral procession from Kensington Palace was doubled, under pressure from Prince Charles, when the organisers realised that a million people might turn out to see Diana's cortège on its way to Westminster Abbey and then on to Althorp, where she was to be buried on the Spencer estate. The Queen finally appeared and made a formal, frigid statement paying tribute to Diana.

19. Funeral

The horses flanked by Welsh Guards slowly emerged from Kensington Palace bearing the body of Diana in a coffin shrouded by the royal standard, and topped by white lilies with a card saying 'Mummy' from her children – a heart-stopping proclamation about the identity of the woman.

The cortège turned into the highway and as it met the crowd, there was the sound of a woman wailing Diana's name. It was the only time the crowd was anything but sober and silent. The only sound along the rest of the long journey to the abbey was the muffled Tenor Bell tolling minute by minute, and the ethereal rustle of a million people standing still, with the metal of the horses' hooves clattering on the street, the snorts and swishes of the horses' bodies, and the wheels of the carriage. A woman whose last great campaign was a protest against the wanton spread of landmines across civilian landscapes was finally mounted on a gun carriage, the 'traditional' bearer of a royal body. The last funeral at which the gun carriage had appeared was Lord Mountbatten's. This was a Windsor parade that exemplified a royal regime that could not imagine its way out of the masculinised and militarised management of death and grief.

When the cortège circled Buckingham Palace and passed the Queen and her family standing – by-standing – they bowed their heads in deference. At St James's Palace up the Mall the cortège was met by Prince Charles, Prince Philip, Earl Spencer and Diana's sons. Throughout the week the boys' presence had been undecided. This day was theirs, yet with whom could they candidly share their bond with their mother? This corps of men was irreconcilable. In the absence of any emotional symmetry, according to Snow, Philip took charge and ordered them to walk together. People wondered why on earth Philip was there with that thin, disconnected line of men. It was more than wonderment – they didn't *want* him there. William never lifted his head.

> Even in her death Diana bore silent witness to the profound ambiguity of women's status in a patriarchal symbolic order. In death as in life she was surrounded by groups of men – who fought over her, protected her, wept for her, sang for her, added postscripts to her biography and analysed the constitutional implications of her death. She died, chased by men, in a car full of men, and was brought home by her former husband. (Barcan, 1997, p41)

The people who spoke for Diana and for the crowd were men. The people who accompanied her body were men. Police patrolling the route were men. The television commentators that day were men. It was as if only men were being allowed to define and describe the lives, deaths and tears of women.

The cortège was joined by the 533 representatives from charities who streamed into the Mall, some carrying lilies, some wearing sweatshirts, emblems of their organisations.

When the coffin arrived at the doors of Westminster

Abbey, the Welsh Guards regrouped and, with the slight, stiff steps of drilled men, shuffled slowly and impeccably around the coffin. They lifted the coffin on to their shoulders, gripped each other and then carried the most fetishised body in the world, now out of sight, up the steps and along the aisle. The coffin swayed, synchronising with the steps of eight young men, a mute dance of death.

There were 2000 people inside the abbey; a million outside in London parks watching the ceremony on vast video screens, and three quarters of a billion more watching on their television screens at home.

Diana's sisters read their chosen elegies, poems beloved by the Spencers; the Prime Minister read from Corinthians (rather too theatrically); Lynne Dawson sang the last text, 'Day of wrath, day of calamity and woe ... let perpetual light shine ... ' from Guiseppe Verdi's *Requiem Mass* – music often heard in Diana's Kensington Palace apartment. After Elton John sang the rewritten 'Candle in the Wind' Diana's brother Charles rose to address her coffin. Without her, he said, we would have been 'immersed in greater ignorance at the anguish of AIDS and HIV sufferers, the plight of the homeless, the isolation of lepers, the random destruction of landmines. Diana explained to me once that it was her innermost feelings of suffering that made it possible for her to connect with the constituency of the rejected.'

Champagne Charlie stood in the long tradition of reckless earls, and became a truth-teller. He might not be able to live the truth he proclaimed, but he knew the meaning of it. He recalled their childhood, their interminable train journeys between their parents, their loneliness, and pledged that Diana's sons would be spared the anguish that had driven her to tearful despair. While respecting 'the heritage into which they have been born', he promised that these boys would continue to be cared for 'so that their souls are not simply immersed in duty and tradition but can sing openly as you planned.'

The crowd outside in Hyde Park stood and soberly clapped and slowly the applause rolled into the abbey, where the congregation also put their hands together in applause. Some members of the royal family, unseen by the cameras, cried quietly and couldn't stop themselves clapping in church. Once again, the crowd filled the space with its feelings.

Democratic Mourning

No member of the aristocracy had enunciated such a personal, public rebuke to the royal family as a family, *and* as a royal family.

The young Welsh Guards lifted the coffin again and swayed slowly back down the aisle to the hearse that would take the body to Althorp. As the cavalcade passed through the streets of London and then swung down the M1, people standing on the bridges and the roadside threw flowers on to the car, 'transforming the hearse itself into a last and vast bouquet, outfacing and outflanking the remembered image of the concertina'd Mercedes smashed against the concrete wall'. (David Edgar, *Guardian*, 10 September 1997). We had never seen anything like this, we had never *been* like this. Or rather we didn't know that we had been like this before.

Just as the sexual politics which shook the monarchy and made a mass movement in 1820 had been erased from folk memory, so Britons' collective capacity for calm, contemplative grief had been traduced from its popular manifestation to patriotic propaganda. The carnage of World War I produced just such a moment of national mourning. Since then the annual Armistice Day ceremony has been shrouded in the mist of militarism, and the activity of collective grieving has been approriated by the military and the church, the guardians of the public expression of sorrow.

David Cannadine has reprised the history of Armistice Day as a national ceremony which eschewed the excess brought to the great, sensual pageants designed by Lord Curzon to celebrate imperial power, fileted of pain and conflict. Cannadine has analysed the function of ritual as 'visual advocacy', the opportunity to cement the links between past and present, to 'impart a message, impress an audience, to reinforce a sense of identity and community'. (1994, p82)

Lutyens' Cenotaph in Whitehall was originally only intended as a temporary monument to the million people across the colonies slaughtered in World War I. Initially Lord Curzon resisted the proposal by Lloyd George to salute the dead because he feared that such a 'Latin notion' might not attract a 'properly reverential attitude' among the people. Lloyd George was adamant: there had to be a tribute to the dead.

On Armistice Day 1920 the new Cenotaph was unveiled. Westminster Abbey proposed that the body of an unknown soldier be brought from Flanders and laid to rest after a funeral at the abbey. The congregation at the service was to be comprised of the relatives of fallen soldiers together with 100 nurses wounded in the course of duty. Making a break with his own traditions, Lord Curzon committed himself to a democratic ceremony, one which excluded 'high society' in favour of the people. The ceremony was to be marked by the thundering bell of Big Ben, followed by silence.

The response of the people overwhelmed the expectations of the organisers: one million people visited the Cenotaph and laid 100,000 wreaths. The ceremony at the Cenotaph was 'Curzon's triumph', and yet it was the only time he had devised a ritual that caught the national mood, by embracing the people and their feelings and eschewing pomposity.

The mass mourning after Diana's death recalled the unexpected dignity of quiet public passion in the 1920 Armistice Day ceremony. It recalled, too, the function of grief as *advocacy* for the 'fallen' and the 'lost' in South Africa and South America; for the victims of disasters at Hillsborough and Dunblane. The improvised demonstrations of mourning represented a determination to remember, to bear witness to lives lost, to demand respect for the dishonoured, to insist upon justice for the wronged.

Royal Rows

After the funeral, repeated rumours of royal rows confirmed the collective wisdom that the Windsors had shown respect neither to Diana nor to the people. On the Wednesday, John Snow at Channel 4 News discovered that the royal family had been embroiled in bitter rows ever since Diana died. It was Charles against the rest of his family, particularly the Queen, who had wanted the body nowhere near any of her palaces, who took no responsibility for organising the flight to return the body to Britain or to gather flowers to greet her when she arrived home. Mrs Majesty was also adamant that this should not involve state arrangements. The broken Spencers were to take her body, privately, to a chapel of rest in west London. Charles mutinied against his mother and insisted that Diana's body be taken to his chapel at the palace. Flying back from France, he had to telephone from the flight deck to order flowers for the coffin's arrival at Northolt.

This was all amazing – but it made sense of the sullen silence from the royal family bunkered in Balmoral. Could the story be corroborated, however? No one in the royal family could or would confirm it. But as the week wore on the royal family were no longer in control of the story. The people were conducting the national conversation without them. And there were too many tributaries to damn the flow of information and innuendo.

There was a funeral to be organised, an abbey to host the service, soldiers to deliver the body of Diana, singers and speakers to be assembled, a route to be planned, press to be informed, a committee to co-ordinate, and a government that expected to be engaged in everything.

The Labour Party had, throughout the twentieth century, been relied upon to protect the royal family from political harm. The Labour presence now provided Charles with an alliance against his family. (The Labour prime minister who had appeared to speak for the people when he pronounced Diana the people's princess seemed, in hindsight, to have been speaking for the royal family, too. New Labour's old royalism spoke up, perky and embarrassing, when Tony Blair marked the jubilee wedding anniversary of Elizabeth and Philip by describing the Queen as 'the best of British'.)

So, by the middle of the week there were too many people who knew that the royal family was at war with itself. The Westminster Abbey order of service was not settled until the end of the week because the royal family could not agree. The idea aired in public that week was that Elton John was too low for the royal family. Actually, Elizabeth's problem wasn't Elton John, it was Verdi's *Requiem*. Although Diana adored it, Elizabeth did not. Although she was a patron of the Royal Opera House, 'the Queen does not tend to favour ballet or opera too much,' said a spokesperson.

The royal family could not agree about the flying of flags because Elizabeth didn't want her flags flying. The royal family could not agree about the procession because they couldn't agree about anying. It was a performance of gross royal pique about a person they had *purged*.

Snow's discovery was corroborated: Channel 4 could make the story stand up and on Monday he reported there had been 'bitter rows' between the Windsors when they heard the news of Diana's death. 'It was made very clear to Prince Charles that Princess Diana's body was, on no account, to be brought to any of the royal palaces. My informant tells me that the Queen's desire was for her to be taken to a private mortuary and on to a private funeral.' But at Balmoral,

Charles resisted his mother and also Sir Robin Fellowes – a senior member of the household and Diana's brother-in-law – whom he told to "impale himself on his own flagstaff". Snow added that it was, 'amidst the worst of the rowing that the family went to church to a service at which there was, as usual, no mention of Diana's name – it was never allowed to be mentioned in the presence of the queen.'

Nothing had been resolved by the time Charles flew to France and the royal family left him to organise everything. It was during the flight that Charles called Tony Blair and together 'they concluded that the body would eventually lie in the Chapel Royal at St James's Palace, but not in state, and that the funeral would be far from private but in Westminster Abbey, on a state scale.'

By Monday the rows were further inflamed by Earl Spencer, who was outraged at Elizabeth's proposal that everything should be private, out of the public eye. 'It was only through Downing Street that inter-family negotiations even became possible,' reported Snow.

With only 55 minutes to go before the funeral procession passed the palace, the families had still not been able to resolve who should follow behind the coffin. 'Hence Prince Philip's sudden and unexpected presence so intimately at the movement of someone who, in life, he is known to have had the most robust reservations about,' Snow told Channel 4 viewers. The royal household belatedly considered reinstating Diana's titles, stripped away after the divorce, 'an offer that all eventually agreed she would never have wanted'.

Snow was pilloried, both for sheer nerve and for the effrontery of Channel 4 in taking a space hitherto occupied by the tabloids: this was tabloid stuff being broadcast by a medium that had shunned royal stories. But despite the calumny, Channel 4 was showered with anonymous telephone calls from people in and around the royal household confirming that they had heard the rows and the raised voices.

Despite the growing reports, the government dutifully denied it; it had looked over the crowd, saw something tumultuous, and decided to tame the temper of the people.

The playwright David Edgar caught the contradiction in his elegiac commentary on Diana's death. Reprising the magical wake of the 1 May general election and its repudiation of the 'brute, metallic logic of the market', he noted that 'this time there wasn't a ballot box in which to post that message' but nonetheless the crowds and their snaking queues waited patiently 'to record their anger and their love'. (Edgar, *Guardian*, 10 September 1997)

The *Observer* commented after the funeral that the palace had benefited from 'a lightning Millbank course in the use of symbols as a means of political communication'. But in the end 'Diana's legacy was taken and transformed by millions of people who, for all their raucousness, corniness and vulgarity, behaved as mature citizens, not servile subjects.'

British society was split not by class or politics, or even gender and generation: it was split into feelings about Diana's death, between those who felt strongly and those whose felt little; those who felt that she was a woman wronged who had emerged as a woman with strength; those who felt she was an undeserving 'rich bitch' who didn't merit our time; those who thought she had taken on the Establishment; those who felt she was the Establishment; and those who felt that although Charles had treated her badly, he was a victim too. Critics complained that people who didn't even know Diana were crying for her and people who didn't even know her sons were worried about their wellbeing.

Paradox

By telling her story Diana did not create republican sentiment, but she did transform the space in which the public could contemplate their feelings about royalty and republicanism, through the filter of her experience as a woman. She had been in danger, but she now became dangerous. Indeed, this woman, who was once such a paradox for modern feminism, came to exemplify its pervasive influence. It helped explain her powerlessness and then her power, it helped her to heal, to begin to know herself and name her enemies. The Establishment's venomous response revealed just how dangerous her life had become.

'Much political talk about women today acts to neutralise once militant ideas,' argues the American feminist Zillah Eisenstein. (Eisenstein, 1997) Paraphrasing her analysis of Hillary Clinton, she writes that Diana's 'shifting borders and ambiguity are much like the contours of gender today. She is used to symbolise the contradictory meanings of motherhood, wifehood and nations as they collide with feminism.' Feminism attaches to her but 'with no private identity allowed' she becomes 'the scapegoat for men and women who fear feminism ... she creates fear and hate because she is both stereotypic of feminism and not enough of a feminist.'

Unlike Hillary Clinton, Diana created a cause and a constituency that not only admired her, they also understood her. Diana's testimony validated her suffering and endorsed the experience of millions of women who had suffered as well. Both men and women did what the Establishment could not do: they empathised with a woman who struggled not to be a victim, but a survivor.

She did something that no woman in the royal family has done in the twentieth century: she called a monarch to account. But in the nineteenth century Queen Caroline set the precedent when she returned from exile in Europe to resist her husband's crusade to discredit her and deprive her of the crown. Her resistance not only exposed his sexual double standard, it also created a cause: women's protest against men's abuse of women. Queen Caroline and her allies created a mass movement that united sexual politics and radicalism. The combination rescued republicanism from the smoke-filled coffee shops of radical men and put it into the service of not only constitutional reform but also the reform of relations between men, women and children. The difference between then and now was the existence of an embryonic republican cause in the House of Commons that connected with women's experience and thus rooted republicanism in mass feeling, rather than in the preoccupations of a marginal minority estranged from the experience of everyday life. Almost two centuries later Britain's becalmed parliamentary politics refused to connect either with Diana's dangerous testimony, which exposed the family discourse of the royals as alien to contemporary culture, or with the republican feeling to which it contributed.

But a mood doth not a movement make. The rise and rise of discontent with the royals in the 1990s could not be attributed to republicanism. However, it did prompt the question: how can we explain the gap between the royals' exponential loss of legitimacy and the lack of a mass movement for reform? The answer lies in the estrangement of parliamentary politics from a discourse scornfully described as mere soap opera when it was actually about the way men, women and children live together – one of the great themes of our time.

It is only in the informal domain of civil society that Diana's atavistic, arranged marriage is registered. It was her suffering, rather than her terrible taste in men, that people cared about and that bonded millions of admirers into critics of her – and our – enemies, the Establishment. A Mori poll published almost a year after the *Panorama* programme revealed that more than half the electorate no longer felt that Charles commanded respect – and since respect is all that the royals command, this was clearly a crisis. No one doubted that the Prince's personal behaviour was the cause of the crisis. But that did not produce a *political* crisis. 'It is because this is about a personal relationship that politicians pull away,' commented Andrew Puddephat, the director of Charter 88, the campaign for constitutional reform. 'The task for organisations now is to work with the zeitgeist,' he said. The problem was that 'the majority of political parties won't allow the debate. This puts an extraordinary demand on civil society.'

It was not so in 1820 when Whigs and Radicals felt compelled to connect with sexual politics and the tumult in civil society. Like the Carolinians of 1820, the people paying their respects to Diana in 1997 were able to move into a public space and say something to each other about how men should behave towards children, how men should treat women and how the royal family should learn something from the rest of us about respect. But no party dared to radiate the insights of civil society and take responsibility for radical reform of our political ideologies and institutions.

Just as the mass movement that ricocheted around Caroline was made to mean less than it might have done, so the response to Diana's life and death occasioned a historic struggle to reveal the sexual politics in both royalism and republicanism. Even if the political parties muted or misinterpreted their meanings, the Establishment believed that Diana's disclosures were an attack on them. They were right.

Bibliography

The material in this book is based on interviews, the mass media, and the following texts:

Abbott, Mary, *Family Ties*, Routledge, London, 1993

Ali, Tariq, *The Nehrus and the Ghandis: An Indian Dynasty*, Picador, London, 1985

Bagehot, Walter, *The English Constitution*, Fontana Library, London, 1963

Barcan, Ruth, 'Space for the Feminine', in *Planet Diana – Cultural Studies and Global Mourning*, Research Centre in Intercommunal Studies, Kingswood Australia, 1997

Beer, Samuel H., *Modern British Politics*, Faber & Faber, London, 1982

Birkett, Dea, 'The Great Pretender', *Guardian* Weekend, 1997

Bowlby, John, *Attachment and Loss, Volume I*, Pelican, London, 1971

Bradford, Sarah, *Elizabeth*, Mandarin, London, 1997

Brand, Olivia, *The Royal Way of Death*, Constable,

London, 1986

Brittain, Victoria, *Death of Dignity*, Pluto Press, London, 1998

Buskin, Richard, *Princess Diana Her Life Story*, Signet, London, 1997

Campbell, Beatrix, *The Iron Ladies – Why Do Women Vote Tory*, Virago, London, 1987

Cannadine, David, *The Decline and Fall of the English Aristocracy*, Yale University Press, London, 1990

—, 'The Context, Performance and Meaning of Ritual: The British Monarchy and the "Invention of Tradition" c1820–1977', in Hobsbawm and Ranger, 1983

Clark, Anna, *The Struggle for Breeches*, Rivers Oram Press, London, 1995

Colley, Linda, *Britons*, Yale University Press, London, 1992

Connell, R. W., *Masculinities*, Polity Press, Cambridge, 1995

Davidoff, Leonore and Catherine Hall, *Family Fortunes*, Hutchinson, London, 1987

Dimbleby, Jonathan, *The Prince of Wales*, Warner Books, London, 1995

Dyer, Richard, *White*, Routledge, London, 1997

Edwards, Arthur, *I'll Tell the Jokes, Arthur*, Blake Publishing, London, 1993

Eisenstein, Zillah, 'Women's Publics and the Search for New Democracies', in *Feminist Review*, no 57, 1997

Evans, Caroline and Muna Thompson, *Women and Fashion: A New Look*, Quartet, London, 1989

Feminist Review, Pluto Press, London, 1980

Formations (eds), *Formations of Nation and People*, Routledge and Kegan Paul, Bury St Edmunds, 1984

Fraser, Flora, *The Unruly Queen – The Life of Queen Caroline*, Papermac, London, 1997

Gallagher, Catherine and Thomas Laqueur (eds), *The Making of the Modern Body*, University of California Press, London, 1987

Gamman, Lorraine and Merja Makinen, Merja, *Female Fetishism – A New Look*, Lawrence and Wishart,

London, 1994

Gillis, J. R., *For Better For Worse*, Oxford University Press, 1985

Grace, Helen, 'The Lamenting Ground', in *Planet Diana – Cultural Studies and Global Mourning*, Research Centre in Intercommunal Studies, Kingswood Australia, 1997

Halevy, Elie, *The Liberal Awakening: A History of the English People in the Nineteenth Century*, Ernest Benn, London, 1962

Hall, Philip, *Royal Fortune*, Bloomsbury, London, 1992

Herman, Judith Lewis, *Trauma and Recovery*, Basic Books, New York, 1992

Hite, Shere, *The Hite Report*, Talmy Franklin, London, 1977

Hobsbawm, Eric and Terence Ranger (eds), *The Invention of Tradition*, Cambridge University Press, 1983

Holden, Anthony, *The Tarnished Crown*, Viking, London, 1994

—, *Charles*, Fontana, London, 1989

Johnstone, Anne M., and Jane Wasworth, Kaye Wellings, and Julia Field, *Sexual Attitudes and Lifestyles*, Blackwell, Oxford, 1994

Junor, Penny, *Charles*, Sidgwick and Jackson, London, 1987

Kelley, Kitty, *The Royals*, Warner Books, New York, 1997

Kuhn, Annette, *The Power of The Image*, Routledge and Kegan Paul, London, 1985

Lamb, Dori and Shashona Felman, *Testimony*, Routledge, London, 1992

Laqueur, Thomas, 'The Queen Caroline Affair: Politics as Art in the Reign of George IV', *Journal of Modern History* **54**, University of Chicago, Sept 1982, pp417–66

Lees, Sue, *Ruling Passions*, Open University Press, Buckingham, 1997

Machiavelli, Niccolo, *The Prince*, Penguin Books, London, 1981

de Mause, Lloyd, *The Untold Story of Child Abuse*, Bellow Publishing, London, 1991

Morton, Andrew, *Diana – Her True Story*, Michael O'Mara Books, London, 1992

—, *Diana – Her True Story in Her Own Words*, Michael O'Mara Books, London, 1997

Mulvey, Laura, *Fetishism and Curiosity*, British Film Institute, London, 1996

Nairn, Tom, *The Enchanted Glass*, Vintage, London, 1994

NCH Action for Children, *The Hidden Victims – Children and Domestic Violence*, NCH Action for Children, 1994

Pateman, Carole, *The Disorder of Women*, Polity Press, Cambridge, 1994

Pimlott, Ben, *The Queen – A Biography of Elizabeth II*, Harper Collins, London, 1997

Pizzey, Erin, *In the Shadow of the Castle*, Hamish Hamilton, London, 1984

Plumtre, George, *Edward VII*, Pavillion Books, London, 1995

Pugh, Martin, *Lloyd George*, Longman, London, 1988

Rutherford, Jonathan, *Forever England – Reflections On Masculinity and Empire*, Lawrence & Wishart, London, 1997

Sarah the Duchess of York with Jeff Coplon, *My Story*, Pocket Books, London, 1996

Shange, Ntozake, *For Colored Girls Who Have Considered Suicide When the Rainbow Is Enuf*, Methuen, London, 1985

Souhami, Diana, *Mrs Keppel and Her Daughter*, Flamingo, London, 1997

Squires, Judith (ed), *Competing Glances*, Lawrence and Wishart, Bristol, 1992

Thatcher, Margaret, *The Downing Street Years*, Harper Collins, London, 1993

Theweleit, Klaus, *Male Fantasies Volume 2*, Polity Press, Cambridge, 1989

Tomlinson, Richard, *Divine Right: the Inglorious Survival of British Royalty*, Little Brown, London, 1994

Trouble and Strife, no 36, Sandypress, Manchester

Trumbach, Randolph, *The Rise of the Egalitarian Family*,

Academic Press, London, 1978

Warner, Marina, *Alone of All Her Sex*, Weidenfeld and Nicholson, London, 1976

—, *Monuments and Maidens*, Weidenfeld and Nicholson, London, 1985

—, *The Trial of Joan of Arc*, Arthur James, Evesham, 1996

Watson, Sophia, *Marina*, Phoenix Giant, London, 1997

West, Rebecca, *1900*, Weidenfeld and Nicholson, London, 1996

Whitaker, James, *Diana v. Charles*, Signet, London, 1993

Williams, Gwyn A., *When Was Wales*, Penguin, London, 1985

Williamson, Judith, *Consuming Passions*, Marion Boyars, London, 1986

Zeigler, Philip, *Mountbatten – The Official Biography*, Collins, London, 1985

The Women's Press is Britain's leading women's publishing house. Established in 1978, we publish high-quality fiction and non-fiction from outstanding women writers worldwide. Our exciting and diverse list includes literary fiction, detective novels, biography and autobiography, health, women's studies, handbooks, literary criticism, psychology and self-help, the arts, our popular Livewire Books series for young women and the bestselling annual *Women Artists Diary* featuring beautiful colour and black-and-white illustrations from the best in contemporary women's art.

If you would like more information about our books or about our mail order book club, please send an A5 sae for our latest catalogue and complete list to:

The Sales Department
The Women's Press Ltd
34 Great Sutton Street
London EC1V 0DX
Tel: 0171 251 3007
Fax: 0171 608 1938